A JOURNEY IN
THE WORLD OF WINE

FROM OPERATING IN THE TRADE TO
FOUNDING A BOUTIQUE WINERY

CHRISTOPHER CANNAN

Independently published in 2023.

Photography credits:

Front cover: Rafael Lopez-Monné
Page 82: Wine Advocate
Page 190: Tokaj Borlovagrend/Tokaj Confrérie
Pages 233, 235, 238: Rafael Lopez-Monné
All other photographs, author's own.

_____

Editorial Sharon Lucas
Cover and book design Anna MacKenzie
Proofread Katharine Walkden
Index Ruth Ellis
Production Michelle Thomas

To all those who take the risk to cultivate the vine,
either by choice or inheritance, in these
changing and challenging times.

CONTENTS

PROLOGUE

As the title suggests, this book is about a journey, a journey that continues after half a century on the road. Such has been the extent of my travelling that often, on returning home from a trip, I did not even bother to unpack, keeping the suitcase half-full and open on the floor.

It's a journey that has allowed me to witness profound changes in the world of wine. As well as my personal experiences, I have tried to convey some of the developments over the years and their consequences on the situation today.

Above all it has been an amazing experience. I have been so lucky to have had the good fortune to combine my great love of wine, geography, geology, gastronomy, and languages with my career.

This book is my small contribution to the recent history of the wine trade. Please join me on my travels and reflect on all that has been achieved in the world of wine over the past fifty years. Moving forward there's also an exciting future for those in the trade and for wine lovers who appreciate and promote quality and authenticity.

PART ONE

EARLY DAYS

*From a First Taste to the Assault
on the US Market*

CHAPTER 1

THE BIRTH OF A PASSION

How It All Started

Milton Abbey School, Blandford Forum, Dorset

16th February, 1966

Dear Mother and Father,

Yesterday evening we had a wine tasting and lecture given by Christopher Stevens, a Master of Wine. It was fascinating and I learnt about Bordeaux, the Medoc and other regions. We tasted some wines and I was especially impressed by a German wine called PIESPORTER GOLDTRÖPFCHEN. It was a bit sweet and quite delicious. I have kept the empty bottle in my study. I feel strongly that wine is a subject I would like to learn more about.

At sixteen years old this was my first exposure to wine. I had spent the previous summer in Normandy, staying in the home of a professor of the famous Ecole des Roches, near Verneuil-sur-Avre. I remember the food being so much better and more exciting than anything tasted before, especially after boarding school in England. In those days, French family life revolved around mealtimes. Wine was served at every meal but I was too young to appreciate it. Besides, it was a rather rough *vin ordinaire* from litre bottles with stars engraved around the neck, which were common at the time, but a rarity today.

In the summer of 1966, accompanied by a friend from Bermuda, I made an epic bicycle tour of the Loire Valley. We cycled from Orléans to Angers, visiting châteaux and other sights along the way. At the time there were few cars on the road and cycling was less dangerous than today, despite the narrow embankment road along the Loire. By then I was hooked on wine, we both were, even to the extent of having two water bottles on our bicycle handle bars, one filled with *vin ordinaire* (all we could afford) and one with water! On reaching Vouvray we were fascinated by the chalk cliffs bordering the Loire, with homes and wine cellars carved into the rock. We decided to visit a cellar in one of the caves. The tasting was a revelation. The Vouvray we tried was

a little sweet and very much to our liking. Vouvray, produced from the Chenin Blanc grape variety, is very versatile, the resulting wines ranging from intensely dry to ultra-sweet, with a capacity to age for many decades. The producer gave us the remainder of the bottle he had opened for us. We installed ourselves on the grassy banks of the Loire and rapidly polished off the wine followed by a long and deep siesta. We awoke to a headache but with the realisation that some wines

Bicycle tour of the Loire Valley, summer 1966.

were better than others. The *vin ordinaire* was abandoned and other stops were made along the river including the discovery of the refreshing, fruit-driven red wines of Chinon and the semi-sweet Rosé d'Anjou.

My family had no connection to wine and, having survived the Second World War, felt it was a luxury they could ill afford. I was born on a sunny summer evening in June 1949 in a manor house at Winson, a tiny Gloucestershire village in the lush Windrush river valley, located in the heart of the Cotswold Hills. My education was at boarding school from the age of eight. First in Bournemouth on the south coast and later at Milton Abbey, built as a beautiful stately home in a remote Dorset valley. My academic efforts did not produce miraculous results but did inspire my lifelong love of geography, history, and languages. For sports my preferences ran to sailing in nearby Portsmouth harbour and skiing after a school trip to the Austrian Alps.

After leaving school in 1967 at the age of seventeen I was all set to study at the University of Perth in Australia. There was a three-month gap before term started, so my father decided to send me to Lausanne to learn French. Three months was not enough to speak fluent French so I pleaded with Father to abandon the Perth project and continue for a further six months in Lausanne. The following year was spent in Cologne and Bavaria, learning German. Finally, in 1969, I spent six months in Madrid to master Spanish. All three languages have been of enormous benefit throughout my career and are still in use almost every day. While wine continued to be of interest, my strict budget meant being less exposed to the pleasures of fine wines. All my spare cash was spent on my ongoing passion for travel, mostly hitchhiking, as far north as Narvik in northern Norway and as far south as Nice and the Côte d'Azur. I do recall the delightful habit of opening a bottle between meals in Germany when visitors were received, also an occasional glass of Valdepeñas in Madrid, the everyday wine during the Franco dictatorship. The wines were rough and ordinary but light and easy to drink. Despite Franco and the wine quality, it was during my time in Madrid, at the age of nineteen, that I fell in love with the country and everything Spanish, consequently an enormous influence on the future of my career.

The wines available in Franco's Spain in the late 1960s were restricted to just a few names from Rioja, Catalonia, and Valdepeñas. No single estates were allowed so the sources were all large companies producing wines of variable quality. Some of the names such as CVNE (Compañía Vinícola del Norte de España), Marqués de Murrieta, Marqués de Riscal, La Rioja Alta S.A., López de Heredia, and Torres were among the best and continue to be among the most revered labels in Spain today. Other legendary names from the 1960s, including Campo Viejo and Federico Paternina (Ernest Hemingway's favourite), are now supermarket labels. The Ribera del Duero, with the exception of Vega Sicilia, was producing indifferent rosé wines and did not exist as a DO (Control of Origin) until 1982. The only decent white wine was Monopole, produced by CVNE in the Rioja and featured on many restaurant wine lists. At the time, this wine, partially aged in American oak, was rather different and more complex than the Monopole on the market today.

On returning to the UK, I ended up working a short time at Willis, Faber & Dumas, a Lloyds insurance broker, specialised in non-marine international reinsurance. The work was boring with little opportunity to use my recently acquired languages. Furthermore, earning only £60 a month, paying the rent was difficult, let alone investing in a bottle of wine. After four months, in spite of much family discouragement, I made the decision to join the wine trade.

Father had always told me there was little opportunity to make money in wine. He was right but he nevertheless agreed to assist me and gave me an introduction to an old friend of his from his school days at Eton. The late John Surtees MW, one of the first Masters of Wine and most charming of individuals, did all he could to help me get started without going as far as offering me employment in his agency company, Percy Fox & Co. Ltd., which represented some of the most prestigious producers in Europe.

John recommended first spending time visiting the main producing regions of Europe and offered to give me introductions to his suppliers. Since so few funds were available, the idea was to work in cellars in order to cover the cost of lodging and meals.

The first objective was Bordeaux. The Percy Fox principals, Cordier, a reputed Bordeaux *négociant*, could not offer a *stage* (an apprenticeship) so, in early December 1969, I purchased a £25 return train ticket to Bordeaux in order to find accommodation and arrange for a *stage* with a *négociant*. I had amassed a number of introductions and spent a productive week in Bordeaux. On the way, stopping in Paris to visit friends, I met Henning Jans, a young wine merchant from Denmark. He was working for Ginestet, another Bordeaux *négociant*, and offered to put me up on the floor of his room in the Ginestet premises on Cours St. Louis, the location of Hotel Château Chartrons today.

The first morning I visited Cordier, who had agreed to show me their prestigious châteaux in the Medoc. On a rainy day, Daniel Vergely, the export manager, drove me to Château Meyney in St. Estèphe, my first château visit. We returned to Bordeaux with stops at Châteaux Talbot and Gruaud Larose. I recall being very impressed despite the damp December weather. The following day I visited Maison Sichel and met Peter Sichel, a legend in the Bordeaux wine trade. He took an immediate interest in my desire to enter the trade. His notorious generosity towards those wishing to become members of the wine trade had no bounds. He offered me employment for a month starting in early January 1970. Remuneration for work in the cellar was half-pension with a family on the rue Vauban in the very centre of Bordeaux. During the same week, a visit to Maison Mestrezat Preller, another well-established *négociant*, was also productive and work was proposed for February and March. Remuneration was four francs an hour with the added opportunity of tastings and weekly visits to the vineyards with the Bordeaux wine brokers. Further encounters during the week included a meeting with Jean Calvet and a visit to Cruse & Fils Frères, both famous and historic names in the Bordeaux trade of the time. Edouard Cruse kindly invited me to lunch at the legendary Château Pontet Canet with a young Australian couple, a pleasant experience in this venerable and impressive property, only somewhat spoiled when we ran out of petrol during the return trip to Bordeaux!

The die was cast and I was all set to start my tour of the European vineyards. On returning to the UK, I purchased a 1959 light-blue Volkswagen Beetle for £99 with indicators that lifted from the gap between the front and rear doors. It proved to be a loyal and useful means of transport until, on reaching Germany some months later, the police told me the car was not fit to travel on their *autobahns*.

On Sunday 11th January 1970 I arrived in Bordeaux and started with Maison Sichel the next day. This included a tasting of 1966 and 1967 Burgundies followed by a long and entertaining lunch with John Salvi, a life-sized character, Master of Wine, and export manager for Sichel at the time. Accompanying us was Peter Crosse, my room-mate in rue Vauban, fellow traveller, and soon to become a lifelong friend. Bordeaux in January 1970 was a rather dismal place. Apart from the dull rainy weather, many of the majestic buildings in the centre of the city were black with soot in spite of being built with the local white, chalky stone. The city was isolated from the river by a chain of pre-war warehouses, many of which were abandoned. In the years after the war, before Spain opened up after the death of Franco in 1975, Bordeaux was very provincial and considered a sort of cul-de-sac with few tourists and consequently lacked restaurants and hotels of any repute. The main activity and focus was the wine trade. The cellars were strung out along the Quai des Chartrons, the wine quarter of the city. The façades of some of the *négociant* houses were very grand, and still are today, although, since the 1990s, most have been converted to luxury flats as the wine shippers moved out of the city to occupy larger and more practical premises for their business. Behind the façades the cellars containing the casks for ageing stretched back some 300 metres (984 feet) away from the river. These areas are now being converted to multistorey flats. Bordeaux today is a very different place with a modern tramway, the buildings cleaned up, the riverside warehouses mostly demolished, and the city open to the Garonne river, encouraging frequent calls by cruise liners and provoking a tourist boom. Numerous restaurants and wine bars have sprung up throughout the city, some of world-class standards.

After three weeks with Sichel, working on the bottling line, filling containers, and participating in numerous tastings, I joined Mestrezat Preller on the Cours de la Martinique, again in the Chartrons district. Working in the cellars with some colourful characters, I learnt about the treatment and handling of bulk wines as well as every slang word in the French language. What's more, the cellar staff advocated that all the wines had to be tasted with outlandish frequency in order to supplement the boredom of work! Visits to vineyards with some of the Bordeaux brokers taught me much about the traditional structure of the Bordeaux wine trade. In those days the shippers purchased most of their wines in bulk and aged them in their cellars in the Chartrons district before bottling and shipping. This included some of the more prestigious Crus Classés wines from the Medoc and St. Emilion before château bottling became the norm. In addition, many of the wines were shipped to northern Europe in cask and bottled by importers on arrival. The brokers played a key role in selecting wines for the shippers. Queues of brokers would line up every morning in the *négociant's* reception rooms with their little sample bottles for the buyer and directors of the company to taste.

Numerous châteaux were visited during my time in Bordeaux including such illustrious names as Margaux, Latour, Lafite Rothschild, Cheval Blanc, Ausone, Haut-Brion, and Yquem, to name but a few. Two visits especially stand out in my memory: Vieux Château Certan in Pomerol and Château Soutard in St. Emilion. During a visit to Pomerol I became lost and was busy looking at a map while parked by the front gate of Vieux Château Certan. The owner, Gérard Thienpont, happened to walk by and offered assistance provided I visit his château and taste his wines. No hesitation was necessary and a long friendly association with the Thienpont family was initiated over a bottle of their exquisite 1964 vintage. A family friend gave me an introduction to Château Soutard, a St. Emilion Grand Cru Classé, and one of the most imposing buildings in the area. The owners, the Des Ligneris family, were delightful if a little eccentric. Monsieur des Ligneris was locally known as the *Comte Rouge* (the Red Count) reflecting his politics. They invited me frequently to lunch accompanied by mature vintages of Soutard going back to 1943. The wines at Soutard, structured and quite tannic when young, had a well-deserved reputation for their ageing potential. Regretfully the property has since been sold and is now in the hands of a large insurance company.

La Frèche

Domaine Boingnères

Appellation Bas Armagnac controlée

LÉON LAFITTE
PROPRIÉTAIRE-RÉCOLTANT
LA BASTIDE-D'ARMAGNAC
(LANDES)
TÉLÉPHONE Nº 128
CH. POSTAUX BORDEAUX Nº 1686-34
MÉDAILLES D'OR
MONT-DE-MARSAN 1953 - 1958 - 1966
BORDEAUX 1966
CONCOURS GÉNÉRAL AGRICOLE
PARIS 1962 - 1964 - 1966

La Bastide-d'Armagnac, le _____

Bourgueil Mr Amirault – St Nicolas de Bourgueil – (Indre et Loire)
Tel. 33

Vouvray* M. Huet. Mairie de Vouvray. 56.10.62

Muscadet M. Bonhomme 44. Mouzillon –

Bourgogne –
MERCREDI 9.30.

* Michel Gouges rue Nuits St Georges. rue du Moulin –

** Charles Rousseau (fils d'André) ✓ Gevrey Chambertin

Pouilly Fuissé
et Beaujolais * | M. Edmond LANEYRIE 71 Solutré Pouilly
Tel : 11 à La Chapelle Pontenevaux

Beaujolais – Madame Geoffray. à Odenas Rhône.

Champagne * Pierre PERTOIS à CRAMANT Marne
Tel. 50.54.55.

Alsace. *✓ M. Kuehn à Ammerschwir 1400 LU
LU 16³⁰ Louis Léon Bayer à Eguisheim (Maire)
MA 16³⁰ ✓ M. Klipfel à Barr. (Ht Rhin, 08 94 85

Bandol Lucien PEYRAUD – Le Plan du Castellet
T. 21 à Le Beausset
(voir)

*Léon Lafitte's list of quality-orientated wine producers
he recommended I visit on his behalf, March 1970.*

During my time in Bordeaux, apart from a few weekends skiing with friends in the nearby Pyrenees, excursions were made with Peter Crosse to Cognac and Armagnac. Both were fascinating. In Cognac we were lodged at Denis Mounié & Co., a small, quality-orientated producer. We were treated like royalty and learnt about the process of distillation and ageing of fine Cognacs complemented by visits to independent distilleries and to the more prominent houses, notably Hennessy, Hine, and Martell. I was most impressed by the sheer size of these operations and the rows of casks with fine Cognacs, some many decades old. Despite the terrible condition of the roads at the time, a number of producers in Armagnac were visited but one remains of special importance regarding my future. This was a stop at Léon Lafitte, one of the most prestigious independent estates. During the tasting of 20- and 30-year-old vintage Armagnacs Lafitte told us about a Swiss-based association called the Académie Internationale du Vin. He knew many of the founding members. He wrote out a list of quality-orientated wine producers *(see previous page)* he recommended I visit on his behalf in most of the French appellations, predominately members of the Académie. The list included Constant Bourquin, the founder of the association and owner of DIVO, a Swiss importer focused on so-called "natural wines", true to their origin and the traditional non-interventionalist winemaking practices of the past. Not to be confused with the natural wines of today, rather the definition of a single-estate wine as opposed to blended, *négociant*-bottled wines. This list was gospel to me and I made sure of a visit to each producer during my travels. These included Henri Gouges, Armand Rousseau, and Ramonet in Burgundy; Geoffroy in Beaujolais; Dr. Parcé in Banyuls; and Jean-Noël Boidron of Château Corbin Michotte in St. Emilion, among others. All were high-quality, family-owned estates, provoking my fascination and desire to be involved with this sector of the trade. Jumping forward fifty years I am now a member of this distinguished Académie. The Académie's terminology "natural wines" has understandably been changed to "noble wines".

Towards the end of March, I attended a fascinating, week-long, intense enology course at the science faculty of Bordeaux University with the renowned and much respected enologist Emile Peynaud. Much was learnt in a very short space of time. Peynaud was very eloquent and easy to understand so the mysteries of winemaking and the art of tasting were revealed with ease. It was during this course that I first met Henry Cavalier, who became a close friend and played a significant role in the orientation of my career.

Moving on from Bordeaux in early April 1970, I stayed a few nights with friends in Tours, visiting some of John Surtees' contacts in the Loire Valley. These included the Caves de la Loire, a cooperative in Anjou, and a memorable visit to the celebrated Domaine Huet in Vouvray where Gaston Huet himself treated me to a bottle from the 1940s, another revelation of the seductive charm of well-matured older wines and the unique ageing capacity of Chenin Blanc.

Like the Bordeaux wine trade, the Loire in 1970 was dominated by a few large *négociant* houses and cooperatives. Nevertheless, the idea of single-estate bottling was already underway and some superb wines were being made with the added benefit of representing their origin. This was especially evident in the wines from Sancerre, Pouilly-Fumé, and Vouvray.

The end of April found me in Champagne staying on the premises of Lanson Père et Fils in central Reims with a small refrigerator in my room full of Lanson Champagne! This stay turned out to be an orgy of succulent meals in the best restaurants around Reims and Epernay. The Lanson family did not really know what to do with me for a whole week so I was tagged on to every visit made by trade customers for lunch and dinner. Nevertheless, I learnt much about the Champagne production process while visiting not only Lanson but other houses including Pommery and Moët & Chandon. I had the opportunity to drive through much of the region, visiting small growers and understanding the structure of the trade between the shippers, growers, and cooperatives. Also, the differences in style between each of the three main production areas. By the end of the week, being so bloated and exhausted from all the rich food, I drove to Paris to recover. Incidentally it was on this visit to Paris I discovered the first edition of the *Gault & Millau* gastronomic magazine. A collection of subsequent editions over many years led me to interesting producers during my search for suppliers for Europvin, the company I founded in 1978. Another incidental event during this Paris visit was my first viewing of the film *Patton* with George C. Scott as General Patton and in which I had participated as an extra while studying Spanish in Madrid, in one scene as an American military policeman and in another as a Russian soldier, dancing on the occasion the two armies met in Germany. The dancing scene took a whole night of filming but appeared for only a few seconds in the final production. I guess we were not much use as Russian dancers, our only attribute being blond hair!

From Paris to Germany and the town of Worms in the Rhine Valley where I did odd jobs at the house of Langenbach, one of the most prestigious producers. Occupations included cleaning out the classic oval wooden casks. Being slim at the time, in spite of the indulgence in Champagne, I could crawl through the small openings of the 2,000-litre (528-gallon) oval *foudres*. Langenbach owned part of the famous Liebfrauenstift vineyard surrounding the Liebfrauenkirche (Church of Our Lady) in Worms. It is from this vineyard that the ubiquitous Liebfraumilch takes its name. Many hours were spent clearing the weeds between the vines, earning my bed and breakfast. Even so, I managed to escape to visit most of the main German production areas and taste at some of the more prestigious estates, including Schloss Johannisberg, the Staatsweingüter in the Rheingau and the Nahe. The Mosel has a special place in my heart, being the source of the first wine I enjoyed back in my school days. The Mosel scenery is extraordinary and the crisp, mineral-scented Rieslings are still among my favourite wines in the world.

After two months in Germany, I returned to England for my twenty-first birthday and to sell my Volkswagen Beetle, ill-adapted for the 1970s roads in Europe. It was sad to say goodbye but it sold for the same price as purchased. The replacement was a more recent light-blue Renault 4 procured in Germany and a good companion for the remainder of my travels around Europe.

In early July I moved south to Alsace and spent a very pleasant couple of weeks in the touristy town of Riquewihr with the well-respected Hugel family. The weather was superb and I visited a number of producers in the region including

Peter Crosse in 1970 with my second car in the background.

Léon Beyer and Trimbach. The notion of single varietal wines in Alsace was easy to understand and I enjoyed the distinctive differences between the various varieties such as Sylvaner, Pinot Blanc, Pinot Gris, Gewürztraminer, and Riesling, the last being my favourite. At the time little attention was paid to the notion of terroir (the microclimate and soil of specific vineyard plots) so the reputation of the *négociant* was crucial when searching for quality. Today, with the Grand Cru designation being established, enormous importance is attached to the soil types and origin of the grapes.

At the end of lunch one day with grandfather Hugel and his wife at his home above the winery shop, he asked if I knew the eaux-de-vie from Alsace. On a negative reply twenty bottles appeared and instruction followed on the merits of each one. There was an eau-de-vie of almost every fruit and plant I had heard of and some I had never heard of at all. It was fascinating but meant that the rest of the afternoon was spent asleep in my lodging across the street.

From Alsace to Burgundy where a *stage* had been arranged with Bouchard Père et Fils, one of the most venerable *négociants* in Beaune. The most memorable moments of the stay were spent in the cellars recorking wines from the late nineteenth century, tasting each bottle for cork taint and topping up from a bottle of the same wine. Recently some of these revered bottles have been offered at auction direct from the Bouchard cellars. The wines seemed to be remarkable at the time – never having left the cellars they were in superb condition with surprising freshness. In October 2020 I had the opportunity to revisit these same cellars with my son. Nothing had changed and the amazing stock of old wines seemed remarkably intact.

Time was also found to visit the vineyards of the Côte d'Or to study the structure of the appellation system. In the early 1970s the Burgundy scene was still dominated by the *négociants*. Just a few single estates were beginning to make their mark in the main export markets, especially the United States.

It was during this time in Burgundy that I drove to Switzerland to visit my brother, who was enjoying life as a student in Lausanne. On a Saturday afternoon we drove up to the village of Chandolin, the highest village in Valais, to meet Constant Bourquin, founder of the previously mentioned Académie Internationale du Vin. Over a glass or two of excellent Swiss wine he told me more about the Académie and the merits of what he called "natural wines" with authenticity, produced by individual estates. This approach has been the guiding light of my career ever since.

Shortly afterwards notice came through that I had been offered a summer job as an assistant in the export department of the house of Garvey, at the time a highly regarded Sherry producer in Jerez de la Frontera. Thrilled with this opportunity I left Burgundy for Spain with a stop in Bordeaux on the way. During the previous months I had been negotiating with Louis Eschenauer, a long-established *négociant* in Bordeaux, for employment as assistant to Yves Fourault, the export director. An interview had been arranged and subsequently the post was confirmed to start in mid-September.

I drove on to Jerez in my little Renault 4 without air-conditioning. Being English, getting used to the 40°C (104°F) heat was a bit of a challenge, but I have fond memories of my six weeks in Jerez. Lodging was in a small room above the restaurant Gaitan. The work in a small office was laborious due to my lack of experience with a typewriter. However, with the assistance of Jaime Fraser-Luckie, the export manager, the mysteries of Sherry production were revealed and a number of visits to other producers including Gonzalez Byass, Domecq, and Luis Caballero were organised. The working hours from 9 a.m. to 3 p.m. allowed plenty of time to enjoy the considerable pleasures of the local beaches and nightlife. Most Sundays I would watch the bullfighting in El Puerto de Santa Maria, not so much for the fight itself but more for the ambiance. I did however witness the celebrated "El Cordobès" in action shortly before his retirement.

I fell in love with the region and the products. Bars and restaurants abound in the Sherry towns of El Puerto de Santa Maria and Sanlúcar de Barrameda with some of the freshest and most sublime seafood in the world, ideal with the Fino and Manzanilla Sherries which were consumed in large quantities. The atmosphere was always relaxed and friendly and I felt I was permanently on holiday. I was fascinated by the unique production process and different Sherry styles with their versatility with and without food. Later, Sherry became an important part of my career.

At the end of my stay a difficult decision had to be made. Garvey offered me a permanent job to assist the export manager, while simultaneously Eschenauer had confirmed my post in Bordeaux. What to do? I loved Spain and the lifestyle in Jerez, and Garvey's offer was very tempting. However, the opportunity in Bordeaux seemed too good to ignore. Finally, it being obvious that Bordeaux was a better option for my career, the decision was reluctantly made to leave Jerez, a wise decision. Ever since the mid-1970s, with a few exceptions, the Sherry trade has suffered from declining consumer interest due to poor decisions on quality control and fortified wines no longer being fashionable. Fortunately, this state of affairs is now gradually being reversed and fine Sherry is at last becoming more popular.

A detour on the return journey to Bordeaux took me to Oporto where John Surtees had arranged for me to spend a week with the Symington family, owners of the renowned Dow's, Warre's, and Graham's Port houses. Ian and Peter Symington made sure I learnt about the singularity of Port production, a wine I have loved, sold, and appreciated ever since. I was very taken by the beauty of the Douro Valley landscape and the fascinating wines. I vowed to become involved with the Port trade in some form in the future. The last evening was spent at the Symington-owned Quinta do Bomfim in Pinhão. Dinner with the production manager was a bit of a challenge with my non-existent Portuguese and the manager's non-existent Spanish or any other language. The following day I made the long drive to Bordeaux to start my career in the wine trade. Believe it or not, on crossing the border to France, I felt sure that somehow my future would involve Spain.

CHAPTER 2

LOUIS ESCHENAUER S.A.

Bordeaux

Initiation in the Trade

A Monday morning in mid-September 1970 was my first day at Louis Eschenauer and the first day of my wine-trade career with proper remuneration. The first three months of my time at Eschenauer were spent moving from department to department learning about the structure of a classic Bordeaux *négociant*. The company, founded in 1821, was of medium size, employing about one hundred people. Its activities included the purchase of bulk wines and their ageing and bottling, as a so-called *négociant-éleveur*. Eschenauer was owned by an English entertainment group, John Holt & Sons, who also owned the renowned Château Rausan Segla in Margaux and Château Smith Haut Lafitte in the Graves at Martillac. They farmed the vineyard at Château Olivier, also in the Graves, taking care of the vinification, ageing, and sales of the entire production of their red and white wines. Both the Graves properties are now part of the more recently created Pessac-Léognan appellation. Today Rauzan Segla, with a change in the spelling, is in the hands of the Wertheimer family, owners of the Chanel luxury group.

Louis Eschenauer, with a respected name in the trade, had a worldwide distribution network. Apart from traditional importers and agents, sales were made to airline companies and through a network of local agents in the French market. In the early 2000s the imposing premises on the Avenue Emile Counord were sadly demolished and replaced by a supermarket. The brand still survives in the hands of a large distribution group, Les Grands Chais de France.

Moving through the various departments I learnt about the different activities. I started in the cellars with Monsieur Dupuy, the amiable cellar master, then worked with the purchasing manager, before moving to accounting and finally to the commercial office. Here was my first exposure to the unique practice of selling Bordeaux Grand Cru Classés *en-primeur* or as futures. In the early 1970s the wines were purchased by *tonneau*, the equivalent of four casks, each of 225 litres (59 gallons), a total of 1,200 bottles. Compulsory château bottling was not yet applicable and in some cases the wines were sold on in cask to be bottled by the importer, usually in the UK or other northern European countries, especially Belgium and Denmark. For those requiring the wines in bottle, bottling charges were invoiced separately. Eschenauer had sizeable allocations for their importers and agents. I recall long meetings with Ab Simon of Austin Nichols in New York concluding with millions of francs' worth of orders. The system worked well for the 1970 and 1971 vintages – in fact so well that some wines were sold *sur souche*, before the grapes were even picked. However, the practice fell apart with the terrible 1972 vintage offered at prices that defied all logic. Pricing for the 1970 and 1971 vintages had been reasonable and made the notion of purchasing *en-primeur* worthwhile, the wines rapidly increasing in value after purchase, to the obvious advantage for the consumer and collector. This method suffered during the financial crisis of the early 1970s exacerbated by a series of poor vintages from 1972 until 1977. From 1978 interest was regenerated but it was not until the 1982 vintage, with the enthusiastic support of Robert Parker, the famous critic from Maryland, that the system was revived with relish. Over the years there have been many fluctuations, depending on the quality of the vintage, the pricing strategy of the châteaux, and the world economy. Recently the practice has faced a new crisis due to the high pricing from the châteaux and little or no increase in value after bottling. The notable reduction in prices for the excellent 2019 vintage has been an exception.

During this period one of my principal roles was to take care of trade visitors and show them the châteaux. I enjoyed this activity and remember driving the dark-blue company-owned Peugeot 404 estate car to Margaux for Rausan Segla and to the Graves for the other châteaux. Lunch at Rausan Segla was always a treat, not so much for the food, which was the ubiquitous entrecôte with *pommes frites*, but for the wines. Rare were the occasions when Rausan Segla and Smith Haut Lafitte from the sublime 1961 vintage were not served. Furthermore, the dessert was invariably accompanied by a bottle of Château Yquem from the legendary 1967 vintage. On one occasion, for a dinner with Edmund Penning Rowsell, the acclaimed journalist and author of many books on Bordeaux, a bottle of Rausan Segla from the late nineteenth century was opened. The wine was still fresh and delicious but Penning Rowsell spoiled the magic by claiming a dose of Port must have been added for the wine to have such freshness. Memorable dinners with similar vintages were also enjoyed with the late Michael Broadbent, founder of Christie's wine auction department, whose tasting experience and humble approach with clear thinking on many wine-related subjects gave me exceedingly valuable inspiration throughout my career.

About two weeks after my arrival at Eschenauer, Yves Fourault asked me to represent him as a member of the Commanderie de Bontemps du Médoc et des Graves for a dinner of the Young Presidents Organization at a leading hotel in Monte Carlo. The Commanderie is a long-standing traditional brotherhood which promotes the merits of the various appellations with colourful ceremonies, hosting famous personalities from the cultural and political world for spectacular dinners. I flew to Nice with some distinguished members of the Bordeaux wine community including Jean-Eugène Borie of Château Ducru Beaucaillou, Anthony Perrin of Château Carbonnieux, and Pierre Tari of Château Giscours. During the dinner a ceremony was performed to induct choice members of the audience to become members of the Commanderie.

Just as we arrived on stage to perform the ceremony, gowned in the heavy, dark-red robes of the brotherhood, I was asked to translate the text for the ceremony into English. This was an extraordinarily difficult task since the text was in eighteenth-century French and I understood next to nothing of what was being said. I did my best to make some sense of the ceremony and later was rewarded for my performance with congratulations and a generous, condescending smile from Princess Grace in person.

From 1st January 1971 I was officially promoted to the role of assistant to Yves Fourault, the export director, who knew little about wine but was a remarkable salesman. He travelled extensively and once a year in October made a month-long trip around the world calling on the more remote markets. At the end of January, I accompanied Yves on his annual visit to customers in the Channel Islands, my first sales trip. At the time, both Jersey and Guernsey had several small independent wine merchants, most of whom are not in existence today.

My first trip to the Channel Islands with Yves Fourault,
export director at Louis Eschenauer S.A., centre.

My first order consisted of twenty-five cases mixed of various Bordeaux wines from Le Riche's Stores, a small local supermarket. We went on to visit several other merchants on both islands, receiving orders from them all without exception. I began to think it was all too easy! The following year I made the same trip on my own. I have fond memories of the Islands, the friendly importers with odd names like Bucktrout & Co., the delightful scenery, and the small six-seater planes that flew us from the mainland and between the islands, sometimes in alarming weather conditions.

The following spring, I was sent to Denmark to work the market with Eschenauer's agent, Einar Wandel of Carl Wandel & Sons, with offices located next to the port of Copenhagen. Time was spent visiting customers, small- to medium-sized merchants, all over the country. Einar drove me in his huge Chevrolet to the various islands and to Jutland. We covered the whole country in the space of a week. We had huge success selling casks of the 1970 vintage *en-primeur*, especially those from Rausan Segla, Smith Haut Lafitte, and Olivier. Einar had a wonderful sense of humour and was well loved by his customers. We were entertained to lunch and dinner almost everywhere. On free evenings Einar would take me to the cinema. Fortunately, the films were in English with Danish subtitles. Other trips to Denmark the following years were all very successful and enjoyable. The Danes seem a happy people on the whole, always welcoming with a ready smile.

Another country I visited regularly was England. The agent was David Stevens MW of Rigby & Evens, based in London. After meetings at the head office I was sent out with the sales staff to visit customers. On one occasion, with the late Christopher (Kit) Stevens MW, who had been responsible for my first wine tasting when I was sixteen years old, a call was made to Tony Davies of J.T. Davies & Sons, owners of pubs and a chain of wine stores based in Croydon. Tony informed me that his son Michael would soon be coming out to Bordeaux to do a year-long *stage* with Borie-Manoux, a leading Bordeaux *négociant*. Michael became a close friend and in winter we would go skiing in the Pyrenees. For the summer he brought out his speedboat from England and many a Sunday was spent water skiing on the Carcans lake in the Medoc.

Later Mike's late wife Lizanne would become godmother to our son Edward and I godfather to their daughter Chloë. On joining his father's company, Michael became a very important customer during my time with Wildman and Europvin; this lasted until his chain of stores was sold in the late 1990s. His support contributed immensely to Europvin's success in the early years. Other trips to the UK included travelling all over the north of England in fast cars with members of the Rigby & Evens sales team. As in Denmark, calls were made on small- and medium-sized merchants with a special focus on the *en-primeur* sales.

Back in Bordeaux I befriended the De Bosredon family, owners of Château Bélingard near Bergerac. They were delighted when I was able to arrange a major purchase by Eschenauer of their Bergerac wine in bulk. Not being allowed to earn a commission on the sale, an invitation was extended to spend a memorable weekend with the family. It was my first exposure to the gastronomic delights of the Périgord. We went from restaurant to restaurant comparing the merits of the foie gras and duck confit from each establishment. Between meals we visited the caves at Lascaux and other sights along the beautiful Dordogne Valley.

Another memorable episode at Eschenauer was the visit of a couple of curious and ambitious merchants from the UK. Over two days Augustus Barnett of the Augustus Barnett chain and Ahmed Pochee of Oddbins tasted and selected wines for their portfolios. These wines were to have an exclusive label that was especially designed for the large quantities they purchased. The lead time was extremely short and it was my responsibility to see that all was ready in time. This was a tight call and was only achieved by upsetting almost all the departments in the company. Two full truckloads left Bordeaux on time. Oddbins continues to operate today but Augustus Barnett is now history.

Other episodes at Eschenauer included several visits to Alsace where the company had purchased Jules Muller & Fils, a producer based in Bergheim. My role was to accompany trade visitors with the additional benefit of enjoying the rich gastronomic tradition in Alsace. A visit to Burgundy and La Reine

Pedauque, a *négociant* associated with Eschenauer for a short while, was my first opportunity to conduct a tasting and make a presentation. The subject was the wines of Bordeaux and the audience the entire staff of La Reine Pedauque. It was a nerve-racking experience at my young age.

Finally, in January 1973 I convinced Yves Fourault to send me to the US to learn about the market. It was decided I spend a month in the country: two weeks with a retailer, and two weeks with an importer. The retailer chosen was Calvert on Wisconsin Avenue in Washington DC, run by Alfio Moriconi, head of the local chapter of Les Amis du Vin, an organisation for wine consumers holding events, including wine tastings and wine education. I was lodged with a delightful family near the store and was able to witness the inauguration of Richard Nixon to his ill-fated second term as president. I also attended a service in Washington National Cathedral, conducted in part by Ted Kennedy and dedicated to the evils of the Vietnam War. Alfio was most generous with his time and made sure I learnt as much as possible during my short stay. This included a brief visit to South Carolina to meet Jean-Pierre Chambas, an enterprising Frenchman with a huge moustache, installed as a retailer in Columbia. Jean-Pierre later became an importer and a customer.

Washington under snow, with wide open spaces, imposing buildings, fascinating museums and monuments, left a lasting impression on me. I have always enjoyed returning to the city. Moving on to New York by train I was welcomed by Ab Simon of Austin Nichols, a major importer at the time, later part of Seagram's, the Canadian distiller. Ab's right-hand man in the company was Gerald Asher, a personality who I greatly admire for his attempt, well before his time, to import into the UK single-estate wines from the lesser-known areas of France. This strategy, and Gerald's entertaining wine column for the now defunct *Gourmet* magazine, were to have a major influence on furthering my career.

Gerald took good care of me during my stay in New York, introducing me to the major retailers including Sam Aaron at Sherry-Lehmann and Peter Morrell at Morrells. Sam took me to lunch in a nearby trendy restaurant twice during my stay, teaching me much about the New York wine scene. His enthusiasm for the wine trade and success as a retailer are legendary. Like Washington, New York with its dramatic architecture and dynamic atmosphere left a lasting impression, with a certain excitement and sense of opportunity that is renewed with each visit.

By this time, at twenty-three years old, I was becoming restless and started to think about the future and a return to Spain. Through the Spanish consul in Bordeaux, visits and interviews were arranged with a number of Rioja producers including Bodegas Franco-Españolas, AGE, and Federico Paternina. These trips to Rioja were enjoyable but came to nothing regarding a future employment. Little did I know how important Rioja would become later in my career.

Having a love for geography and a passion for wine, I was becoming more and more interested in wines that offer a sense of place. Henry Cavalier, who I had met at the enology course with Emile Peynaud, had started a company based in Washington DC called Morrison Cavalier. Henry had worked with Gerald Asher in the UK and, sharing a similar passion for wines from lesser-known regions, had taken this concept to the US, launching Cavalier Selections. Henry had a fascinating portfolio full of gems from the less familiar appellations of France, including little-known areas of the South West, the Jura, and Savoie, all regions unknown to American consumers at the time.

I remember my first trip to the Southern Rhône to meet Henry and talk about joining his enterprise. We stayed in a small hotel in Sorgues near Avignon. After a pleasant dinner with Henry and his first wife, Milagros from Chile, I tried to sleep. This did not come easily as a strong mistral wind was intent on destroying the plane tree just outside my window, my first contact with the singularity of the Mediterranean climate. The next day Henry moved on and left me to visit one of his suppliers in Châteauneuf-du-Pape, Clos du Mont Olivet. After this first visit, I needed no convincing that Châteauneuf-du-Pape would become one of my preferred red wines.

A few weeks later, in June 1973, Henry made me a proposition for a post within his organisation and shortly after I handed in my resignation at Eschenauer. My employment with Eschenauer continued until 31st August that year but I became disturbed by the lack of communication from Henry during the summer, suspecting that something was wrong. Indeed, there was a problem but not so acute that Henry did not discourage me from taking a flight to Washington DC in early September. Fortunately, my intuition made me delay my departure and see how matters would develop with Henry's company. It turned out that his partner, Morrison, was involved in real estate and was unwilling to inject the capital required for the venture to be a success. I had left my lodging and sold my car but decided to wait until early October, staying with a lifelong friend, Robert Nicholson, at Ludon-Medoc. Robert, who had worked with Gérard Jaboulet in the Rhône, took over my post as assistant to Yves Fourault at Eschenauer and today lives in California, running a hugely successful mergers and acquisition business specialising in wine and spirits.

John Salvi, with whom I had kept in touch since my first day in Bordeaux, also lived in Ludon-Medoc and one day in early October encouraged me to call on Anthony Sargeant at his isolated house in the vineyards just north of Margaux. I was not hopeful about finding employment since the oil crisis of 1973 and the Yom Kippur War were in full swing. Nevertheless, I arranged a meeting with Anthony who was managing director of Frederick Wildman & Sons, a prestigious New York–based importer founded in 1934 by Frederick Wildman Sr. soon after the end of prohibition. Anthony, based in Margaux and New York, was looking for an assistant. To my chagrin he asked me a trick question during my first short interview: are red wines produced in Meursault? I said no and later, on finding out the truth (Meursault is known for white wines, but an almost insignificant quantity of red wine is made there, which very few people know about), imagined my chances of employment with Wildman were nil. Anyway, I cannot have made too bad an impression since Anthony decided to employ me anyway, giving me the opportunity to start the second stage of my career in an exciting and stimulating environment.

CHAPTER 3

FREDERICK WILDMAN & SONS

New York and Margaux

Challenging Times

The autumn of 1973 was fraught with international political upheavals, the Yom Kippur War and the resulting oil crisis, kicking off a major world depression. Nevertheless, I was allotted a number of challenging assignments for Wildman. The first was to find an office that was to be the European base for Frederick Wildman & Sons. Anthony lived just outside Margaux and wanted the office nearby. For several days I searched every corner of the locality and eventually found an attractive, isolated semi-detached single-storeyed house called Domaine Campion in the vineyards of Château Margaux. This was refurbished and became our office for the duration of Wildman's presence in Europe. I found myself an apartment in Blanquefort, just north of Bordeaux, about twenty minutes from Margaux. Having lived in furnished flats in Bordeaux I had no furniture for my unfurnished apartment. Happily, John Salvi lent me a bed and a table. I drew up the bed to write at the table, until a young English couple, living in the residence opposite, sold me their furniture on their departure from the region.

My first trip was to the Loire Valley. The company represented a number of prestigious estates but in the Loire they purchased a range of generic wines from a *négociant* in Saumur and had them bottled under their own Wildman label. The 1972 vintage in France was a disaster, with a cold summer followed by a wet harvest. In short, the grapes were unripe and the wines were tart, acidic, and as near as undrinkable as any vintage in the latter half of the twentieth century. My first mission for Wildman was to go to Saumur and taste the wines with the producer in question. Not one of the appellations was acceptable on tasting, giving me the difficult task of informing the *négociant* that Wildman would not take up their annual allotment. As a result, we decided that Wildman would purchase their Loire wines directly from producers in each of the principal Loire appellations: Muscadet, Anjou, Vouvray, Sancerre, and Pouilly-Fumé; an activity with which I became much involved during my five years with Wildman.

For the next trip Anthony lent me his Peugeot 505 for a drive to the Rhône Valley and Burgundy. This was to be my first tour of the Wildman suppliers in areas I was excited to learn more about. Part of my brief was to search out top-quality single-estate wines, especially from Châteauneuf-du-Pape. Wildman already represented Chapoutier in the US but shared the agency with another importer, a rather unsatisfactory arrangement since, like for all American importers, exclusivity for the market was important, if not essential. I stayed in a small room above La Mère Germaine restaurant in Châteauneuf-du-Pape with a magnificent, unhindered view over the Southern Rhône. I visited a number of estates including the famed Château Mont-Redon. Among others I discovered Domaine du Père Caboche, which became part of the Wildman portfolio for a time. Moving on to the Northern Rhône, I was overwhelmed by the views of the steep vineyards of Hermitage and Côte Rôtie, not to mention the superb Syrah wines.

After a visit to Chapoutier, I drove on to Burgundy with George Watt, vice president and sales manager for Wildman. This first visit to Burgundy for Wildman was a true eye-opener. They represented a number of the most prestigious estates as well as the *négociant* Louis Latour. The domaines included the legendary Romanée-Conti, Maison Leroy in Auxey-Duresses, the recently created Domaine Dujac in Morey St. Denis, Domaine Rousseau in Gevrey Chambertin, Domaine Leflaive in Puligny Montrachet, Domaine Jacques Prieur in Meursault, and Château Fuissé to name but a few. Many of these relationships with Wildman dated back to the end of prohibition in the 1930s. Burgundy had always been Colonel Wildman's great love.

There were few estates bottling their own wines in the 1970s. Wildman represented many of the best with Robert Haas, Alexis Lichine, and Frank Schoonmaker representing others. Needless to say, I was thrilled with the opportunity to visit these estates and taste their wines with the owners. I was in Beaune over the weekend of the Hospices de Beaune wine auction. Being curious to see how the proceedings were conducted, I stood at the back of the auction hall. Behind me was a young English couple taking notes for the American press. We began a conversation and compared notes. The couple turned out to be Tim and Stephanie Johnston, who became close friends for life, and later the inimitable Tim became godfather to my daughter. Tim now owns, with his daughters, the famous Paris wine bar Juveniles, a mandatory stop for ex-patriots and visiting Americans. Later that day, at the Hotel de la

With Tim and Stephanie Johnston
in Sanlúcar de Barrameda.

Poste in Beaune, I had the privilege of meeting Colonel Wildman, founder of the company in the 1930s. It was his last trip to Burgundy; he passed away shortly afterwards.

Another trip that first autumn was to Rioja in Spain. Since 1962 Wildman had belonged to the Canadian-based distiller Hiram Walker, owners of Canadian Club Whisky, Ballantine's Scotch Whisky, and Courvoisier Cognac. Hiram Walker had a Spanish subsidiary producing a whisky called "W", run by Ramon Mora-Figueroa Domecq from Jerez. Ramon had negotiated the export rights to CVNE (Compañía Vinícola del Norte de España), one of the long-established and emblematic Rioja houses. Both Anthony Sargeant and Ramon wanted sound advice on the quality of the wine and had engaged Emile Peynaud, Bordeaux's most famous and sought-after enologist. I was fortunate enough to accompany Peynaud on his visit to CVNE. We spent the entire day tasting wines from vats, casks, and bottles all the way back to the 1928 vintage. At the end of the day Peynaud told the gathering that, although he had been paid fees to consult for Hiram Walker, he had much enjoyed his day, had an excellent lunch, but could offer only three words of advice: "Don't change anything" and off he went to consult for the recently born Marqués de Cáceres winery. My connection to CVNE became considerably closer after this occasion because I was asked to take care of European sales for the duration of the contract with Hiram Walker. Much later, for a short period, CVNE was to become a partner in my company, Europvin.

Hiram Walker had other investments in Europe, notably a 50% share in the prestigious Chablis producer J. Moreau et Fils. The other 50% belonged to the Moreau family and the company was under the capable direction of Jean-Jacques Moreau. It was not long before I was sent to Chablis and asked to help out with the European sales of their wines. This project became a dominant role during my time with Wildman. Even though the European economic crisis was continuing to hamper wine sales, importers were beginning to realise the advantage of buying their Chablis from producers in Chablis rather than from the large Beaune-based *négociants*. I covered many thousands of kilometres on the roads of Belgium, Holland, Germany, even as far north as Denmark and Sweden, in my small Peugeot 204, visiting importers and making new contacts for both Moreau and CVNE. In spite of the economy, these were stimulating and exciting trips on which I made many new friends and contacts. Everyone needed Chablis in their portfolio and was keen to buy from a Chablis producer. Prices were low and availability, after the abundant 1973 vintage, was plentiful. I shall never forget visiting the buyer at Albert Heijn, a large supermarket chain in Holland. He wanted to purchase a full truck of Chablis, about 1,000 cases, but only wanted to pay 6 francs per bottle when the normal price was about 9 francs. I phoned Jean-Jacques Moreau from the Albert Heijn office and with reluctance he agreed to make the sale. Imagine selling 1,000 cases of Chablis today at less than 1 euro per bottle!

During my association with Moreau the company became more and more successful and the work more time consuming and challenging. I visited Chablis every month staying at the Hotel de l'Etoile, the only hotel in the town and long overdue for refurbishing. I recall the lumpy beds and feasting on the ubiquitous *Sole au Chablis*, a rather stale sole in a white wine sauce, the only saving grace being an ample supply of reasonably priced Premier and Grand Cru Chablis from Raveneau, the most celebrated of the Chablis producers. Jean-Jacques Moreau was ambitious and, availability becoming limited in Chablis, he was soon offering his clients wines from other regions, notably the Loire, Beaujolais, and nearby St. Bris, famous for the crisp and captivating Sauvignon de St. Bris. I became involved in finding new sources, especially in the Loire. During my time with the company expansion was dramatic, and soon new cellars had to be constructed to accommodate over 150,000 hectolitres (3,962,580 gallons) of wine. Today the company belongs to Boisset, a large Burgundian *négociant*, but the Moreau family kept their vineyard holdings and have created two separate quality-orientated estates, Domaine Christian Moreau and Domaine Louis Moreau.

During the journeys throughout Europe, I was finding new markets for CVNE and Moreau, but the icing on the cake came from another source. Times were so difficult in the US during the mid-1970s that Wildman was having difficulty in selling the allocations of their most prestigious Burgundy estates. In order to maintain their commitment to the estates concerned, I was asked to find buyers for the wines in Europe and was given samples from Dujac, Rousseau, and others. I had no trouble in finding wildly enthusiastic buyers, especially in Holland, where a number of top restaurants snapped up all that was available. Needless to say, with some lucky newfound friends, I enjoyed some memorable meals with a number of these bottles.

As the economy improved, and surplus Burgundy stocks became rare, we started selecting a number of Bordeaux wines to complement the wines from Moreau and CVNE. The first order I received in Europe was for one hundred cases of Château Sénéjac, a Cru Bourgeois from the Haut Medoc, from the Brussels-based division of the Champagne house Lanson Père et Fils. This was during the summer of 1974 when the economy was at its very worst and orders were hard to come by for any wines, let alone a mid-priced Cru Bourgeois from the Haut Medoc. I was proud of this achievement although Dominique Lanson, director of the Belgian division of Lanson, never gave me another order. I believe they were still selling the stock of Château Senéjac four years later.

Over the coming months our Bordeaux activity developed with the assistance of Courvoisier who financed the purchase of top-quality Bordeaux châteaux, including Grands Crus Classés, at very reasonable prices. During the crisis years of the mid-1970s it was possible to purchase First Growth Bordeaux for about 60 francs and other Classed Growth wines for 40 francs and less. This situation turned out to be a huge asset when the time came to establish Europvin in 1978.

Another exciting aspect of my European role for Wildman was the negotiations with their suppliers or prospective suppliers. Some were successful, some not, but all were rewarding and interesting experiences. With the difficult situation in Bordeaux in the mid-1970s, a number of châteaux were beginning to question the classic distribution system through the Bordeaux trade and were looking for exclusive importers in specific countries. I remember visits to several châteaux including La Tour Carnet and Léoville Las Cases. However, it was at Lynch-Bages that we came close to a deal. Jean-Michel Cazes had just taken over the estate from his father and I recall a number of agreeable conversations with him on having Wildman as their exclusive importer in the US. But as conditions on the Bordeaux open market improved, the deal never came to fruition.

Negotiations with Gérard Jaboulet in the Rhône Valley were, however, successful, and Wildman became the exclusive distributor for the prestigious house of Paul Jaboulet Aîné, owners of the renowned Hermitage La Chapelle. This agreement remained in place until 2015. Furthermore, after the creation of Europvin, Gérard became a close friend and great supporter of my future activities, giving us a number of leads to interesting importers in several countries, some of which continue to work with Europvin to this day. His premature death in 1997 was a great loss to all who knew and worked with him. His enthusiasm, generosity, and loyal friendship were boundless.

Business in Burgundy was not easy during this period either but Wildman was able to hang on to most of their exclusivities except for Romanée-Conti and Leroy. Probably the most awkward moment of my career with Wildman, perhaps of my whole career, was being sent, against my judgement, to visit Lalou Bize-Leroy to try to persuade her to allow Wildman to continue as agent for Romanée-Conti without having to purchase the wines from Maison Leroy. I knew it would be a lost cause before the meeting and, in the end, Wildman was unable to continue with either Leroy or Romanée-Conti due to the restrictive payment terms for the large sums involved.

Since German is one of my languages I was put in charge of the supply of German wines for Wildman. At the time German wines were popular in the US and Wildman listed many of the top estates. They were also agents for the famous Maximin Grünhaus property in the Ruwer tributary of the Mosel. Since most of the estates were available on an open market there was always the problem of exclusivity. Following several fascinating visits and tastings at Schloss Schönborn in the Rheingau it was decided to create a special label exclusive to Wildman for the Schönborn wines. Freddy Wildman Jr., son of the founder and author of books on Spain, where he lived, was asked to create the label. He came to Germany with Anthony Sargeant and I recall a fascinating couple of days. Freddy was a great talker and intellectual and would hold forth entertainingly on numerous subjects for hours without stopping. There was never a dull moment. The label was finally produced and was superb but was never used since Wildman's strategy in Germany changed soon afterwards.

I was also asked to source a line of generic German wines with Wildman's own label. The wines were to come from Dr. Werner Wenckstern, owner of the Hotel Schwann in Oestrich-Winkel. I much enjoyed several visits to this charming hotel overlooking the Rhine, busy with barges carrying all kinds of merchandise to ports of call between Switzerland and Holland. In spite of the creation of an attractive label, this project never came to fruition either. Instead, Wildman continued to purchase a range of wines from the house of Kendermann, specialising in top estates.

It was in the summer of 1976 that I first met my future wife, Charlotte. One evening I was driving in the Medoc, when I spotted a small car with a rather distressed young lady standing beside it trying to work out how to fix a flat tire. It turned out I had met her many years previously in Germany and later in Madrid – we were studying German and Spanish in the same language school. She was from Bordeaux but I had lost touch with her over the years. She told me she was to be married a few weeks later and I was invited to the wedding. My first meeting with my future wife was at the reception buffet. She was tucking into the cakes while I was contemplating the cheeses. Realising I was on my own and knew no one at the party, she introduced me to her friends and then disappeared. A few days later I was passing the bank where she worked. She was standing outside talking to colleagues. I stopped and invited her to join me for dinner. She accepted and we met on a few occasions before losing touch. Two years later she phoned me out of the blue and our romance took on a new dimension. We were married in a small Saxon church in my parent's home village of Beverston, near Tetbury in the Cotswolds, in late October 1979.

Also, during this period, I would take a holiday in winter joining my friend Peter Crosse and other friends in the Alps for an intensive two weeks of skiing, by far my favourite sport. Lodging was in a rented chalet where students would take care of the cooking and upkeep. This was a very satisfactory and enjoyable arrangement. Subsequently, a skiing holiday every year was compulsory. After my marriage we used to frequent the Club Méditerranée, also a good arrangement, especially when our children were small. The staff would teach the children to ski while we were able to spend the day on the slopes. Later we found a small friendly hotel at Wengen, a car-free resort in the Swiss Alps. The scenery, with some of the highest mountains in Europe, was hard to beat. The skiing was excellent, and the food in the hotel and in a mountain inn on the slopes was of Michelin-star level. We returned to this idealistic spot frequently over many years until the hotel was sold and the welcome no longer what we had experienced.

One amusing anecdote during my time at Wildman was our daring attempt to introduce some top Californian wines into the French market. This was before Steven Spurrier's famous Judgement of Paris tasting in 1976 and sadly met with little success, despite the prestige of the properties concerned. A very few cases were shipped from Ridge Vineyards, Mayacamas, and Schramsberg to the *négociant* Dourthe Frères in Bordeaux. I believe most were consumed by the directors and staff of the company! We were ahead of the times, long before such well-known names were only available on an allocation basis.

It took some persuading to obtain permission to visit the US, the purpose being to offer distributors a selection of wines outside the normal Wildman portfolio. Finally, in January 1978 I flew to New York and visited the classic New York town house at 21 East 69th Street, location of the Wildman headquarters. Afterwards I called on distributors in Washington DC, New Orleans, Texas, California, and Seattle. During the trip, I began to feel more and more under the weather and, by the time I reached Vancouver, my eyes were yellow. I was diagnosed with hepatitis and had to return to Bordeaux before completing my tour. The cause was a bad oyster in the Loire Valley and the outcome was six months with no wine! It was a sorry conclusion to my career with Frederick Wildman, but there were no regrets. I had time to read *War and Peace* and other heavy tomes.

During my days with Wildman, besides having a good time and learning an immense amount, I had met and worked with many fascinating personalities and key members of the world of wine. Apart from Colonel Wildman these included Aubert de Villaine, Alexis Lichine, Michael Broadbent, Hugh Johnson, Peter M F Sichel, Jean-Michel Cazes, Gérard Jaboulet, Marcel Guigal, Max Chapoutier, Louis Latour, Charles Rousseau, Vincent Leflaive, Andreas von Schubert, Graf von Schönborn, Christian Pol Roger, Pierre Dourthe, Gaston Huet, and many others, including most of the top châteaux owners in Bordeaux. Furthermore, I had created a network of contacts in Europe which would prove invaluable after I created Europvin.

CHAPTER 4

EUROPVIN

The Early Years

High Stakes and Early Rewards

In the spring of 1978, after Anthony Sargeant's departure from the company, Hiram Walker decided to close the Wildman office in Margaux. This provoked the creation of Europvin on 1st May 1978. The inspiration for the name of my new company came early one morning in April 1978 after a near sleepless night. I leapt out of bed and wrote down the words "Société de Séléction et Distribution des Vins Fins d'Europe" before I could forget them. This being quite a mouthful the word "Europvin" was soon adopted, becoming the more familiar name of the company. Next was to find a logo. At the time I was reading about the pilgrim road to Santiago de Compostela and the numerous wine regions traversed by the various paths to the city. I came across a drawing of an attractive compass, which continues as Europvin's logo to this day. Another task was to find a motto. John Ruskin came to the rescue with: "Quality is never an accident; it is always the result of intelligent effort."

On 1st May 1978 we were open for business. Thanks to my short experience in the trade and influence from the likes of Gerald Asher and Robin Yapp,

Europvin was founded on the idea that I would select the finest wines I could find in every appellation in France and Spain, and later in Portugal and Italy, focusing on family-owned estates and producers we felt we could work with comfortably. The ambition of the project was to set up a worldwide distribution network for the wines we had selected. The backbone of our work was to provide a service both to the producer and importer. The producer had access to our network, the specialised press, and our knowledge of the legislation in each country. Frequently they did not speak foreign languages, relying on Europvin to sort out any difficulties that might arise. For the importer it was foremost a service of selection and subsequently the logistics of grouping together small quantities from a wide range of estates from all regions in order to fill a container for export overseas. Once the wines reached their destination, we supported our importers with market visits, tasting events, and winemaker's dinners, especially significant when we were accompanied by the owner of the estate. With some minor modifications, including the marketing of brands owned by the current owners of the company, this strategy and philosophy continues today. Initially Europvin worked as a commission agent but we soon realised it was complicated to maintain the loyalty of the suppliers and control the payments. We subsequently switched to invoicing all the shipments, thus protecting our suppliers from the possibility of an importer going out of business with unpaid invoices. This happened on a couple of occasions. We took the loss, the producers the full amount.

Luck was with me during the early days. First our excellent secretary at Wildman, Marie-Paul, decided to join me and we became partners in the adventure. We opened our first office in a small room in her home in Castelnau-de-Medoc, just ten minutes from Margaux. The furniture consisted of a large table, two chairs, and a telex machine, as there was no room for more. The table soon became cluttered with papers and the telex machine chattered away. Marie-Paul took care of all the bureaucratic formalities of founding a new company, no small accomplishment, while I started to drum up some business. At the outset this proved to be relatively easy. We were coming out of the prolonged recession of the 1970s and Bordeaux had good wines from the 1975 and 1976 vintages to sell.

On my departure from Wildman, Courvoisier, part of the same group as Wildman, was holding stocks of over 5,000 cases of Bordeaux wines. These cases were destined to be sold in Europe and the US through the European arm of Frederick Wildman & Sons. Wildman no longer existed in Europe and Courvoisier was not a wine merchant, restricting their business to the production and sale of Cognac. They offered me the entire stock on consignment at their cost price. Since prices were on the increase at the time this was of enormous benefit in the early days of Europvin and enabled us to auto-finance the company almost from the very first day.

Although we published a small price list with wines from all regions of France, it was Bordeaux that accounted for the bulk of our initial orders. Our early supporters were mostly in the UK and included Michael Davies at J.T. Davies & Sons, Laurence Hayward, Ehrmanns, Stevens Garnier, Laytons, Bibendum, André Simon Shops, Grants of St. James's, Berkmann Wine Cellars, Bordeaux Direct, Stowells of Chelsea, to name but a few. Furthermore, I had maintained a good ongoing relationship with Wildman's New York office. They purchased container quantities of Bordeaux for a year or so until they took on the US agency for Borie-Manoux, an important Bordeaux *négociant* and châteaux owner.

During my days with Wildman, I had developed a strong relationship with a company in Germany called W. Ph. Kiefer. Based in Saarbrücken, this company was run by a dynamic husband-and-wife team who had strong links with the top department stores in Germany. They were huge supporters of Moreau in Chablis and purchased large quantities of Bordeaux from Europvin, mostly from the Mazeau family in the Entre-deux-Mers but also from Château Larose Perganson in the Haut Medoc. At one point they needed another wine from the Entre-deux-Mers. Monsieur Mazeau sent me to meet Bernard Greffier, who wanted to start bottling his own wines. I was given samples of their first bottling, an extremely tart and acid wine from the 1976 vintage. I remember taking Monsieur Greffier an armful of other white wines from the Entre-deux-Mers for him to see what the market required. Since then, the Greffier family has not looked back and still produces excellent white wines from the region. Forty years on, Europvin continues to sell Château Tertre de Launay from this property with ongoing success. For a time, the wine featured as the first (and least expensive) white wine on the list at Taillevent, the prestigious Parisian restaurant.

It was not long before we realised the office in Castelnau was too small and not practical for the development of the business. Then the chimney in the office collapsed during a storm, rendering the premises unusable. We decided being located in Bordeaux would be more practical. During a visit to an estate agent on the Place Paul Doumer, on the edge of the Chartrons district, he pointed to a building across the square where a first-floor apartment was available. It was an attractive building from the late nineteenth century and we spent time and energy making it suitable both for business and for receiving visitors. In this I was assisted by my long-suffering wife, almost causing the demise of our recent marriage! From 1980 to 1985 number 120, Cours de Verdun, was ideal for our purposes. We had a large-enough office, a room for tastings, and eventually were able to take over the top floor of the building where we could lodge our customers during their visits to Bordeaux.

Our business continued to develop during this period and it came to the point when we needed more staff, particularly as Marie-Paul resigned her position and left for Biarritz for family reasons. One of our suppliers was

controlling the sales for a group of châteaux who decided to change their strategy. The person running the operation was Luc Savatier, a graduate of the Bordeaux Ecole Supérieure du Commerce. With a little persuasion he decided to join me and became a minority

Organising a tasting with Luc Savatier in the early 1980s.

partner in the business. He remained loyal to his post until 2012 when the company was in the process of being sold. We made a successful long-term team lasting thirty-two years, his expertise being financial control and the everyday running of the company, mine being sourcing and sales.

During this period, I started to develop the portfolio of suppliers with a goal to offer the trade a selection of the finest estate wines from every corner of France. I had two main sources of inspiration. The French gastronomic magazine *Gault & Millau* had an excellent team of tasters and was constantly recommending rising stars from lesser-known regions. The other was Robin Yapp, a dentist-cum-wine-merchant from Wiltshire in the UK, who specialised in the wines from the Loire Valley and the Rhône. He and his wife Judith wrote a delightful book, *Vineyards and Vignerons*, accompanied by some captivating drawings of his various suppliers in these two up-and-coming regions. Much time was spent during the winters visiting producers in each region and signing them up for the markets where they were not already committed.

Bordeaux being the bulk of our business, we focused on carefully selected Petits Châteaux and Crus Bourgeois. Some of the more successful were contacts from my Wildman days. Château Sénéjac, a Cru Bourgeois in the Haut Medoc, owned at the time by Charles de Guigné, an American aristocrat, was particularly successful. With the 1976 and 1978 vintage we sold half the total production. Furthermore, for some unknown reason, Charles still had considerable stocks of the legendary 1945 vintage in perfect condition. Another important property for us was Château Siran, one of the leading chateaux in the Medoc, from Margaux, owned by the Mialhe family, and Château de Malle, a Grand Cru Classé in Sauternes, also the owner of Château de Cardaillan, an excellent red Graves. We enjoyed close relationships with these family-owned châteaux over many years.

Very soon we had an increasing demand for Bordeaux Classified Growths. These wines are purchased on the open market in Bordeaux through a network of brokers. We were a new company and at the outset were not allowed direct access to these sought-after wines but managed to work out a deal with Pierre Dourthe of Dourthe-Kressmann, an important *négociant* on what is known as the Place de Bordeaux, whereby he would purchase the wines for us and we would split the commission. This arrangement lasted a couple of years, by which time we had established a strong enough reputation to be able to purchase these wines on the Place like any other *négociant*. This activity became an important part of our trading in the years to come, especially from the 1982 vintage onwards when we became involved with the more speculative *en-primeur* or futures market for the top wines. The key to success with this activity was to have good relationships with the château owners in order to obtain allocations of the most sought-after wines. This entailed frequent tastings at the châteaux as well as discussions with the assistance of the specialised brokers or *courtiers* as they are known.

During this early period, we made contact with some customers who would become an important contribution to our sales in the formative years. During 1980 we received a visit from Henri-Claude Quinson who owned the highly successful mail-order business Le Club Français du Vin, based in the Beaujolais. We started in a small way shipping a few cases of various Bordeaux wines. Soon he asked us to become involved with his Vin du Trimestre project. This entailed sending a case of the selected wine to his customers automatically every three months. If the customer did not want the wine, he could return the case. Few of the 15,000 members of the programme sent back the case, so the challenge was where to find the 15,000 cases of an interesting and exciting wine. This was not so difficult in Bordeaux and the Rhône Valley but was a problem in the smaller appellations of South West France. We participated in several of these operations, in Bordeaux selecting a Montagne St. Emilion, in the Rhône Valley a Lirac and an excellent Côtes du Rhône Villages. In the South West a Cahors we found from Georges Vigouroux, a Côtes de Buzet from Château de Padère, and the most complex of all, a Madiran from Alain Brumont of Domaine Bouscassé and Château Montus. Alain did not have enough wine to fill the 15,000 cases ordered. Undaunted, we visited a few of his neighbours and with difficulty were able to prepare a magnificent cuvée for the required quantity.

With each new release a magazine called *L'Etiquette* was published and launched at a Michelin-starred restaurant in various locations. Well-known personalities of the specialised press and gastronomic world were always invited. I recall one superb lunch at Chez Chabran, a two-star Michelin restaurant in the Rhône Valley, animated by the dynamic presence of the late Alain Chapel, founder and owner of his own three-star Michelin restaurant near Lyon. Alain Chapel was a pupil of Fernand Point and had achieved a worldwide reputation for his cuisine but sadly died prematurely in 1990. Le Club Français du Vin was eventually sold to a publishing company, bringing to an end what turned out to be a huge contribution to our early success.

Another important aspect of the early days of Europvin was my close friendship with the late Theo van Broekhuizen, owner of a small wine shop in the centre of Amsterdam. I first met Theo back in the early 1970s while working with Eschenauer. On founding Europvin I invited him and his partners to take a share in Europvin and help finance our early days. The partnership and financing never came about but he agreed to purchase substantial quantities of wine for his shop and import company. The wines were mostly from Burgundy and the association helped cement our relationship with a number of prestigious producers including François Germain, Jacques Prieur, Hubert de Montille, Aubert de Villaine for his wines from Bouzeron, Marcel Vincent from Pouilly Fuissé, and Henri Boillot, who was introduced to us through Gérard Jaboulet and subsequently became one of Europvin's most important suppliers.

Dinner in Holland, with Theo van Broekhuizen second left.

Every winter in the late 1970s and early 1980s I would spend a week in Burgundy visiting producers with Theo, sharing a room on the top floor of the Hotel Le Cep in Beaune. One of Theo's contacts was a small estate in Meursault called Domaine Pitoiset Urena. The wines were superb and so was the personality behind them. Madame Pitoiset, an energetic and vivacious lady, lived alone in a small house in the centre of Meursault. We had huge success with her wines and were able to purchase a sizeable proportion of her production. She kindly invited us to lunch in her home on one occasion but on arrival we found a big sign telling us to beware of the large and dangerous dog. Madame Pitoiset answered the bell and, to our intense amusement, out came a tiny little dog as friendly as could be, unlikely to even scare the postman! Sadly, the Pitoiset Urena estate no longer exists but I preserve fond memories of her sublime Meursault Poruzots and her sweet little dog.

In 1985 our office in Cours de Verdun was becoming too cramped and, as the company grew, we needed to find bigger premises. We were receiving more and more visits from the trade and wine-related press so a proper tasting room was compulsory. We were regularly receiving Robert Parker for extensive tastings and on one occasion we also received Harry Waugh, earning us a brief mention in one of the diaries he published regularly. We eventually found a town house on the Cours St. Louis in the Chartrons district, not far from our previous location. We proceeded to convert it for office use and today, more than thirty-five years later, it continues to be the headquarters of Europvin. The building, from the nineteenth century, is attractive and ideal for tastings with plenty of natural light, thanks to a small courtyard at the back of the house. It also had space for the construction of a large air-conditioned cellar for our samples. The tasting room became the hub of the operation but we also had a dining room and were able to offer lunches to our customers during their visits, a welcome break during the extensive tastings. During Vinexpo, the big biannual trade fair in Bordeaux, we would have open house every evening for dinner, often receiving up to forty customers and suppliers. These were always animated affairs and many of our more prized bottles were opened for the occasion.

The Europvin office in Cours St. Louis, Bordeaux.

The Europvin stand at Vinexpo, Bordeaux.

CHAPTER 5

CANNAN & WASSERMAN

A Strategic Alliance

The late Becky Wasserman, an ex-patriot American, arrived in Burgundy with her artist husband in the late 1960s. Living at the time in Saint Romain near the well-established cooperage François Frères, she began exporting quality French barrels to Californian vintners. Later she became more interested in the contents of the barrels and began exporting wines from a few prestigious domaines. After meeting Becky in 1980, we soon discovered that, apart from a mutual love of wine, we had a shared goal for developing exports of select family-owned estate wines to the US. It was not long before we made our first trips together to visit importers and distributors in several key states. Becky had numerous contacts and a portfolio of very fine Burgundies and Champagnes. From Europvin we offered wines from Bordeaux, the Rhône, the Loire, Alsace, and a few lesser-known appellations. We could supply importers with a complete portfolio of the finest estate-bottled French wines. The key to our success, like in other overseas markets, was logistics; the ability to group together small quantities from a wide range of producers for shipment in one container – in short, one-stop shopping.

At the time the US wine market had consolidated considerably, dominated by just a few powerful distributors. However, sommeliers and wine enthusiasts were beginning to look for interesting new wines of the highest quality. A few start-up distributors picked up the ball and began importing such wines with success. In those days it was relatively easy and not too costly to set up a distribution company. Today the market is once again dominated by just a few huge distributors focusing on important brands, and it is much harder and much more onerous to set up a new distribution company. Nevertheless, they are being created with some success, since the demand exists for more eclectic wines, especially from enthusiastic and knowledgeable sommeliers.

Becky's company, Le Serbet, is based in an attractive old farmhouse at Bouilland, a charming village in a narrow-wooded valley 16 kilometres (10 miles) north-west of Beaune. Operationally we shared the commission, with the larger share going to the company who sourced the wine. We never created an official company but traded under the name Cannan & Wasserman for a number of years during the 1980s. Europvin took care of the logistics and invoicing, but both companies shared the sourcing and sales.

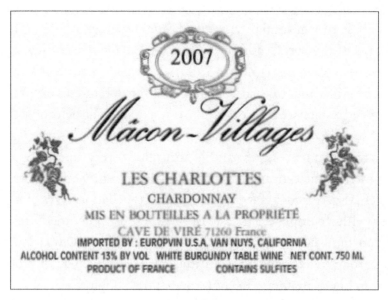

*Les Charlottes, the white Macon Villages
named after my wife.*

Becky's selections included such prestigious names as Domaine de la Pousse d'Or in Volnay, Coche-Dury in Meursault, Michel Lafarge in Volnay, Daniel Rion in Nuits St. Georges, Joseph Roty in Gevrey Chambertin, Duc de Magenta in Chassagne Montrachet, Jean-Paul Droin in Chablis, Domaine des Comtes Lafon in Meursault, and Pierre Morey also in Meursault. For volume we selected our own cuvée at the competent cooperative at Viré in the Maconnais. It was a white Macon Villages Les Charlottes named after my wife. For a time in the 1980s container quantities of this wine were shipped to New York with listings in many of the best restaurants. In the same spirit a Chablis selection was made at the reputed cooperative La Chablisienne, with the appropriate brand name Chablis La Porte d'Or.

Becky had a friend based in Paris, Jean-Baptiste Lechère, a passionate Champagne lover. He negotiated with the owners of the Venice Simplon-Orient-Express, the luxury train, to supply them with their own house Champagne with an attractive dark-blue label reflecting the logo and color of the carriages. The Champagne was made by Union Champagne under Jean-Baptiste's control. It was a delicious cuvée, more in the Blanc de Blancs style, turning out to be a huge success in the US, where we had exclusive distribution rights.

Becky also maintained a good relationship with the Troisgros family, owners of the famous three-Michelin-starred restaurant near Roanne. They sold a few wines and a Champagne under their own Troisgros label and Becky was asked to take care of sales in the US. Most of the wine came from the Cave du Haut Poitou, from a little-known region just north west of Poitiers and south of the Loire Valley that produced pleasant dry white wines, specifically an excellent Sauvignon Blanc and a Chardonnay. It was the Troisgros name that helped sell these wines successfully, not the appellation.

From Europvin's side, apart from a selection of Bordeaux châteaux, we concentrated on the Rhône with Domaine du Vieux Télégraphe in Châteauneuf-du-Pape, Domaine Auguste Clape in Cornas, Domaine Gilles Barge in Côte Rôtie, Georges Vernay in Condrieu, Albert Dervieux in Côte

Rôtie, Emile Champet in Côte Rôtie, Domaine St. Gayan in Gigondas, and many more. From the Loire we worked with Domaine Chatelain for Pouilly Fumé, Domaine Jean-Max Roger in Sancerre, Prince Poniatowski in Vouvray, Château de Fesles in Anjou, and Monmousseau who produced our own volume-orientated brand called Vouvray La Coulée d'Or. From Alsace we listed Jerome Lorentz, Schlumberger, and later Josmeyer. In short, together we were pioneers for the selection and export of single-estate wines, especially from Burgundy and the Rhône. In Burgundy, many of the great domaines already had importers but we were behind the success of a number of fine estates that had not previously been exported to the US.

In 1983, after lengthy negotiations with Albert Vuillier, owner of Château Rieussec, Première Cru Classé in Sauternes and Gérard Gribelin, owner of Château de Fieuzal, Cru Classé in the Graves (now in the Pessac-Léognan appellation), we signed up for the exclusivity of these two prestigious properties for the US. Neither château relied on the Bordeaux open market to sell their wines, preferring to have a direct relationship with their customers by granting the exclusivity to specific importers in each country. We arranged a few trips to the US, one for Gérard Gribelin accompanied by Dominique Lafon of Domaine des Comtes Lafon who was working at Le Serbet at the time. We had some success but these were not inexpensive wines and, despite their notoriety, they were not easy to sell. When the market changed in 1985, after the exchange rate became less favourable, we discontinued the project and Château de Fieuzal reverted to the Bordeaux open market. Château Rieussec was purchased by the Rothschild family of Château Lafite Rothschild. One day I was summoned to Paris by Albert Vuillier who introduced me to Eric de Rothschild at the offices of his family bank. Afterwards we went to lunch at the nearby Crillon Hotel. The outcome was Europvin would lose the exclusivity for Château Rieussec in the US but would receive a larger allocation *en-primeur* of all the Rothschild properties. A satisfactory arrangement that continues today.

Later we included Europvin's Spanish selections in the C&W portfolio. The best known were Bodegas Muga and Remelluri in Rioja, Bodegas Mauro in the Duero, Marqués de Griñón's wines from Rueda and Toledo, Scala Dei from Priorat, and other wineries from Toro and Navarra. In those early days we were only partially successful as we did not appreciate the expectations for volume from some of the producers. I still remember an argument with Jaime Rodriguez of Remelluri who could not understand why New York could not absorb more wine than his native Basque Country. Muga was another winery that was impatient for more volume and consequently went to another importer. As a replacement we were fortunate in being able to sign up La Rioja Alta S.A. for the US and gradually established a very successful long-term presence for the winery.

Our first trips included stops in Boston, New York, Chicago, Detroit, Seattle, Portland, and San Francisco. We met with a number of motivated young importers who were enthusiastic about our project. It was not long before we were shipping mixed containers to several states. The market was very open to French wines at the time with a favourable exchange rate and, apart from Italy, little competition from other countries. Distributors were obtaining import licenses and bypassing the long-established national importers, selecting wines not yet available in the US. Many of these new operations were extremely

Europvin tasting room with Chip Delsener from Detroit.

successful and ended up being taken over by larger importers in the 1990s. A few of the new importers are still operating today and continue as customers for Europvin and Le Serbet. Others have been absorbed by large importers or have simply gone out of business.

I remember receiving our first order from Chip Delsener of AHD Vintners in the top-floor bar of a Detroit hotel, a full-mixed container from all corners of France. Chip is still a customer for our own Clos Figueras domaine. I also recall my first meeting with Phil Diamond, a San Francisco–based lawyer who founded his own wine import company with Becky's help in 1977. The relationship with Diamond Wine Merchants flourished over the years to the extent that Europvin almost purchased the company in the mid-2000s. A very large proportion of their portfolio was from Cannan & Wasserman and later from Europvin.

Our first trip to Chicago included a meeting with Peter Rudiger, the colourful director of Orange Wine Merchants who owned an unforgettable 1960s green car which he called his "mean green machine"! Later we met the owners of the Chicago Wine Company, an auction house who put us in touch with Sam Leavitt, who was in business to import wines for them. The company was called the Direct Import Wine Co. and became one of our largest customers despite a few upsets, the worst being the loss of a container of expensive Burgundies falling off a train and an uncooperative insurance company making their cash flow problematic. One memorable moment in Chicago in early 1983 was visiting Sam's, an immense liquor store in a warehouse basement. Robert Parker's notes on the legendary 1982 vintage in Bordeaux had just been published and Sam's wine buyer, Mr. Silverman, ordered a full container of the prominent wines, no doubt the largest order in value we had received to date.

Another Chicago contact was Pete Stern, a wealthy local resident with a superb apartment on Lake Shore Drive and a wine store called Connoisseur Wines. His passion and enthusiasm for wine was boundless and he made regular purchases from the entire C&W portfolio in small quantities. It so happened his wife, Florence, had the same birthday as me, albeit not the same vintage. I remember a superb dinner in his apartment overlooking Lake Michigan with a bottle of Lafite Rothschild 1949 in pristine condition, my birth year and my first opportunity to taste a First Growth of that legendary vintage. Pete and Florence came to France regularly and on one tour in the Loire Valley his love of sweet Chenin Blanc wines became the main theme. After a visit to Prince Poniatowski in Vouvray we were welcomed at Château de Fesles in Anjou where a bottle of the sublime 1947 vintage was opened. Pete was in heaven.

Indeed, we met several colourful personalities and had numerous memorable moments, one when we were invited to an ice-hockey match with Peter Rudiger, a unique experience and ambiance that could only be Chicago. Another was when we visited Seattle with the Duc de Magenta. We were met by a restaurant owner and wine merchant, Harry Alhadeff, in his new Jaguar. At the time a phone in a car was a novelty and Harry was on the phone before we left the airport to check he had a table for us in his restaurant. On arrival we were the only guests in a huge restaurant with eighty empty tables!

In time our markets matured and we set up strong relationships in most of the important states. In Boston we had an embarrassing start. Becky arranged for us to meet the owners of the Winecellar of Silene, Jim and Lucie Hangstefer. They decided to visit us in Bordeaux on the same day and the same time as Carmine Martignetti, their closest competitor. Somehow it all worked out and we were able to cooperate very successfully with both companies. Later we linked up with M.S. Walker, a long-established spirits producer run by the Shaw family. I had met Doug Shaw in Bordeaux in 1977 and we became close friends. The company started importing fine wines in the early 1980s and almost their entire French portfolio reflected our catalogue. In Washington DC we had a broker, Todd Ruby, another colourful character and a brilliant salesman, provided he liked the wine he was selling. His enthusiasm for the wines he liked was infectious and irresistible. As well as DC he looked after our interests in Maryland, Virginia, and North Carolina.

One evening I received a phone call from Steven Spurrier, at the time owner of the Caves de la Madeleine in Paris. He told me about a wealthy widow called Connie von Schultess in Fort Lauderdale, Florida, who was looking to find an occupation for her companion. She had decided to import wines and was looking for assistance in France. It turned out that Connie did most of the work and succeeded in befriending influential restaurant owners in the area. She purchased important quantities of expensive wines until finally the companion left and she became bored with the hassle of the wine business. I still have fond memories of my visits to her in Florida and the Sunday fishing trips in the open Atlantic she arranged with her cousin. Later she introduced us to two brothers from Nicaragua, Roberto and Aldo Serrano. They had a small import business in Miami handling almost exclusively the Italian selections of Neil Empson. After some hesitation they took on our portfolio with considerable success. Over the years the Serrano family became close friends and our Clos Figueras continues to do business with them to this day, even after their company was taken over by the giant Southern Wine & Spirits. Aldo Serrano eventually left Southern but continues to act as our ambassador. In November 2015 my wife and I accepted an invitation to visit the family in Nicaragua, where we spent a delightful and fascinating few days admiring the spectacular scenery and tourist-free ambiance.

In Colorado we linked up with the Tindall Family Wine Company. Mr. Tindall had nine children, many of whom were involved with the company. Over a period of a few years, they purchased serious quantities of wines and spirits from our entire portfolio. This added up to about three or four full containers each year until the relationship suddenly stopped and the company disappeared without explanation in the late 1980s. In Oregon, on the trip with the Duc de Magenta in 1981, we called on the Lemma Wine Company in Portland after spending the night at the recently established Adelsheim Vineyard. Lemma was another independent family distributor, with all four children involved. We worked with them until late 2018 when they decided to close their doors after suffering strong competition from large distributors in the Northwest. In Washington State we worked mainly with retailers who imported our wines through various importers. The owners of the stores used to visit us every year and select their wines during their trips – a phenomenon that was becoming increasingly rare in the 1980s as retailers relied more and more on the power of the press to make their purchases, neglecting their true vocation as a wine merchant making their own selections.

In California, our relationship with Diamond Wine Merchants was especially strong in the San Francisco area. As time went on Diamond, in spite of a few ups and downs, became one of our largest customers in the world, with substantial purchases of Burgundy and Rhône wines and later with our Spanish portfolio. Indeed, Phil Diamond and his collaborators became close business partners and friends over the years. Sadly, Phil died in 2014 having sold the company a few years earlier. Today the company no longer exists.

In the early days we also shipped considerable quantities of various wines to Kermit Lynch, a successful retailer in Berkeley, California. These included Bordeaux Petits Châteaux, Clos Ste. Magdeleine from Cassis, and Domaine de Durban, famous for their Muscat de Beaumes de Venise. As Kermit's company expanded out of California, he became more and more a competitor and finally decided to purchase all the wines directly. Kermit going national caused us considerable difficulties since Kermit convinced the producers of his requirement of national exclusivity for the distribution of a number of estates important to us, including Lassalle Champagne, Auguste Clape in Cornas, and Domaine du Vieux Télégraphe, all of which we were distributing outside California.

In New York we initiated our relationship with Barry Bassin who had recently founded what was to become a dynamic and exciting importer with an outstanding portfolio of prestigious wines. Barry was from Washington DC, from the same family that owns MacArthur Beverages, one of the most successful retailers in the country. For our small company he was a very important client, purchasing container quantities of high-value wines. His enthusiastic sales team introduced our selections to many of the most popular restaurants of the day in New York City.

Apart from Cannan & Wasserman his catalogue consisted of a number of prestigious names including Aubert de Villaine for his Bouzeron wines and Jacquesson Champagne. Tragically the success story was not to last. In 1986, due to a number of factors, the Bassin company ran into financial trouble and could no longer pay their outstanding invoices. This represented an important amount for Europvin and Le Serbet. Luc Savatier took charge of the situation and did everything he could to recuperate as much as possible of the assets (mostly unsold stock) not only for Europvin and Le Serbet but also for other producers in France. This was only partially successful and the strain was such that the situation caused the demise of the Cannan & Wasserman association. The companies continued their separate ways as Europvin and Le Serbet, ultimately surviving successfully to maintain their long-term commitment to the fine wine trade.

This was a sad moment because it was becoming evident that our association with the selection and logistics of shipping wines from small producers was very much in demand. Furthermore, we represented some prestigious brands that acted as a locomotive for the overall success of the portfolio. Had we been able to remain together I feel sure we would have continued to become a very important source and brand on the imported wine scene in the US. Nevertheless, our few years of working together were exciting times and, apart from the Bassin demise, very successful.

PART TWO

MARKETS

Travelling the World

While at Europvin we gradually developed our international network to cover over fifty countries in all the continents. After founding Clos Figueras in Priorat in 1997 and Laurona in Montsant in 1999, I had to rework the network to integrate these two new projects, at times with the assistance of Europvin. Later, in Europe and the US, we sold the wines directly to the importers. Europvin continued offering the wines in parts of Asia. By 2022 Clos Figueras was present in twenty-five countries in spite of the small volumes produced. Laurona has since been sold.

CHAPTER 6

EUROPE

Laying the Foundations

UNITED KINGDOM

In the early days of Europvin, England was by far our most important market. Over the years the situation has changed with a tendency for importers to buy directly from the producers. This said, Europvin has allocations of Bordeaux Classified Growths *en-primeur*, estate-bottled Burgundies, and some sought-after Rhône wines that continue to be of interest to British importers. Loire wines, especially from Sancerre and Pouilly-Fumé, have always been very successful. Compared to the US, trading in the UK is relatively simple. We supply the importers directly and they sell on to their respective customers whether they be private consumers, retailers, or restaurants. Many have their own retail outlets and import their own selections: the classic role for good independent wine merchants.

The list of our importers is long and includes many that continue in business today. Among other well-known names, exports were made to Harrods and Fortnum & Mason, both high-profile stores in London. We also had a special relationship with my friend Michael Davies, who owned a number of wine shops called Davisons. Michael gave me great support from the very first days of Europvin, buying large quantities, mostly from Bordeaux, Burgundy, and the Loire. We would meet regularly at his Croydon offices and during his annual trip to Bordeaux with his father. Frequently we would have lunch with the De Bournazel family at Château de Malle, an architectural jewel and Cru Classé in Sauternes. Mike purchased large quantities of their red Graves, Château de Cardaillan.

In the early days I used to drive to the UK. Traffic in London was bearable and parking quite easy, although on one visit I had to collect my car from the pound in Elephant and Castle, paying the corresponding fine. I drove all over London visiting our various customers and at weekends I drove to my parents' home in Gloucestershire. We had a customer in the Cotswolds called Broadwell Vintners. One day in 1979 I took my father, who had retired from the electrical engineering industry, for lunch with Ian Maitland-Hume and his team at Broadwell Vintners. By the end of the day, they had signed up my father for a role as their agent for South Gloucestershire. The company only sold wines to private consumers and, for four years, my father delivered numerous cases to his friends and acquaintances in the area. Every year a tasting was arranged at Chavenage House, a beautiful sixteenth-century manor house nearby. On doctor's orders he had to abandon this activity in 1983 due to problems with his war wounds. He much enjoyed his short period in the wine trade, meeting many people and making new friends.

Our small sales team at Europvin was almost exclusively English or Irish. For a time, Julia Wilkinson was our permanent representative based in London. She took care of the sales in the UK, Ireland, and Scandinavia and continues today, but now based in Bordeaux. Julia became the buyer for the Rhône Valley and Burgundy, taking over the responsibility from me, negotiating the allocations from highly sought-after domaines. Many of these allocations are destined for the British and Irish markets. Apart from a short stint with Fortnum & Mason, Julia has been a loyal employee at Europvin since 1988. She is much respected by producers for her tasting skills and a huge asset to the company in the fickle environment of Burgundy.

Another importer who contributed to our success in the early days was Tony Laithwaite's Bordeaux Direct, now one of the largest direct-to-consumer importers in the world. They purchased large quantities of Vieux Château Landon in the Medoc and a Rioja from Marqués de Cáceres we were selling under our own registered brand name called Grandeza. This worked well until it was discovered that an English merchant had also registered the name Grandeza in 1911 but hardly ever used it. The Spanish patent authorities had not done their homework but they took our money anyway.

Back in 1980 I first met Jasper Morris when he was working in a Fulham Road wine shop called Birley and Goedhuis. Mark Birley owned the London nightclub Annabel's, arguably one of the most elegant clubs in the world, and Jonathan Goedhuis was at school with me at Milton Abbey. Jasper became the world's youngest Master of Wine and founded an import company, Morris & Verdin, initially based in Oxford then relocated to London. He purchased almost all of his selections from Europvin, including Burgundies supplied by Becky Wasserman. I recall an extensive tasting of Domaine Daniel Rion from the Côte de Nuits in Jasper's London flat with the legendary Harry Waugh. The range of wines purchased by Jasper was considerable, including several from the Loire Valley, Bordeaux, and elsewhere. Over the years the selection changed but Jasper remained loyal to Europvin and purchased wines from the same producers year after year until he finally sold the company to Berry Bros. & Rudd, England's oldest wine merchant, originally established in 1698. Jasper was their Burgundy buyer for a time before moving to Burgundy and becoming an independent consultant and writer. His books *Inside Burgundy* (the first and second editions) are masterpieces. Recently Jasper told me that the first order he placed for Morris & Verdin was with Europvin for one hundred cases of Pouilly Fumé from Jean-Claude Chatelain.

Today our wines from Clos Figueras are imported by Fortnum & Mason for their store in Piccadilly and by Georges Barbier, a cousin of René Barbier of Clos Mogador in Priorat. Georges and his family specialise in selling to prestigious hotels and restaurants in London, giving our wines excellent international exposure.

IRELAND

Ireland was always important to Europvin. In the 1980s Gérard Jaboulet introduced me to Sue O'Connell, an energetic character from an old Irish family who wanted to join the world of wine. She became a huge asset to the company, helping me with the travelling, principally in the US, and accompanying customers to visit producers. We also visited Ireland together. In the 1990s Sue moved on to found a public relations company in London, representing prestigious wineries.

One of our importers went by the very Irish name of Paddy Callaghan. He lived in Dublin but specialised in selling wines to private clients and country hotels in the west of Ireland. He had a small car full of samples and would drive from hotel to hotel taking orders. For many years he purchased the same wine selection, remaining loyal to his list. With every shipment there was our Sancerre and our Châteauneuf-du-Pape; no decent wine list could be without these two appellations.

Other importers included Grants of Ireland and Karwig Wines. The late Joe Karwig, based in Cork, was of German origin and spoke with a strange mixture of Irish and German accents. He imported an eclectic range of wines and showed great loyalty. His company was founded in 1979 and was closed in 2019 after his sudden death in 2015. We supplied him throughout the entire existence of the company.

Not long ago I received a call from an Indian friend, Harshal Shah. I first met Harshal while promoting Guigal in India. A little later I met him, again promoting Guigal, this time in Australia. After helping successfully found Pembroke Wines in Dublin, voted as the best fine wine merchant of the year in 2019 by the Irish press, Harshal had a short stint in the restaurant business before deciding to set up another wine import company. During his time at Pembroke, Harshal took on the distribution of our Clos Figueras, selling to hotels and restaurants across the country. The company organised impressive tastings in the autumn, giving me the opportunity to stay with Peter Crosse, my old friend from my earliest days in Bordeaux, who lives near Dublin with his Irish wife and three daughters.

HOLLAND

Holland was another country that contributed extensively to the early success of Europvin. I have already mentioned my friendship with the late Theo van Broekhuizen and his support from the very first days of Europvin's existence, purchasing sizeable quantities from our selection of Burgundy estates. Included in the lineup was a Sancerre from Domaine du Nozay, belonging to the brother-in-law of Aubert de Villaine, co-proprietor of the Domaine de la Romanée-Conti. The first shipment was in 1980 with further exports continuing to this day, more than forty years later. Theo also supported our family winery, having included our Clos Figueras in his portfolio.

Later Theo introduced us to another small independent wine merchant in Utrecht called Van Wageningen & de Lange founded in 1886 and owned by Menno and Dinike ten Berge. They became close friends and loyal customers during my entire time at Europvin. On my first visit to their historic wine cellar, beside a canal in the centre of Utrecht, they offered me a glass of Sancerre. It was delicious, quite rich, and not too acidic as some Sancerre is inclined to be. It was from a grower called Jean-Max Roger, whose vineyards and cellar are located in the village of Bué on the southern edge of the appellation. Subsequently, Jean-Max became one of Europvin's largest suppliers. We shipped thousands of cases, mostly to England and Ireland. Menno had such perfect conditions for ageing wines in a labyrinth of fourteenth-century underground cellars: his strategy was to purchase wines young and age them until they made perfect drinking for his customers, an admirable practice so seldom applied today. Shortly after the 125th anniversary of the company, Menno retired and sold his shares. The couple were passionate golf players and insisted we play with them during their visits to Bordeaux. A disaster since, with my wife, we were no match for Menno and Dinike.

BELGIUM AND LUXEMBOURG

For Europvin, Belgium was never a big market. Being so close to France, and many speaking the same language, most purchases were made directly from producers. Over the years we did, however, have a few regular customers for Bordeaux and Loire wines. When we started we had a broker called Ludwig Cooreman. He sold various wines to the smaller traditional importers in the Flemish part of the country. Today we use this same model for our Clos Figueras wines. Our agents, Steve Michaels and his French wife Karine, have listed our Clos Figueras wines with seven different small, family-owned distributors and retailers. Every year I visit these customers with Steve. Some are specialised in selling to top restaurants, giving me the opportunity to enjoy some outstanding lunches and dinners.

The Belgians love their food, and gastronomy being important, Belgium is one of the largest markets for fine wines in the world. Back in the 1970s almost exclusively Bordeaux was consumed, especially from St. Emilion and Pomerol, where a number of Belgian families have invested. Burgundy was important in Wallonie, the French-speaking part of Belgium; consumers can drive to Burgundy in three hours and to Champagne in less than two. Today the situation has changed radically, Italian wines now having a strong foothold with the spread of Italian restaurants. Spanish wines are also more sought after. In short, Belgium, like England, is a dynamic mature market where quality wines from all parts of the world can be found easily and are consumed with enthusiasm.

Luxembourg, being a small country, is not a big market, but due to its geographic position and many European institutions, there is plenty of demand for wines in the upper price category. We had little business in the early days but did, however, make regular shipments of Coulée-de-Serrant made by the biodynamic maverick Nicolas Joly to the Caves Bernard-Massard, a large sparkling wine producer. Joly's wines needed long ageing and were not easy to sell, and soon the importer's stocks backed up and he discontinued his purchases. Through my connections with Romanée-Conti

I met Gérard Wengler, their importer for Luxembourg. Gérard has among the finest portfolios in the country with a very strong emphasis on Burgundy, as well as high-profile estates from all over the world. He agreed to take on our wines from Clos Figueras for Luxembourg, where we were in illustrious company until he decided our wines were not adapted to his clientele. Instead, Johan Tisserand, a young and enthusiastic Catalan from Barcelona, is making successful placings for our wines in the finest restaurants.

FRANCE

France was never a priority for Europvin but we did have some interesting clients. When we started exporting Lustau Sherries and Churchill's Ports we kept some stock in our Bordeaux warehouse. This allowed us to supply small quantities to customers in France. In Paris we had an independent agent called Philippe Céalis. He sold these wines on a regular basis to restaurants and independent wine merchants with some success. Occasionally I would go to Paris and accompany Philippe to visit his customers and conduct tastings, notably at Lafayette Gourmet, the wine department at Galleries Lafayette.

Our most influential encounter was with Jean-Claude Vrinat, the owner of Taillevent, at the time a three-star Michelin restaurant in Paris. The introduction was from Robert Parker. Vrinat came to visit us in Bordeaux when he was looking to source wines for a new wine store he was about to open on the Rue du Faubourg Saint-Honoré in 1987. He did not have time to ferret out a selection of wines for the opening so he came to taste a wide range in our office. Indeed, the first selection for Les Caves Taillevent was almost exclusively from Europvin. This changed over time as various sommeliers became involved with the selection. Some of the wines featured on the restaurant wine list, and for a number of years our Entre-deux-Mers, Château Tertre de Launay from the Greffier family, was the first wine on the list. Other wines and spirits we supplied to Taillevent included Churchill's Port, Cossart Gordon Madeira, Dolin Vermouth from Chambéry, Vega Sicilia, Malt Whisky, Van Winkle Bourbon Whiskey, Early Landed Vintage

Cognac from Hine and Delamain, and Caribbean Rum aged and bottled in the UK. We even sold a 25-year-old Lustau Sherry Vinegar for the kitchen!

Apart from the selection for Les Caves Taillevent, Vrinat asked me to find some interesting spirits for the store and restaurant. Specifically, he wanted a Cognac from the Hine cellars and an Armagnac, both under his own Taillevent label, with the previously mentioned selection of malt whiskies and rums from my contacts in Scotland. Our relationship with Taillevent lasted well into the 1990s, but now that Jean-Claude Vrinat has passed away and the restaurant been sold, we have lost contact. It was, however, a very rewarding experience since Vrinat, like any great restaurateur, was a stickler for detail and never compromised on quality. More about our relationship with Vrinat follows in relation to Japan.

GERMANY

Germany is no doubt the largest European market for imported wines. We have been present since the very first days of Europvin. I have already mentioned our relationship with importer Kiefer in Saarbrücken who gave us tremendous support until the mid-1980s when the Kiefer couple divorced and eventually retired, closing down the operation. During that period, we worked with other large importers, the best known and most powerful being Schlumberger who purchased full truckloads of good-value Bordeaux. In central Cologne there was a reputable wine store called Fegers & Unterberg who was always on the lookout for well-priced Classified Growths and other prestigious wines. In Northern Germany we had dealings with Adolf Segnitz, one of Germany's oldest and most traditional importers, founded in Bremen over 155 years ago.

As in Holland, our business in Germany declined over the years as German companies steadily started sourcing their wines directly from the producer. At the same time, Europvin's business became more and more orientated to countries outside Europe, where we could be of more service to importers.

Today, Germany is of renewed importance due to the need to establish a good presence for our Clos Figueras. The market is fragmented, with numerous regional importers and few national importers. This degree of fragmentation into regions has the advantage for the producer of having several importers, with many of them being small to mid-sized family concerns who carefully select their portfolio. We currently have a presence in Berlin, as well as in the areas around Stuttgart, Munich, Frankfurt, and Düsseldorf. With a strong belief in the future of fine wines in Germany, we are trying to expand to other regions.

SWITZERLAND

In past years Switzerland was always a small market for Europvin. We only had one regular customer, called Les Crus d'Origine, based in Lausanne. The company specialised in selling directly to private consumers through an army of representatives who would visit customers in their homes. This was an expensive way to operate which meant, in order to avoid conflicts over pricing, Les Crus d'Origine needed to have the national exclusivity for the wines they were importing. Consequently, they purchased the same wines from us, all from Bordeaux, over a period of thirty years.

Switzerland has always been a successful market for Spanish wines. After the creation of Laurona and Clos Figueras, the country immediately became our most important European market. Today for Clos Figueras we have several importers that are specialised in different sectors of the trade. Geographically they are widely spread out with a particularly strong presence in Zürich through Gerstl, who maintain an impressive inventory of one of the most serious collections of European fine wines in the country. They purchase all our wines as well as our olive oil and honey. In Berne, Lausanne, and Valais we work with smaller companies who regularly purchase small quantities.

AUSTRIA

Our presence in Austria had more to do with glass than wine due to our one-time association with Georg Riedel. Nevertheless, we have always had customers in Austria, especially a well-stocked wine store on the St. Stephen's Cathedral Square in the centre of Vienna called Vinothek St. Stephan. Later, on a visit to Riedel with Pablo Alvarez of Vega Sicilia, I met Peter Morandell, importer for Vega Sicilia. Peter is also the importer for Romanée-Conti, which gave me several opportunities to meet him at the Domaine. This long-established company is based in Wörgl in the heart of the Austrian Alps and specialises in servicing the hotels and restaurants in the ski resorts. They have an office and sales team in Vienna as well. Clos Figueras is now part of their portfolio, giving us exposure to some prestigious accounts.

On this same trip with Pablo, we met Georg Riedel at his glass factory not far from Wörgl. It was not the first time I had visited Georg and on the first occasion, over a bottle of Austrian Riesling, we discussed his theory that wine tasted different in different glasses. He then invited me to join a tasting for the choice of the ideal glass for the Syrah grape, which took place a few weeks later at the three-star Michelin restaurant La Maison Pic in Valence, with Robert Parker in attendance and a number of the most celebrated Rhône producers. Twelve glasses were put in front of us from large to quite small but all different. Throughout the three-hour tasting, some outstanding Northern Rhône wines were served and the glasses gradually eliminated as their suitability was questioned. Finally, we were down to just two glasses. During a superb dinner at Pic, Georg explained to us that he would send us prototypes of the most suitable glasses and we were to test them over time to see which one we preferred and eventually send him our observations. A choice was made and the Syrah glass created in the same way as others for a range of red and white grape varieties and appellations. This dynamic approach has put a whole new perspective on tasting wines. It is evident that the shape and size of the glass considerably impacts the aromas and taste of wines of all descriptions and origins.

During the meeting with Pablo we discussed the idea of a visit to Spain, where Riedel had no presence in the mid-1990s. Having strong connections in Rioja and Oporto we put together an extensive trip to select specific glasses for Rioja, Vega Sicilia, and Port. With my wife we drove to Bilbao to pick up Georg at the airport and take him first to Rioja. The trip started badly since Georg had left his wallet on the counter at Barcelona airport while connecting from Austria. Some considerable time and hassle were needed to retrieve the wallet. The Rioja glass tasting was held in the dining room at La Rioja Alta S.A. in Haro, with members of various bodegas and a representative of the Rioja Control of Origin also invited. We went through the same process as for the Syrah glass and decided on the perfect shape for the specific style of classic Rioja. In the end the glass was not adopted, perhaps because the focus on single grape varieties, notably the Tempranillo, was better suited to the project. Also, there are various styles of Rioja, ranging from a modern international style to the classic American oak aged wines dating from the pre-phylloxera period.

After such a big tasting, followed by a substantial lunch at the generous invitation of La Rioja Alta, driving to Vega Sicilia was quite a challenge. We stayed overnight at the Vega Sicilia property and the following morning repeated the process of glass selection for the famed Unico wine from Vega Sicilia. The conclusion, after a superb tasting of several vintages of Unico, was that the Bordeaux red wine glass was the most suitable. Georg designed a glass with a longer stem and the Bordeaux shape exclusively for Vega Sicilia. After another hefty lunch we drove on to Ciudad Rodrigo on the Portuguese border. We stayed at the Parador and the next day drove to Oporto in time for a lunch and another glass experience with the Port trade community at the Factory House.

The Factory House is a historic building constructed back in the late eighteenth century by the British nationals trading and living in Portugal. Today it is used exclusively by the British Port producers as a club with a traditional lunch every Wednesday when the trade, visitors, and Portuguese nationals working in the British-owned companies meet and discuss matters of mutual interest. It was at one of these Wednesday lunches that Johnny Graham of Churchill's Port organised the usual glass elimination exercise for Georg Riedel. After much deliberation a glass was chosen and later produced but the British in Oporto, being very conservative, mostly preferred to keep their small balloon-shaped glasses for their Port. Nevertheless, a few houses, including Churchill's, invested in the new Riedel Port glasses.

Georg left us after lunch to fly back to Austria and following this trip it was decided that Europvin should represent Riedel in the Iberian wine trade. This worked for a short time but soon we realised it was not our business to sell glasses. Georg found an alternative solution with our friend Jordi Segura in Catalonia, who continues today supplying Riedel glasses very successfully throughout Spain.

SCANDINAVIA

At Europvin we did some business in Denmark, Norway, and Finland but it was small and irregular. Sweden was by far our most successful market in Scandinavia largely due to our friend Janake Johannsson. I initially met Janake in Bordeaux back in 1972 when he was working for the Swedish retail monopoly Systembolaget and I was just starting my career in wine with Eschenauer. Later on, to my surprise and pleasure, I received a phone call from Janake in the early 1990s. He told me he had left the monopoly and was now working with an independent agent. Not long before, the import monopoly in Sweden had been disbanded at the request of the European Community but the retail monopoly was allowed to continue. The agents could now handle the importation for the retail monopoly and sell directly to restaurants.

Thanks to Janake's special relationship with Systembolaget we were able to establish a strong presence in Sweden. He changed companies a few times, eventually founding his own company called the Janake Wine Group, and of course we followed him. Additionally, we arranged for Janake to obtain the agency for Vega Sicilia and other important brands. Janake also represented our own Clos Figueras, selling Serras del Priorat directly to restaurants, creating a loyal following. Janake's company has now been sold to a larger group who continue to represent our wines with success.

It was not all work as we had some fun too. On one visit with my wife, a trip was organised with Janake and his wife along the Göta Canal which runs all the way from Stockholm to Gothenburg on the west coast. For two days we travelled on a narrow one-hundred-year-old wooden boat in relative comfort. The cabins were tiny, necessarily so, because the canal is so narrow with numerous locks. During the journey we conducted tastings for our few fellow travellers. It was not hard work, so we had plenty of time to enjoy the quiet country scenery and superb weather.

It is a pity that Sweden continues to have a monopoly on all alcohol sales since it greatly restricts the choice for consumers. It is a wealthy country with a huge potential for fine wines. The monopoly is becoming even more restrictive due to the tender system which is complex and expensive for small producers, giving them little chance to penetrate the market successfully. Some consumers have found ways to circumvent the system by buying directly online or by crossing over to Denmark where there is no monopoly and a wide choice of excellent wine merchants. Norway and Finland also have monopolies and are even more difficult markets to penetrate successfully. We did have some success in Iceland where, for some time, our importer from Europvin days, Jon Armannsson, supplied the few hotels and restaurants on the island with wines from Bordeaux, the Loire, Rhône, and Languedoc.

EASTERN EUROPE AND RUSSIA

As the Eastern European countries become wealthier, interest in fine wines is gradually growing. In fact, some countries, notably Hungary, Romania, and Bulgaria, are important producers making rapidly improving wines of great value. Poland has also become a wine-producing country, largely thanks to global warming.

For imports, Poland is our largest market in Eastern Europe, although we do send some wines to the Czech Republic. In Poland we have a loyal importer in Warsaw and in Sopot on the Baltic coast near Gdansk. To visit Sopot, the train from Warsaw used to take nearly five hours to cover just 320 kilometres (200 miles). Today I believe new trains cover the distance in three hours. But still, it used to be a pleasant ride on an almost empty train. Festus, our importer in Sopot, has several wine shops and a guest house at the disposal of visitors. It was always a pleasant visit to a delightful family-run wine merchant and an opportunity to admire the beautifully reconstructed city of Gdansk, after almost total destruction during the Second World War.

We began shipping wines to Russia in the early 2000s, initially to a company called Whitehall through Brett Crittenden, an Australian wine broker who was consulting for them at the time. The company was the importer for the Moët Hennessy group among others. I recall my first visit to their premises just opposite the Kremlin. Lunch in their offices, with an uninterrupted view of the Kremlin, was memorable for the never-ending copious servings of the very best caviar. This company has since fallen off the radar screen.

Our main partner for Russia was Fort Ltd. run by Sergey Kotov. From Europvin we shipped a wide range of wines, mainly from Bordeaux. They also took on our Clos Figueras for a time. I made a few trips to Moscow and had a chance to visit part of the city including an evening at the Bolshoi theatre, the magnificent Metro, and Red Square. There, on a cold snowy night with Rod Hull from Europvin, much to our chagrin, we were questioned by the police and feared they would take us to the nearby sinister Lubyanka prison! I also visited St. Petersburg with Fort's sales team and, on another occasion, with my wife, never ceasing to admire the magnificent architecture of the Tsar-era palaces.

However, the most memorable trip was to Nizhny Novgorod, a large city on the Volga some 400 kilometres (250 miles) east of Moscow. With Sergey, I took the train from Moscow to visit the local agent. What I thought was going to be a formal meeting turned out to be a very informal picnic. Six of

Sturgeon caught in the Volga at Nizhny Novgorod, Russia.

us were embarked on a small fishing boat and taken out to the middle of the wide Volga. There we started fishing and almost immediately caught as many sturgeons as we could manage. These are not the same sturgeons that provide caviar but a rather coarse but just edible fish. We then headed for the river bank, started a fire, and grilled the freshly caught fish for immediate consumption with a whole crate of beer as accompaniment. It was a long afternoon, since some members of the party decided to have a siesta. Others were talking in Russian, so I had to while away the time wandering along the river bank. Finally, we crawled back to the boat to cross over to Nizhny Novgorod and a substantial dinner before taking the train back to Moscow the next day. A strange and memorable experience for a wine merchant.

Russia is not an easy market. Although there are some fine restaurants and a demand for good European wines, the administration and logistics is not far short of a nightmare. No doubt as a form of protectionism, the government makes life very difficult for importers. Each new wine has to be registered and then issued with a special label that includes a traceability chip. The wines have to arrive in Russia with this chip. Since few producers are equipped to take care of this procedure the wines are sent to the Baltic countries where special warehouses finish the labelling before transport to Russia. If, for some reason, no chips are available, no wines can be imported. This happened on one occasion and I recall visiting wine stores in Moscow with empty shelves. Despite these difficulties, serious quantities of fine wines were being imported. Russia is a market to be cultivated for the future, however the recent war in Ukraine has, at least temporarily, halted imports of fine wines from Europe.

SOUTHERN EUROPE

For obvious reasons the wine-producing Mediterranean countries were not good customers. We did some work in Italy with the successful introduction of the Lustau Sherries. We also shipped small quantities of mostly Spanish wines to retailers looking for diversity in Piacenza; and to the legendary Trimani Enoteca in Rome, founded in 1821. We had an importer in Greece, and more recently an importer for our Clos Figueras in Portugal. In Spain we had, and still have, a strong connection to Vila Viniteca in Barcelona, to whom Europvin supplies allocations of top Burgundies and Rhône wines, also a few Bordeaux Classified Growths *en-primeur*. Spain, especially Catalonia, has today become an important market for our Clos Figueras wines, with listings in many of the best restaurants, especially in Barcelona and the Costa Brava. My daughter, Anne-Josephine, takes care of this activity with very positive effect.

CHAPTER 7

UNITED STATES AND CANADA

Challenge and Exhilaration

UNITED STATES

It is no secret that the US market is of the utmost importance in the world of wine, being the country with the largest potential for growth, and a strong economy. China may become more important one day but the US is a much more mature market, especially for fine wines. After the demise of Cannan & Wasserman in 1986 we continued to operate in the US using more or less the same network of distributors. Of course, after the separation from Becky, we sold less Burgundy and more wines from Bordeaux, the Loire, and Rhône Valley. However, what put Europvin soundly on the map in the US was our involvement with Spain, and the prestigious agencies we were able to sign up. Initially we represented a handful of wines, some of them becoming household names in time. As mentioned in the chapter on Cannan & Wasserman, these included Bodegas Muga and La Granja Remelluri from Rioja, Marqués de Griñón for his wines from Rueda and his estate in Toledo, and Cellers Scala Dei, one of only two single estates in Priorat in the early 1980s. With some of these agencies we underestimated their ambitions for the US market. This was especially the case with Muga and Remulluri and, to our disappointment, we lost both agencies due to their lack of patience. Both brands were unknown and needed time to become established.

Matters improved enormously when we established relationships with three important Spanish wineries, Emilio Lustau in Jerez in 1984 and by 1986, La Rioja Alta S.A and Vega Sicilia. For the US market, at the initiative of Rafael Balao, managing director of Emilio Lustau, we negotiated an agreement in 1990 for promoting the three bodegas together. We founded a joint venture called Europvin Iberia and hired a full-time representative, based in New York, to take care of the sales and promotion.

Our first delegate was Louis Broman who had previously worked at the now defunct Barry Bassin import company. Louis was passionate about all things Spanish. He had studied Spanish literature and spoke the language without an accent. He was an enormous asset and greatly contributed to our success with these brands. Later he left us to lead "Wines from Spain", the government-sponsored organisation that promotes all Spanish wines. Tragically, in the late 1990s, he contracted Aids and died far too young. Our next delegate was Todd Helmus, based in Boston, also a hard-working wine professional, who suddenly disappeared after a few years with Europvin Iberia. His disappearance remains a mystery – in spite of frequent enquiries, nobody in the trade has ever heard from him since. Later, in 2004, Jake Halper joined Europvin as our East Coast representative, after a few years with our New York distributor, Michael Skurnik Wines. Today Jake has his own import company.

During this period a Paris-based organisation called the Adhesion Group rented rooms for producers in the legendary Hotel Martinez on the seafront in Cannes. They invited American importers, all expenses paid, and arranged appointments for tastings with the producers in their sea-view rooms. Lunches and dinners with the importers were also arranged. This was ideal for Europvin, enabling us to make new contacts and open up a few new markets. The presence of a few colourful personalities made these events enjoyable and fun until disputes broke out between the retailers and the importers on issues concerning pricing. But still, the location and luxury of the Hotel Martinez made for a memorable experience.

Thanks to our efforts with numerous visits to the markets and reviews from the specialised press, notably from Robert Parker and the *Wine Spectator*, our principal Spanish brands gradually became more sought after. In the early 1990s none of these producers had a track record in the US; even Vega Sicilia was almost unknown apart from in pockets of New York and Florida. This also helped Europvin sell other brands, notably our success with Churchill's Port and our range of French wines, mostly focused on the Rhône Valley, Alsace, and the Loire. Later we added a selection of Italian wines to the portfolio and one German estate, the prestigious Dr. Bürklin-Wolf in the Pfalz. Having a reputation now for Spanish wines, Europvin started to represent some other estates. These included Bodegas Mauro owned by Mariano García, ex-winemaker at Vega Sicilia; René Barbier's Clos Mogador in Priorat; our own Clos Figueras in Priorat; and Espectacle in Montsant, a joint venture with René Barbier.

Every year in October we would participate in the New York Wine Experience, a prestigious event organised by the *Wine Spectator*. Over two evenings many of the most celebrated wineries in the world poured their wines for hundreds of wealthy consumers. We participated, serving wines from Vega Sicilia and La Rioja Alta, a worthwhile event for the promotion and prestige of the wineries.

Furthermore, the partners in Europvin Iberia owned other brands. In 1991, Vega Sicilia founded Bodegas Alión, a modern and elegant Ribera del Duero wine aged in new French oak barrels. In 2001 they launched Bodegas Pintia, a classic wine from century-old vineyards of Toro. They also acquired Oremus in Tokay, producing exquisite sweet wines from this celebrated appellation. La Rioja Alta owns Lagar de Cervera, producing dry, aromatic Albariños in Galicia and Aster in the Ribera del Duero. Lustau owns Viña Herminia in Rioja, Marqués de Irun in Rueda, and the celebrated La Ina Fino Sherry brand in Jerez. All of this, of course, kept us busy.

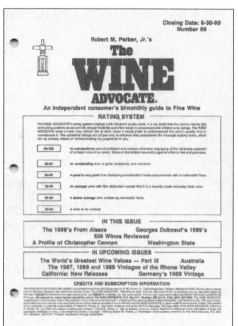

For a white wine in this price range, the 1989 from Sarda-Mallet has surprising body, roundness and generosity. A light intensity bouquet of flowers is followed by a wine with excellent concentration, good balance, and an ampleness that is reminiscent of some of the dry white wines of the Rhône Valley. Drink it over the next 1-2 years. The 1988 **Black Label** offering represents the top red wine cuvée from this producer as it is aged in oak casks. Consequently, the wine exhibits a big, roasted, ripe, blackcurrant bouquet, backed up with generous amounts of toasty new oak. In the mouth, there is considerable intensity, long black-cherry flavors, full body, and a serious, muscular finish. This is a big wine by any standards, and should continue to drink well for another 3-5 years.

| DOMAINE DU TARIQUET | 1989 CÔTES DU GASCOGNE | WHITE | ($4.69) | 85 |

In previous vintages, I have consistently recommended this wine as an excellent value. Produced from the Ugni Blanc grape, Tariquet is better than ever in 1989, no doubt because of France's torridly hot summer. There is more ripeness and opulence in the wine, but it remains a light to medium-bodied, crisp, deliciously fruity, fragrant wine. The price makes it a **sensational value**. Drink it over the next year.

| VEGA SICILIA UNICO | 1975 SPAIN | RED | ($82.00) | 96 |

It is irrefutable that Vega Sicilia produces Spain's greatest red wine. Further evidence of this is provided by the 1975 **Vega Sicilia Unico**, which has just been released. The price is high, but when you consider (1) less than 4,000 cases of this wine are made, (2) the winery will often age their Vega Sicilia Unico for 15-20 years before they release it, and (3) the quality is brilliant, then the price appears justifiable. The 1975 is still an amazingly young wine with a purple hue to its deep ruby color. The young, backward bouquet offers up sweet aromas of ripe plums, licorice, and plenty of toasty new oak. In the mouth, there is phenomenal concentration, unbelievable extract, and a fabulously long, ripe, voluptuous finish with gobs of tannin. After a decantation of several hours, this wine can be drunk with great pleasure, but it promises to continue to evolve for at least another 20-25 years. As a postscript, the winery has just released another allocation of their 1962 **Unico**; ($116.00), which I would rate 93 points. It is in amazing condition, has a deep ruby color, with a big, plummy, spicy, oaky bouquet, as well as exceptional concentration. Of course, it is more supple than the 1975, but I would fully expect it to continue to drink well for another 10-15 years. These wines are remarkable, and collectors of Vega Sicilia should be making reservations now to latch onto a few bottles of their 1968 and 1970, which have never been released, and which are considered by the winery to be the greatest wines they have made in the post-World War II era. The winery has intimated that these two vintages will be released in either 1991 or 1992.

The above selections represent only a small proportion of the wines selected by Christopher Cannan. I intentionally avoided covering his burgundies since I have reviewed many of them in previous issues of The Wine Advocate. His extensive selection of outstanding Rhône and Provence wines will be reviewed in the October issue, along with other wines of that region. Christopher Cannan also represents numerous estates in Bordeaux, many of which were reviewed in Issue 68's comprehensive look at the 1989, 1988, and 1987 vintages.

These are the wines of an exceptionally talented man, driven by his desire to represent the most interesting estates he can find in France and Spain. He is one of only a handful of wine brokers who truly holds the consumer's interest close to his heart. Both Cannan and his selections should be given serious consideration and enormous respect. With the exception of the well-known Spanish bodegas of Vega Sicilia and La Rioja Alta, the wines I have focused upon are all from relatively unknown estates. I hope responsible merchants make them available, and that consumers take the opportunity to stock up on some individualistic, flavor-filled, pleasure-giving wines.

"A Profile of Christopher Cannan" in the Wine Advocate, *June 1990.*

Europvin team with Robert Parker (centre) in the Bordeaux office.

Of special importance, and a large contributor to our success, was our relationship with Robert Parker, the world-famous, if controversial, wine critic. I met Bob back in 1981 when I arranged for him to visit Domaine du Vieux Télégraphe. From 1983, when he became famous thanks to his praise of the 1982 vintage in Bordeaux, he visited our offices regularly. We organised extensive tastings with wines from all parts of France, Spain, even Portugal and Italy on occasion. He liked this formula since he was able to taste a large number of different wines in one place. Sometimes up to 150 wines were tasted and the record was 200 wines during one very full day. Since he never visited Spain, it was also an opportunity to introduce him to Pablo Alvarez of Vega Sicilia; Carlos Falcó, Marqués de Griñón; and other important Spanish producers who joined us for the tastings. These tastings were memorable and continued over twenty-five years, sometimes in other locations, especially at Alain Graillot's cellar in the Rhône Valley and at The Oregon Grille restaurant, near Bob's home in Maryland. Bob always arrived on time, full of enthusiasm for what we had to show him. His positive notes and scores enabled us to put numerous wines on the map in the US and world markets. In 1990 he dedicated a wide section of his bi-monthly reviews to our selections. There is no question, whether one agreed with his evaluations or not, his influence was a huge contribution to our success and to the remarkable developments in quality over the past forty years. The style of wines he liked best were concentrated and intense, rather in the manner of the great Napa Valley Cabernet Sauvignons. Today the trend is towards more elegant and fresher wines, certainly more approachable and friendly for the consumer.

The growing importance of the Europvin Iberia brands began to put a lot of pressure on our small team. We had fixed sales targets that had to be met each year. This ultimately led us to open up the capital of Europvin to enable us to invest in the market and take sales to the next level. This was a difficult decision but we had little choice. In August 2003, after lengthy and complicated negotiations, Lustau invested in Europvin with Vega Sicilia. Initially Europvin maintained the majority shareholding but this changed over time. Later CVNE, the long-established Rioja house, purchased some of Lustau's shares. This caused a fundamental change since CVNE had very ambitious sales targets. Over two or three years, sales in the US of CVNE wines went from 3,000 cases to over 50,000 cases. This was a big strain on the company and led to other brands being neglected, and finally to the departure of CVNE from Europvin. Today Europvin is owned by Emilio Lustau and Vega Sicilia with an equal shareholding.

Going back a few years, the bureaucracy in the US became more and more complex. In order to have the correct licences in each state we needed to become an official importer. For many months we negotiated with our California distributor, Diamond Wine Merchants, for the purchase of the company. Eventually this did not work out so we settled on purchasing Golden State Wine Co., a sub-distributor of Diamond Wine Merchants based near Los Angeles. This has proved an excellent choice since Golden State Wine Co. has all the licences for importing, distribution, and retail.

Since the end of prohibition in 1933 the distribution of alcohol has been handled by each individual state. Each one has different regulations, many of which are still in place. Some states such as Pennsylvania are monopolies controlled exclusively by the state. Most of the other states opted for what is now called the three-tier system. This means wines and spirits must first pass through the hands of an importer, then a distributor before reaching the retailer or restaurant and eventually the consumer. Golden State is one of the very few companies that has all three licences. In other states Europvin is able to avoid one of the tiers by working directly with distributors who have import licences. This enables the company to remain competitive in the market. Furthermore, Golden State was previously owned and run by Mike Miller, an ace sales person who has close relationships with the top restaurants, retailers, and collectors in the Los Angeles area. Mike continues to make sure Europvin's priorities are well taken care of.

The difficulty today is that there are too few distributors, because most of the good medium-sized companies have been purchased by the larger groups. Just four of these mega-sized companies now control approximately 80% of the market, leaving little space for smaller companies to operate. This said, there is room for small, specialised companies catering predominately for the restaurant trade, and sommeliers looking to have diverse and eclectic wine lists. Many of these companies are fragile and have a hard time up against the giant operators.

Over the years this has meant that little effort is made by the larger distributors to sell the wines they have in their portfolio. They concentrate on taking orders for high-profile brands that often require little effort. They therefore rely on the producers, and exporters like Europvin, to come to the market and support the sales by visiting retailers and restaurant customers with their sales teams. These visits include trade tastings, workshops, winemaker's dinners for consumers, and staff training for the sales teams. It can be rewarding work but it is expensive and often impossible for small wineries. It is in this activity that Europvin excels, with a large portfolio of different wines from France and Spain. Consequently, Europvin had to increase their staff. Initially by more of the team travelling from Bordeaux and later, putting in place a full structure with a national sales manager based in the US and regional sales managers for the key markets.

I have participated in this activity since the 1980s and have been immensely fortunate to make many friends in the trade who loyally support our wines and activities. Today, no longer owning Europvin, I am able to take care of the sales for our own family winery, Clos Figueras, working directly with distributors in the US. Being present in a dozen states, I continue to visit the market regularly with a special focus on the key states including Massachusetts, Washington DC, Florida, Texas, Chicago, Michigan, Ohio, Minnesota, and California.

During my visits to California, I took advantage of opportunities to visit the Napa Valley and other prestigious regions. I have always admired the excellence of the wines and the enthusiasm of the producers. It is a remarkable success story in spite of a relatively short history. One of the most memorable visits was a lunch with the legendary Robert Mondavi and his wife, Margrit, on the terrace at their winery during a trip with Pablo Alvarez. This was followed by a visit to Opus One, founded as a joint venture between Robert Mondavi and Baron Philippe de Rothschild.

Another memorable visit was with my hospitable friends Paul Woolls and Betty O'Shaughnessy, owners of the O'Shaughnessy winery on Howell Mountain and Progeny on Mount Veeder. On one occasion they arranged a tasting for imported wines at the O'Shaughnessy winery which included our wines from our Clos Figueras and a number of the Europvin imports. This was a huge success but I understand the local authorities did not take kindly to imported wines being shown in the Napa Valley! Other notable visits included a visit to Au Bon Climat near Santa Barbara, belonging to our late friend and Burgundy enthusiast Jim Clendenen. More recently I visited several Napa and Sonoma wineries with my son, Edward, during his employment with Moët Hennessy. The group's most spectacular estate, Newton on Spring Mountain, was devastated by the fires of 2020. Hopefully this trend of catastrophic fires will become part of history as so much depends on overcoming this plight.

Charlotte and me with Ian and Marit Hanna (back left and back right),
our longtime agent in Ontario, Canada.

CANADA

Europvin's presence in Canada dates back to 1981. One morning we received
Jack and Pamela Hanna in our offices in Bordeaux. They were sent to us by
Gary Grosvenor, a mutual friend and broker for German wines based in the
Rheingau. The Hanna family owned an agency company in Toronto. The
Canadian market for wines and spirits is controlled by import and retail
monopolies in each province. It is essential to have an agent who has a
good relationship with the monopoly to take care of the sales and complex
bureaucracy involved in dealing with these huge organisations. In Quebec and
Ontario, they are the largest purchasers of wines and spirits in the world. We
signed up with Jack and Pam Hanna, the late founders of the company, and
have enjoyed a happy relationship with the family ever since. Today it is the
next generation, Ian and Marit Hanna, who are running the company with
their son, Andrew.

In the 1980s we had huge success with the LCBO (Liquor Control Board of
Ontario), the Ontario monopoly, shipping a wide range of wines from France

and later from Spain. The monopoly is not normally loyal to brands at the fine-wine level so shipments declined over the years, but we were able to maintain an ongoing presence for Lustau and some other brands. Today the competition for listings has become very tough but Europvin continues to send shipments of various wines on an ad-hoc basis according to opportunities in the different monopoly divisions and catalogues. There are also occasional openings to make small shipments of the agent's choice to sell directly to consumers. The whole process is strictly controlled by the LCBO, applying the usual taxation and import duties, leaving little margin for the agent. Our wines from Clos Figueras are frequently imported thanks to this system.

The legislation in other provinces is somewhat different. In Quebec the SAQ (Société des Alcools du Quebec), the monopoly, is inclined to be more loyal in their purchasing. We have had limited success over the years but with good agents we were always able to maintain a presence. More exciting for us was our relationship with a journalist and wine critic, Michel Phaneuf, who became famous for his annual wine guide for all the wines listed by the SAQ. We met Michel through Gérard Jaboulet and enjoyed a rewarding relationship with him over many years until his retirement. Apart from his journalistic activities he ran a wine club called Les Amitiés Bachiques. Every few months he would send us a list and purchase order of often very esoteric wines from our portfolio. These were all wines with no presence in Quebec and an ideal opening for lesser-known appellations. We would group together, often quite small quantities, and ship them to the SAQ, who would pass the wines on to the club taking their cut in taxes and import duties. With each shipment we would send samples of other wines so the selection could be made for the next shipment. This arrangement lasted many years until Michel retired in the early 2000s.

In Western Canada we had some success with the British Columbia monopoly, the BCLDB (British Columbia Liquor Distribution Branch) through the 1980s and 1990s. We had a special relationship with the purchasing manager, David Scholefield, who was very knowledgeable and would taste with much enthusiasm, buying most of the wines we showed him. After his departure from the BCLDB our presence became more difficult to maintain, although we had relationships with some wine stores who had licences enabling them to buy directly from us. In early 1999, the BCLDB felt that vast quantities of Champagne would be consumed during the night of 31st December 1999. They ordered at least a pallet from each of our Champagne suppliers. I understand their Champagne stocks, purchased at that time, lasted for many years. In the 1980s, we won the business-class wine listing for the Vancouver-based Canadian Pacific Air Lines. The wine was "R" de Rieussec, a dry white wine from the legendary Sauternes, Château Rieussec. This lasted for a few years until the fortunes of the airline declined and they eventually went out of business.

Alberta was another province of importance to us, especially after the retail monopoly was disbanded and the newly established importers and retailers could buy directly from us. We developed a strong relationship with some of the retailers. The economy was booming in the 1990s and early 2000s due to oil production but today, with US oil production on the increase, there is less demand for Canadian oil, and consequently the local economy is suffering.

Additionally, there is some limited activity in the smaller Canadian markets including the Maritime Provinces and Manitoba.

CHAPTER 8

JAPAN

The Land of
Rising Wine Expertise

My first encounter with Japan was in 1984. I purchased a round-the-world ticket in First Class with Air France and Northwest Airlines, my first and only trip in First Class of a 747. Direct flights to Japan were rare in those days. We stopped in Hong Kong and Taipei before arriving in Tokyo. It was a short visit since we only had a couple of clients in the country at the time – one was the President's Club of Japan; the other was located in Osaka and reached on the Shinkansen, Japan's high-speed train, the first of my many rides on this modern-day marvel. After a brief meeting in Osaka and a short trip on a local train I arrived in Kyoto where my Osaka client had arranged for me to stay in a ryokan, a traditional Japanese inn. The experience was a plunge into Japanese culture; the large wooden bath, the common bathing room, the classic Japanese dinner seated cross-legged on the tatami floor, served by a kimono-clad Japanese beauty. Finally, a thin mattress was rolled out on the tatami floor with a pillow as hard as a wooden bench. The next morning a Japanese breakfast was delivered to my room with miso soup, salmon fillets in soy sauce, and the ubiquitous sticky rice, served at an early hour.

Following my return to France, during a visit to the Brunier family at Domaine du Vieux Télégraphe in Châteauneuf-du-Pape, I had the good fortune to meet Doctor Iwano, a Japanese wine consultant, teacher, and a remarkable chronicler of information and statistics on wine, who travelled everywhere possible by train. At one point he was employed by the Chinese government to advise on viticulture in Southwest China, at a very high altitude on the borders of Tibet. A few weeks later he came to visit us at Europvin accompanied by two wine importers, Hatta Shoten and Seijo Ishii. After an extensive tasting, substantial orders were placed by both companies for a wide range of wines from all parts of France. This was in 1985, the start of the Japanese import boom for fine wines thanks to a strong economy and favourable business conditions, lasting until the financial crash in 1990.

During this period, I made numerous trips to Japan and created a very strong presence for a number of Europvin's suppliers in this difficult and unpredictable market. The most remarkable was the relationship with Hatta Shoten. This very traditional importer had a young consultant called

With Doctor Iwano in Japan in the 1980s.

Minoru Kanai. Minoru is a gastronome and has contacts with many of the best and most prestigious French, Chinese, and Japanese restaurants in the country. He was enamoured with the wines from Alsace. I recall an overnight stay in a ryokan near Hakone where, over breakfast, he ordered large quantities from the producer Rolly Gassmann. Later we introduced him to the wines from Josmeyer, a celebrated producer of some of the most sought-after Alsace wines. The late Jean Meyer, owner of this family estate, was a perfectionist and made wines of great elegance and purity, ideal for the Japanese taste. I was able to persuade Jean to visit Japan to help introduce his wines to the market. What followed was one of the worst moments in my career. Samples for the visit were sent in advance, but on arrival at our hotel in Tokyo we met Minoru, who announced that the samples had not arrived and that they were being held up by the Japanese customs. What to do and how embarrassing! Visiting customers without samples did not make sense. Luckily, Jean had brought three bottles of his finest wines with him. With these samples we conquered the market and Hatta Shoten soon became the number-one importer for Alsace in Japan, shipping hundreds of cases at a time. I believe the relationship between Josmeyer and Minoru continues to this day but not at the same volume level.

As is well known, Japanese restaurants strive for perfection in every domain, whether it be the freshness and presentation of the food, the service, or ambiance. I remember enjoying some of the finest meals of my entire life in French and Japanese restaurants accompanied by the exquisite Rieslings, Pinots Gris, and Gewurztraminers from Josmeyer.

The other adventure with Hatta Shoten was with Champagne. Through our relationship with Robert Parker, we were contacted by Jean-Claude Vrinat of Taillevent. As previously mentioned, Jean-Claude was looking for a source of supply for the opening of his wine shop on the rue Saint-Honoré near the restaurant. During our discussions, Jean-Claude mentioned his interest in exporting to Japan his own label Champagne, Cognac, and Armagnac. I thought Hatta Shoten would be interested and indeed, they were, since the name Taillevent is revered in Japan. The success and enthusiasm was phenomenal, so much so that they tried to convince Jean-Claude to visit Japan. Since he was unavailable, I was asked to come to Japan in his place to participate in tastings and events to help promote the brand and increase the sales. On arrival at the airport, I was treated like a VIP. It was the first and only time I was met at the airport, a distance of more than 50 kilometres (30 miles) from Tokyo. The Hatta Shoten team drove me to a printing house between the airport and Tokyo and, to my horror and surprise, presented me with visiting cards defining me as export director for Taillevent with the logo and address in Paris. This was some way from the truth and the cards had to be destroyed. The success with Champagne Taillevent continued for a few years and was complemented by the Taillevent Cognac and Armagnac, among other products. The arrangement continued until Jean-Claude linked up with Sapporo Breweries to found the spectacular Taillevent Robuchon restaurant in Tokyo.

The other activity that had significant success in Japan was our Spanish portfolio. The Sherries from Lustau initiated their presence in Japan with their elite range, the so-called Almacenista Sherries. Minoru Kanai organised Almacenista parties, events where Spanish tapas were served with flamenco dancing. It was strange to see Japanese women dancing the flamenco but, like in all fields, they did so to perfection. The export manager from Lustau, Manuel Grimaldi, would come to Japan from time to time with his guitar and sing to a raptured Japanese audience, all in the cause of introducing the Japanese to the beauty and versatility of fine Sherries. The lighter Fino and Manzanilla Sherries are ideal with such dishes as sushi and sashimi and, unlike table wines, can dominate the soy sauce, providing a perfect match.

We also represented Vega Sicilia and La Rioja Alta in Japan. Some of the trips with Lustau included Pablo Alvarez and Mariano García of Vega Sicilia as well as Guillermo de Aranzabal of La Rioja Alta. These trips were complex to arrange with numerous trade and consumer tastings as well as some delicious meals in Japan's finest restaurants. On one occasion we were received by the mayor of Sendai. Pablo had arranged a special gift for the mayor which he sent in advance. The anxiety was extreme when we feared the package would not arrive in time for the visit to the mayor with the consequential loss of face. Fortunately, all was well when the gift arrived a few minutes before the meeting in the town hall. These trips were memorable and entertaining, with constant good humour and lively conversation, especially with Mariano García, winemaker at Vega Sicilia at the time. Pablo was particularly enamoured with the high quality of Japanese beef from Kobe and Sendei. He always took some home to Spain in his luggage. Also of interest to Pablo were the local trees and plants that inspired him to create a Japanese garden at Vega Sicilia. With his concern for perfectionism this is now among the finest examples of a Japanese garden in Europe.

As previously mentioned, my gastronomic experiences in Japan were numerous and memorable. The quality of food and attention to detail is second to none. Among the most delightful was sampling sushi in the Imperial Hotel in

With Pablo Alvarez (front left) and Xavier Ausàs (front second right), in Japan.

Tokyo and in a small 10-seat bar in old town Kyoto, of such a quality that, in my view, sushi from anywhere else is relegated to second class. I also recall the quality of the beef in Sendai and the unagi or eel on sticky rice served in a large workers' restaurant under the railway arches in Tokyo with the Shinkansen rolling noisily overhead. I was the only foreigner in a 200-seat restaurant. Another time I had tofu in Fukuoka at ten in the morning. This tofu was renowned all over Japan. The owner had a refrigerated container full of First Growth Bordeaux in his courtyard. On requesting my birth-year, a bottle of Château Lafite Rothschild 1949 was produced and enjoyed with the superb tofu at that early hour! Other experiences included lunches at Fook Lam Moon in Tokyo, part of an exclusive high-end Hong Kong–based Chinese restaurant chain. There, we were treated to enticing dishes that accompanied the older Oloroso Sherries from Lustau to perfection. No doubt the most memorable occasion was at a restaurant in Tokyo when I was introduced to the delectable and dangerous *fugu*. Part of this fish is fatally poisonous and the chef has to have special certification. The remainder of the fish is a sublime example of the delicacy and perfection that is only reached in Japan. Indeed, I was slightly nervous about eating *fugu* but remained on my stool and enjoyed the fine flavours served in various tiny portions from this small-sized fish.

Japan continued to be a good market for Europvin over the years. The importers are traditionally very loyal to their suppliers. For example, we introduced a little Bordeaux château wine called Château Briot to an importer called Toa Shoji back in 1985. Today, more than 35 years later, the company continues to ship full containers of this wine. Of course, after the financial crash in 1990, the market was somewhat less active and visits less regular. We did however go on a skiing trip near Nagano in 1991 with Minoru and his wife, Kumiko. Skiing on the side of a volcano after dark on a fully illuminated ski run was a novel experience.

During the 1990s shipments were regular but rather lacklustre until 1998, when suddenly there was a huge demand for single-estate Burgundies. The popularity of this category continues to this day, although shipments of large quantities is no longer a factor due to high prices and lack of supply. This said, Japan is by far the most mature wine market in Asia with a thorough understanding of what fine wine is all about and often an even more objective assessment of quality than the mature European markets. Many countries in Asia are catching up and our experiences in other countries were also rewarding and at times exciting.

CHAPTER 9

THE REST OF ASIA

The Birth of Emerging Markets

TAIWAN

Not long after my first trip to Japan I received a letter from an importer in Taiwan requesting I visit him to discuss the possibility of importing a selection of French wines. In early January I set off on what was to be a fruitless journey although, luckily, I combined the trip with a stopover in Japan. In short, for Taiwan I was before my time.

The importer met me at the airport and drove me to a small town near Kaohsiung in the south of the island. It was a hair-raising drive during which we passed a couple of burning vehicles on the side of the road. It turned out the importer was a specialist in bonsais, which he sold all over the island. His knowledge of wine was zero and his interest only marginal. I did however persuade him to take me to a wine shop in Kaohsiung. On the shelves were just a few solitary and dusty bottles of oxidised white Bordeaux surrounded by bottles of whisky of an unknown and doubtful origin. I took the next train back to Taipei with a gift of the finest Oolong tea and never heard from the bonsai merchant again.

In the 1990s the picture changed completely. Numerous importers set up business and bought large quantities of Classified Growth Bordeaux. Europvin was in the forefront of this wave of red Bordeaux that unfurled over Taiwan for a short period of time. We exported container after container of expensive wines to half a dozen importers, all based in Taipei. The situation greatly assisted our presence on the Bordeaux open market and, for a time, improved our chances of obtaining lucrative *en-primeur* allocations from the more prestigious châteaux.

I made a number of trips to the market to consolidate our position and recall numerous fine Chinese meals accompanied by copious quantities of First Growth Bordeaux châteaux. The Taiwanese importers were not collectors and relished in every opportunity to open bottles of First Growth Bordeaux. One meal I shall never forget was most embarrassing. I was served a giant oyster taking up the entire space of a large plate. It was impossible to eat in one piece and inclined to escape when trying to cut with chopsticks! It was quite a predicament but was overcome with difficulty while my hosts looked on with amusement, enjoying my embarrassment while consuming a bottle of Château Mouton Rothschild 1982 which, needless to say, did not go well with the oyster.

A highlight of my trips to Taipei was regular visits to the magnificent National Palace Museum with its over 700,000 pieces of ancient Chinese artworks. Most of the collection is of extremely high quality, put together by a long line of Chinese emperors. Not every piece is on display, far from it. So, with the rotation of the displays, each visit was a newly rewarding experience.

The frenetic enthusiasm for Classed Growth Bordeaux went too far and for many ended in disaster when the Asian economies took a dive in 1998. Hundreds of containers were abandoned in the port of Taipei and some never claimed. Fortunately, all our shipments had been paid for in advance but we did lose a very lucrative market overnight. Later, after the year 2000 the market for expensive wines revived a little, not only for Bordeaux, but the excitement of the 1990s has never been repeated.

THAILAND

The situation in Thailand in the 1990s was somewhat similar to Taiwan. Huge quantities of Classified Growth Bordeaux wines were shipped to a variety of importers. Import taxes were low and the King of Thailand was an enthusiastic consumer. All came to a sudden halt with the Asian financial crisis in 1998. Massive taxation was imposed on imported wines, a symbol of luxury and affluence in a very unequal society. To justify the huge taxes the government initiated a campaign to vilify wine, even to the extent of hinting that wine was part of the cause of the economic collapse. Since then, the imported wine market has been focused on price rather than quality, although the situation has improved somewhat recently.

I made regular visits to Bangkok during the 1990s. At that time, it was a city so congested that gridlock was a daily occurrence. In order to plan a day's visit to various importers, an immense amount of time had to be allowed to be sure of arriving more or less on time for an appointment. There were of course many attractions, including the sights and the excellent spicy food, not to mention the welcoming kindliness of the Thai population. I used to stay in the Regent Hotel with attractive rooms, all panelled with tropical woods, and a splendid swimming pool, ideal for an early morning swim. The hotel was a perfect oasis before facing the gruelling, noisy traffic out in the street.

The consumption of wine in Thailand is increasing thanks to the notion that wine is good for health. Recent changes have also led to slightly lower taxation, down from almost 400%. From a population of about seventy million just over 10% consume wine, mostly middle- to high-income individuals and of course ex-patriots and tourists who converge on the country in ever larger numbers. Another aspect is the free trade agreement with Australia and New Zealand, resulting in lower taxation and more affordable quality wines from those countries. We are however still a long way from the heady days of the 1990s when we shipped container after container of expensive Bordeaux.

SOUTH KOREA

Memories of my early visits to Korea in the 1990s were somewhat clouded by the tension between North and South Korea and the possibility of an attack from the nearby North at any time. I always seemed to arrive at moments of high tension, making the population nervous and less welcoming than usual. Although less focused on Bordeaux, Korea was a lucrative market for Europvin, importing a wide spectrum of European wines. When we became agents for the renowned Rhône producer, Etienne Guigal, for parts of Asia, Korea became even more relevant.

I made a number of visits to Seoul, an agreeably open city that gives a unique sense of space, with numerous parks, well-spaced hills, and few high-rise buildings, something rare and delightful for a capital city. I regret however never having the opportunity to explore the country as the scenery is notoriously spectacular. Occasionally I was accompanied by producers who we represented, notably Pablo Alvarez of Vega Sicilia and Marcel Guigal with his son Philippe. We were of course given VIP treatment in the finest hotels and restaurants.

The most memorable and troublesome occasion was a visit accompanied by Rod Hull, the recently joined export representative for Europvin. One of our customers was slow to pay his invoices but after much insistence he agreed to come by our hotel on the day of our departure. To our surprise and consternation, he came with a supermarket shopping bag full of Korean won in cash. At the time it was impossible to exchange Korean won outside the country. We had no choice but to change the entire amount into US dollars at the airport. It was a huge sum, so we split the cash in two parts, one for Rod and one for myself, monopolising the only two exchange booths at the airport for more than half an hour, much to the disgust and fury of fellow travellers wanting to use the same service. We travelled back to France separately, weary that customs would give us trouble over the mountains of cash. Fortunately, we looked innocent enough for customs not to question us.

Other recollections of Korea include the generous hospitality of the importers, one of whom is an art collector. An invitation to dine at his home with Pablo Alvarez was equivalent to a visit to a modern art gallery, with works by some of the most recognised twentieth-century artists. On the down side, I had trouble with the digestion of the ubiquitous kimchi made with long-fermented vegetables and hot peppers. On the other hand, the classic barbecued beef and pork were delicious. Wine does not complement kimchi at all, in fact it is probably one of the worst combinations imaginable. However Korean consumers are increasingly enjoying fine wines with their excellent meat dishes.

MALAYSIA

Being a Muslim country, Malaysia is not a huge wine market, however the smaller overseas Chinese population and tourists are enthusiastic consumers. There are a number of small importers but one of our most loyal clients was the Hilton Hotel in Kuala Lumpur, who regularly purchased a selection of French wines from Europvin.

It is in Malaysia that we had one of our thankfully rare issues with non-payment of an invoice. After many months of waiting and numerous insistent communications we decided to send in a debt collector. We never quite knew his methods but for a sizeable fee he was finally able to extract the outstanding amount from the importer. It was probably better not to ask too many questions about his technique.

Although a small market, our visits with producers in tow frequently included a winemaker's dinner in some of the finest restaurants in Kuala Lumpur. I never had the chance to visit much of the country but do remember a very uncomfortable drive from Singapore to Kuala Lumpur in an old Alfa Romeo with poor suspension. The scenery was monotonous with never-ending rubber-tree forests and a few banana plantations.

SINGAPORE

I have many fond memories of Singapore. Over the years this small, wealthy island state became one of Europvin's most important markets. My first visit was back in the 1980s, a short stop on the way to Australia. At the time there was only one specialised fine wine importer of note called Escoffier, run by Bobby Lim, a rather loud individual who was the pioneer for quality wines, with little competition. He had a very fine selection of prestigious estate-bottled wines and châteaux. Today there are more than one hundred importers competing fiercely in a relatively small market. Escoffier purchased a few of our selections, becoming our first client in South East Asia.

Later I met Richard Paine, one of our importers based in Hong Kong. He suggested I contact the late Doctor NK Yong, a retired surgeon and very enthusiastic wine collector based in Singapore. Over the years we often met up with NK both in Europe and at his home where his wife, Melina, cooked the most magnificent dinners, agreeably accompanied by the contents of NK's spectacular cellar. Often up to twenty people attended these regular dinners and included any well-known producer who happened to be in town as well as other local collectors and, on one occasion, Alain Ducasse, the multi-Michelin-starred French chef. In Europe we arranged for NK to visit numerous producers, including regular visits to Vega Sicilia, Priorat, and our office in Bordeaux for extensive tastings. NK enthusiastically purchased wines for his collection, which at one point had to be lodged in a refrigerated container in his garden! Later he bought a house where the swimming pool was converted to accommodate the collection. Through NK we met many members of the local and international wine trade.

Over the years we had a number of different importers in Singapore. Perhaps our strongest relationship was with Desmond Lim, a stockbroker and owner of the famous Les Amis restaurant. When the establishment opened over twenty years ago it was the only fine-dining venue outside a hotel. Desmond was also a wine importer and collector. He gradually put together one of the largest networks of restaurants in South East Asia. The restaurants vary in themes but Les Amis remains a classic French restaurant that today has finally and deservedly been awarded the coveted three Michelin stars status. I recall many memorable meals and tastings at Les Amis including a vertical tasting of Penfold's Grange and superb lunches with Pablo Alvarez and a lineup of top Bordeaux to compare with his Unico from Vega Sicilia. On one occasion, in February 2006, I, along with five other guests including my son, Edward, who was training with Desmond at the time, and Pablo, consumed or partially consumed a lineup of very special wines. This was an entertaining occasion. Desmond was supposed to have lunch with us but at the last minute had to leave us for an important event in another room. Hardly had we started on a bottle of Comtes Lafon Meursault Désirée 1999 when two mysterious glasses per person were brought to the table filled with what turned out to be Haut-Brion 1998 and La Mission Haut-Brion 1998 to be tasted blind. Pablo then asked for the wine list and ordered the Margaux 1996 and Vega Sicilia Valbuena 1997 and had glasses sent blind to Desmond's table. Thirty-five minutes later another two glasses appeared which turned out to be Haut-Brion 1989 and La Mission Haut-Brion 1989. Pablo then ordered Vega Sicilia Unico 1989 and had glasses sent to Desmond once again – an expensive game played by two immensely generous personalities! This event had a profound effect on my son, who looked at wine from a different angle from that day on. It was his first exposure to some of the world's greatest wines. All the wines were served with a sumptuous lunch including an Alaskan king crab salad, a chargrilled turbot from Brittany, and a consommé of poultry with black truffles and foie gras ravioli. A siesta was a must after this light refreshment!

My son spent several months working with Desmond but a stint in the kitchens managed to convince him that he did not want to own a restaurant. He was always happier being a foodie, rather than preparing and serving the food. Desmond is the most delightful character, whose generosity sees no bounds. Frequently he brings his chefs and staff on tours of Europe, always including stops at the finest restaurants, inviting his suppliers to join the conviviality. There were also numerous invitations during visits to Singapore, often to his favourite Cantonese restaurant where guests brought treasures from their cellars.

Europvin is the Singapore agent for Vega Sicilia and Guigal, among other big names. There was consequently much demand for our conducting of tastings and wine dinners as well as participating in gastronomic events. Singapore, being an island with a very hot, humid climate and not much other entertainment, has become a gastronomic haven with restaurants and hotels of the highest standard.

Other importers included the late Derek Lee, a veteran in the trade who had worked for Seagram in Singapore for many years. He set up his own company called Grand Vin, importing the wines from Guigal and the Romanée-Conti, among other famous names. I conducted many wine dinners for collectors to promote Guigal. Derek was keen on karaoke bars and on one occasion invited Pablo Alvarez and me to a high-end location but the singing was catastrophic and only the Dom Perignon Champagne saved the evening. Derek also gave my daughter, Anne-Josephine, her first taste of the wine business during a three-month *stage* with his sales team.

Another character was the late Michel Bouverat, an ex-patriot Frenchman who directly imported a small selection of French wines from lesser-known regions including wines from the Jura. We worked closely with him for many years, participating in his Friday lunches where he would choose a casual restaurant and invite his customers for a convivial meal with his wine selections. These entertaining lunches habitually lasted most of the afternoon. A delightful way of doing business.

During one of my early visits to Singapore I had lunch at the famous Raffles Hotel and met the head sommelier, Ignatius Chan, who became a lifelong friend. His career took him to partner with Desmond Lim at Les Amis when the restaurant first opened. He was the wine manager and put together probably the most admirable wine list in Asia. Later he founded his own restaurant called Iggy's with his wife Janice. It was an immediate success. Very small but a cuisine of the highest standards with a strong Japanese and Italian bias. The wine list features almost exclusively his favourite regions, especially Burgundy and Riesling from various sources, both ideal with his refined cuisine. Initially the restaurant was in the Regent Hotel and it later moved to the Hilton on Orchard Road. It is a "must go to" destination for all wealthy gastronomes of the region. We often hosted Ignatius in France, usually in Burgundy, his great love. I have had the privilege of enjoying a number of superb dinners at Iggy's, often at the bar with Ignatius and his choice of dishes.

Another encounter was the introduction to another future friend and association. About the same time as I met Ignatius, I was having lunch alone in Maxime's restaurant in the Regent Hotel. There I met Andy Tan, the principal sommelier. Andy is wildly enthusiastic about wine in general and especially Burgundy. After the Regent he worked with various importers and later moved to China where he joined ASC Fine Wines, responsible for wine education. More recently, living in Shanghai, he became a consultant for restaurants and, for a time, was Europvin's representative in North East Asia. His enthusiasm has no bounds. He is now regarded as the leading expert on Burgundy in China and elsewhere in Asia.

To this day Singapore remains an exciting wine market focused mainly on restaurants. With the advent of a few high-end Spanish restaurants, it is one of the few Asian countries that is doing as well as can be expected with our Clos Figueras, currently imported by a company called Monopole run by the friendly and efficient Michael Chong.

HONG KONG

Hong Kong is today at the centre of the fine wine trade in Asia, all taxation on wines having been reduced to zero. In the 1980s, for my first visits to what was then a British colony, the market was small with very few importers and almost no independent restaurants serving western food. All the good restaurants were in the top-rated hotels. The wine lists were all similar, featuring Burgundian *négociant* brands and Bordeaux Classified Growths. Nevertheless, our wine selections met with some success, especially with chain retail stores such as Watson's Wines. We also served a few small importers with predominantly Bordeaux wines.

Later, when Europvin became the agents for Guigal in a number of Asian countries, we had more success. On one unfortunate and unforgettable occasion, a consumer dinner had been arranged at Alain Ducasse's restaurant at the Intercontinental Hotel. On arrival at Hong Kong airport with the Guigal family we received a phone call asking where we were since the guests were waiting for us to introduce the wines. To our horror we realised there had been some confusion over the date of the event. We had arrived a day too late. Gérard Mangeon, Ducasse's head sommelier, never forgave us or our importer for this faux pas. However, we rushed to the restaurant and both Marcel and Philippe Guigal were able to talk about their wines before the end of the dinner. I have rarely been more embarrassed and mortified in my entire career.

Vinexpo was held in the territory every other year and was always an occasion to appreciate the best on offer in Hong Kong from a gastronomic point of view. Over the years the choice of fine restaurants became more and more inspiring. Again, we enjoyed a number of fine meals with the Guigal family, Pablo Alvarez and customers, including dinner in Pierre Gagnaire's restaurant in the Mandarin Oriental Hotel and tasting events followed by dinner at The Hong Kong Jockey Club.

However, Hong Kong was never a big market for Europvin. We were successful with our agencies such as Guigal and Vega Sicilia but for other wines it was always a difficult to establish a presence until the 2000s when China started to take an interest in fine wines. The lack of knowledge among Chinese wine merchants meant that they relied on the Hong Kong market for the supply of brands that had a following, especially some of the Bordeaux Classified Growths, notably Château Lafite Rothschild which rapidly gained a cult following in China. Europvin had some success with the most sought-after Bordeaux wines during this period. Our own Clos Figueras is now capably imported by Liber Wines, partly owned by Billecart-Salmon, the prestigious Champagne house, for both Hong Kong and China.

Today, with no import taxation in Hong Kong, the territory has become the hub for fine wine in North East Asia and especially China. Auctions take place on a regular basis and English merchants have set up shop for access to wealthy Chinese consumers and collectors. Recent events in Hong Kong, with more political involvement by China, could damage this unique position and possibly favour Singapore, even though some import duties are levied there. However, the unique geographic situation and deft handling of the economy could still save the day for Hong Kong.

CHINA

Our experience in China was always somewhat limited and mostly focused on the largest importer at the time, ASC Fine Wines. The company was founded by Don St. Pierre Sr. and later run by his son Don St. Pierre Jr. who became the leading spokesman for the Chinese wine market until he sold the company to the Suntory group from Japan.

From our Europvin portfolio ASC represented Guigal and Emilio Lustau. With over 1,000 employees and offices all over China they were successful in covering this huge territory. We were frequently invited to conduct wine dinners and tastings, often with the Guigal family, in the leading restaurants in both Shanghai and Beijing.

On one occasion we were asked to fly to Changsha where we visited a factory making air-conditioner apparatus on a large scale: the entire air-conditioning equipment for Madrid Airport being an example. The factory was immense and functioned twenty-four hours a day, seven days a week. For their staff and guests, they purchased an entire container of Côtes-du-Rhône from Guigal and another after our visit. We were lodged and fed by the company and attempted to explain the wines. This was difficult since few of the attendees spoke English. Nevertheless, they enjoyed the wine and a good time was had by everyone.

Apart from short trips to various cities with the ASC team, including Xiamen and Hangzhou, I had few opportunities to see much of this huge and fascinating country. However, on one occasion after an event in Beijing, I took a bus with Charlotte to visit the Great Wall. It was a cold, clear day and the views were magnificent, but the walk on the wall perilous since it was covered in ice. We survived and I can certainly recommend an excursion to this wild scenic landscape.

We did work with a few smaller importers but with limited success. The Chinese wine market is complex and immature with knowledge negligible but growing. Over the years counterfeit wines have been and continue to be a problem. During a visit to a sommelier in one of the finest Beijing restaurants in the mid-afternoon, an individual came in and placed a bottle of Château Lafite Rothschild on the table telling the sommelier he would like it opened and decanted for dinner that same evening. After his departure the bottle remained on the table. I soon realised something was wrong. Indeed, the capsule was not the normal Lafite capsule. The sommelier shrugged and said the bottle was no doubt counterfeit and this kind of incident happened all the time. Over the past few years better control has meant the counterfeit problems have improved, but a few years ago it was calculated that half the Lafite bottles in circulation in China were not genuine.

CHAPTER 10

AUSTRALIA AND NEW ZEALAND

Stimulating Enthusiasm
Down Under

AUSTRALIA

Australia has always been a strong market for imported wines, consumption of wine being part of daily life. The friendly, informal Australians love their beer but wine also has its place in their daily diet. I remember being so proud on receiving our first order from Down Under in the early 1980s, before we became involved in Asia. Shortly afterwards I made my first trip to Australia to visit a number of importers. I was enthusiastically received everywhere and the country soon became an important destination for our wines.

One of my early contacts was the undauntable Len Evans, an ex-patriot Welshman with an unfettered sense of humour and a passion for wine. His strong opinions and his writing made Len the leading personality on the Australian wine scene. On my first visit he was an importer; he was also involved in production, specifically in the Hunter Valley. Receiving me in his office in Sydney, he gave me an order for a full container of Marqués de

Cáceres, a leading if fairly recent Rioja producer. On future occasions Len took me to the Hunter Valley where he was involved in various projects, the best known being the Rosemount Estate. Over the years I met the indomitable Len on several occasions, the last being a superb day he organised for the visit of Pablo Alvarez. A lunch with several other Hunter Valley producers, among others Brokenwood and Tyrrell's, was followed by a tasting of a magnificent range of aged Hunter Semillons at his home. The day concluded with the planting of a Vega Sicilia tree in his garden, a tradition for all celebrated visitors. Sadly, Len died a few days later while visiting his wife in hospital.

Another personality was Paul de Burgh Day, an extremely knowledgeable Melbourne-based importer specialising in sales to private customers through a beautifully written newsletter published every month. Paul came frequently to Europe to visit his suppliers and make his selections. While visiting Bordeaux he would stay in the flat above our office. He became a loyal customer until he sold his company in the 2000s and moved to Tasmania.

One project Paul and I tried to launch in 1987 was to make a selection of the finest Australian estate wines for distribution through the Europvin network, specifically in the US. For a full week we drove through Victoria and South Australia visiting estates that were unknown at the time but have now become household names in the world of fine wines. The estates visited included Jasper Hill, whose wines Paul sold to Yapp Brothers in the UK, Mount Langi Ghiran in the Grampians, TarraWarra Estate in the Yarra Valley, Heathcote Winery, Tim Knappstein in Clare Valley, Leconfield in Coonawarra, and others. The historic wineries we called on were Best's Great Western, Bleasdale, and Chambers Rosewood in Rutherglen, famous for their exquisite, sweet Muscat wines. It was a most rewarding and educational journey, often for long stretches on unpaved roads but with the added benefit of observing a large number of leaping kangaroos and koalas high up in the eucalyptus trees. Regrettably we were before our time and were unable to generate enough business to justify the continuation of the project. But still it was an enjoyable interlude. Today all these estates are well established on the export markets.

Australia used to be better known for commercial supermarket wines, especially oaky Chardonnays and rather sweet Shiraz. There is however a growing recognition that, in certain parts of the country, with a suitable climate and altitude, world-class single-estate wines are being made and are gradually gaining their rightful place on the international wine scene. It was in 1951 that Max Schubert launched Grange and the potential for great wine was first recognised. At the time Australia was making mostly fortified wines of a style similar to Sherry and Port. It was a number of years before Grange received any competition from other estates. Today there are numerous outstanding wines being made, encouraged by a dynamic system of competitions and awards.

In Melbourne we had another colourful importer called Nick Chlebnikowski who owned a few successful wine outlets, including a rather chaotic store in downtown Melbourne containing many treasures at reasonable prices. The stores are called Nicks Wine Merchants, with the evocative motto, "Nicks nose knows"! Nick was again a loyal customer over a period of at least twenty-five years, focusing mainly on Bordeaux wines.

One of our stronger relationships was with the company Samuel Smith and Son, owners of the historic Yalumba winery in the Barossa Valley and importer of some of the world's most illustrious wines under the name Negociants Australia. During my first trip to Australia, I met Brenton Fry, responsible for imports. Over the years we developed a strong relationship with the company which continues today, helping them promote some of our most important agencies including Etienne Guigal, Emilio Lustau, Vega Sicilia, and our own Clos Figueras. In addition, the company purchased quantities of Bordeaux Classified Growths and some top-rated Burgundies. Strange though it may seem today, Sauternes was very popular in the 1980s and 1990s. A sizeable proportion of the production of Château Coutet and Château Rieussec was sold and consumed in Australia. Not infrequently I was welcomed at Yalumba, often with our principal suppliers. In 2005 I sent my daughter to Australia to learn the trade and help with the harvest at Yalumba. She spent two gruelling weeks at the large Yalumba-owned Oxford Landing winery and a further four weeks with Louisa Rose, the technical director at Yalumba, famous for her work with the Viognier grape variety. Negociants also had export activity for other producers which gave me the opportunity to visit the nearby reputed Henschke winery and their famous Hill of Grace vineyard.

A trip to Barossa in the early 2000s would not be complete without a visit to Dave Powell at Torbreck Vintners. Dave is a larger-than-life personality who did much to enhance the image of Australian wines in export markets. Regrettably he had to sell the winery after falling out with his partners but has now founded a new winery in the area with his son. Another memorable visit with Yalumba was to Seppeltsfield with their exceptional array of fortified wines, the star being the 100-year-old Para Liqueur. The first cask of this wine was laid down in 1878 and casks have been put aside every year since. As they age the wines are transferred to 500-litre (132-gallon) puncheons before bottling. Benno Seppelt, the founder, specified that the wine should not be released before it was one hundred years old, hence the first release was in 1978 and subsequent release has continued on an annual basis. I have had the privilege of tasting the 1878, an extraordinary wine, not unlike an old Oloroso Sherry but with great complexity, a wide range of enticing aromas and flavours, followed by a never-ending aftertaste.

Every two years Negociants organises highly successful tasting events in the main Australian cities called "Working with Wine." I participated in two of these events, one with Emilio Lustau and other Spanish wines, and later with the wines from Guigal and Australian Syrah producers, notably John Duval, Brokenwood, and of course Yalumba. We started in Brisbane and continued to Sydney, Melbourne, Adelaide, and Perth. These were educational events bringing together the cream of the Australian wine trade to taste and discuss the theme of the tasting in the presence of the producers.

Another strong relationship in Australia was with Jon Osbeiston, the knowledgeable owner of Ultimo Wine Centre in Sydney. He did not take kindly to the summer heat in Australia, so every January he would spend the full month travelling and tasting in France, mostly in Burgundy and the

Rhône Valley. Since we were his principal supplier, we accompanied him on these tours. He would subsequently purchase his yearly requirements from Europvin. As part of her sojourn in Australia, my daughter spent three months in the run up to Christmas 2004 working at Ultimo Wine Centre.

During a visit with my wife over Christmas that year we drove with her from Sydney to Adelaide, with a stop in Melbourne, in a dilapidated old Ford we had purchased for her time with Yalumba during the 2005 harvest. It was the time of the catastrophic tsunami in South East Asia, and everyone was in a state of shock since many Australian tourists had lost their lives.

Being so geographically close, my trips to Australia would often be combined with a visit to relatively nearby New Zealand, although the distance between them can be deceptive.

NEW ZEALAND

I always loved going to New Zealand: the country reminds me so much of my native Cotswolds with green meadows, rolling hills, and countless sheep. The wine scene is very dynamic since the country produces some of the finest Sauvignon Blanc and Pinot Noir in the Southern Hemisphere. There is also a keen interest in imported wines.

At Europvin our main partner was called Eurowine. I still recall Ken Moon, a patent lawyer and one of the founders, visiting me in Bordeaux in 1986 to ask if we minded if they used the name Eurowine for their new import company, hoping it would not cause a conflict of interest. Of course we assented and the company became a significant client for Europvin, specialising mainly in Burgundy and Lustau Sherries.

Another important client was the New Zealand arm of Negociants Australia called, not surprisingly, Negociants New Zealand. They are the importers for the Guigal portfolio. A noteworthy occasion was a visit to New Zealand with

Philippe Guigal. After a few tasting events in Auckland, we visited a number of interesting wineries including the Te Mata estate in Hawke's Bay, Craggy Range, and Ata Rangi in Martinborough. Pablo Alvarez was also travelling with us on this occasion. It was just after this trip, while on holiday in Corsica, that Philippe met his future wife, Eve.

Visits to South Island wineries were made on another trip with Brett Newell, co-founder of Eurowine. We drove from Canterbury to Wellington, stopping to taste with the Donaldson family at Pegasus Bay and on to Marlborough where we stayed the night and tasted at the Fromm winery.

I have made several visits to the Buck family at Te Mata. At one time we were negotiating for the distribution of their wines in the US. John Buck is something of a pioneer on the New Zealand wine scene, Te Mata being one of the first single estates to export their wines. He produces remarkable Cabernet-based wines that can rival many a fine name in Bordeaux.

Another great relationship we have in New Zealand is with James Healy, owner of Dog Point Vineyard. He produces some of the brightest and most refreshing dry Sauvignon Blancs from his organically certified vineyards in the Marlborough district. James regularly visits us at Clos Figueras in the Priorat and is an enthusiastic ambassador for our wines, which are imported by Alastair Pope of Wine Direct.

New Zealand is most famous for its Sauvignon Blancs, names such as Cloudy Bay springing to mind at the mention of the more eminent wineries. A leading restaurant in Auckland, in the process of reviewing their wine list, invited me to an extensive tasting of Sauvignon Blanc on one day, and another of Pinot Noir the following day. I was somewhat disappointed with both tastings, finding many of the wines very commercial, with the Sauvignons being rather too sweet for my taste and the Pinots too light, lacking depth. Nevertheless, there are some remarkable producers making outstanding wines, highlighting the importance of the name on the label.

CHAPTER 11

SOUTH AMERICA

Wine in the Realm of
Samba and Tango

BRAZIL

One morning in our Bordeaux office in 1980 I received a visit from a young Brazilian sent by Steven Spurrier who at that time owned the Cave de la Madeleine wine shop in Paris. Young and ambitious, Otavio Piva de Albuquerque from São Paulo was already selling wine, mostly inexpensive wine from Germany and a rosé made in Brazil. Steven knew we could offer a service to Otavio by supplying him with mixed containers of wine from various origins. His company was initially called Mosel and later changed to Expand. He was our first importer in the Southern Hemisphere. We started by shipping a selection of Bordeaux wines. In July 1981 I visited Brazil for the first time with my wife. We combined business with tourism and visited Rio de Janeiro, Salvador de Bahia, the falls at Iguazu, and of course São Paulo.

At the time wine imports were negligible, especially for fine wines, but the gastronomic scene was improving and with it the demand for extensive wine lists. Over the years I made several visits to Otavio, who became a very significant customer.

The trade in Brazil was polarised; only the most inexpensive or the most highly priced wines were of interest. Otavio placed large orders for Bordeaux Classified Growths. I recall using the phone on a business class flight from Dallas to Los Angeles and noting down one of the most valuable orders in the history of Europvin. It took almost the entire flight to complete the list of top Bordeaux Otavio wished to purchase.

In the early 1990s we negotiated the exclusivity for the Domaine de la Romanée-Conti for Brazil and some other countries. I made a memorable visit in 2001 to Rio de Janeiro and São Paulo with Aubert de Villaine, co-owner of the domaine. During the tour, special winemaker's dinners were organised in the finest restaurants with a fabulous array of Romanée-Conti wines. An unforgettable flight from Rio to São Paulo in Otavio's private jet with an unlimited supply of Champagne and incredible views will long be remembered. In São Paulo, after so many substantial lunches and dinners, some sport was called for, so a tennis game was organised with four players. None of us were any match for Aubert and a total disaster as far as I was concerned. On that same visit we were lodged in a hotel that had been inaugurated the previous week. On opening the sheet-glass shower door, it collapsed into a thousand pieces and badly cut my hand and foot, which did nothing to help my tennis.

Another visit was made with Frédéric Engerer, estate manager at Château Latour. Vertical tastings with about twenty vintages were arranged in Rio and São Paulo. The dinners for about forty guests were preceded by an entire afternoon of double decanting all the wines to give them some air and look for cork taint. Frédéric insisted on doing the task himself. It was a remarkable lineup of great vintages and a real privilege to be able to participate.

Another anecdote with Otavio took place one day while sitting in his office waiting for him to arrive. He had just landed from Italy carrying a large sports bag, which he subsequently opened. It was full of white truffles of the season, brought straight from Alba. The aroma that filled the room was incredibly intense and overpowering, really too much, and I have never ordered white truffles since. That same evening many of the best restaurants in São Paulo received their allocation of white truffles delivered by Otavio and his staff.

Visiting Brazil in the 1980s and early 1990s was always a bit of a challenge. Inflation at over 100% meant that prices changed every day. Coming down from my hotel room every morning I was informed of the new price for the next night. It was during this same period that the restaurants in São Paulo improved to become world class, notably those specialised in Northern Italian cuisine. I participated in a number of outstanding dinners at Fasano, the leading restaurant of the day.

During one of my visits to São Paulo I met a wine collector, Ciro de Campos Lilla, whose main activity was to make coffee machines. His enthusiasm for wine had no bounds. He showed me the list of his incredible collection of the finest Bordeaux and Burgundy vintages. Soon afterwards he founded his own wine import company called Mistral. At Europvin we were one of his main suppliers from the first day. His portfolio of fine wines was, and still is, much more eclectic than Otavio's at Expand. He purchased wines from our key agencies in Burgundy, the Rhône Valley, Spain, Italy, and elsewhere in France. Today Ciro continues to import wines from Europvin and our own wine from Clos Figueras.

Every second year Ciro arranges a tasting event with his suppliers called "The Mistral Encounter". These were very well-organised affairs for the trade and consumers in São Paulo and Rio de Janeiro. The first day, usually a Sunday, was an informal day for producers at Ciro's house in the country, about 50 kilometres (31 miles) from São Paulo, with some excellent food and wines from his collection. Over the following three days we would show our wines to hundreds of guests in the enjoyable company of fellow producers and merchants.

In spite of the adverse economy and high taxation, Mistral has now become the leading importer for fine wines in Brazil, the catalogue including many of the world's greatest wines. Ciro survives the various import restrictions with an excellent staff and strong connections to the government, allowing him to attempt to make the import procedure a little less arduous and restrictive. The paperwork and labelling requirements are undoubtedly the most complicated in the world, the government no doubt making life difficult for importers in Brazil as a form of protectionism, under the influence of a strong lobby of Brazilian producers.

One particular difficulty for importers is that each individual is allowed to bring 12 litres (3 gallons) of alcoholic beverages tax-free into Brazil. This has meant that many collectors purchase their more expensive wines abroad, even to the extent of paying the airfare for friends and acquaintances for flights to Miami and New York to purchase wines for their cellars.

Despite the various difficulties, Brazil is today a highly dynamic and mature wine market. Brazil was always a country I enjoyed visiting for the easygoing generosity of the people and amazing scenery, especially in and around Rio de Janeiro. I also appreciated listening to Brazilian music and the local version of the Portuguese language, softer and easier to understand than in Portugal.

CHILE

In Chile my experience was more with production than sales. In fact, at Europvin, we never shipped one bottle to Chile. High import taxes and their own production of well-made wines has more or less sealed the country from imported wines.

One of our suppliers in France, Henry Marionnet, a well-known producer from the Touraine in the Loire Valley, was contacted in the late 1980s by an investor who had purchased land in the Maule Valley, over 160 kilometres

(100 miles) south of Santiago up against the majestic Andes mountains. He was appointed as a consultant for a new vineyard and winery called TerraNoble. He advised them to plant Merlot for the red wine and Sauvignon Blanc for the white. During a short trip to this spectacular country, I met Winfried from Germany who was coordinating the project. We drove from Santiago to the Maule Valley, a long drive to the south where we also visited other wineries including Los Vascos, belonging to the Rothschild group of wineries. At TerraNoble they were launching their first wines, very much in the Loire style, quite light but full of flavour and charm. Carbonic maceration had been used for the Merlot, much in the same way as Marionnet vinifies in the Loire. We purchased a full container of Merlot and Sauvignon Blanc which was shipped to Bordeaux. In spite of the quality, wines from Chile were not easy to sell in those days. It took us over two years to deplete the stocks. The wines held up well and eventually sold in the US but we did not repeat the transaction. Today TerraNoble is a very successful winery with a larger portfolio of wines.

I was surprised and shocked by the wines I tasted in Chilean restaurants at the time, also tasting at Tarapacá, a large and long-established winery near Santiago. They were nearly all oxidised and I suppose this is how the local population used to enjoy their wines. Of course, over the past thirty years, this has changed radically. The country and Tarapacá are now producing world-class wines. I guess that, once again, we were ahead of our time.

During this visit one anecdote springs to mind. Over dinner with Winfried and his French wife, Fleur, I brought out my Montblanc pen to take a note. Suddenly, Winfried's wife asked if she could have the pen. Since I thought it was in jest, I gave it to her and, to my surprise and consternation, it was not returned. Two years later, during Vinexpo, Winfried came to a reception we gave in our Bordeaux offices. On his departure my wife noticed a Montblanc pen in his shirt pocket. She remembered my story and politely removed the pen from his pocket saying a debt was being paid!

PERU

Our connection to Peru was through a wealthy Peruvian surgeon named Doctor Jorge Cáceres based in the US, in Birmingham, Alabama. He was also an enthusiastic collector who had decided to create a wine import company in Lima.

For the same reason as Chile, with high import taxation, Peru is a very small wine market. However, even at the time, some twenty-five years ago, the restaurant scene was improving rapidly and with it a demand for good wine lists. I visited Lima and brought home purchase orders for both French and Spanish wines, both countries' wines being highly regarded in Peru. During my stay I much appreciated the Peruvian cuisine, especially the ceviche and freshness of the fish. One restaurant we visited, Astrid y Gastón, has become a household name among gastronomes. At the time in Lima, they listed a number of our selections, including their house white. It was a crisp, dry white wine from the Greffier family in the Entre-deux-Mers, delivered with their own Astrid y Gastón label.

ARGENTINA

Argentina is another country with extremely high import duties on wines. On my first visit to Buenos Aires, about thirty years ago, it was most unusual to find an imported wine in a wine store. I was looking for an importer for Vega Sicilia but came away without success.

Subsequently I made two trips to Argentina visiting wineries and vineyards. The first was with Angela Muir, a Master of Wine and a longtime friend. She had founded a small company called Cellarworld Argentina in Mendoza consulting for various wineries and assisting them with exports. In the back of my mind was the possibility of investing in Angela's project with the ultimate aim to include some Argentinian wines in the Europvin portfolio, a project that did not come to fruition.

It was winter in Mendoza and we were able to enjoy the fabulous scenery. Everywhere we went the magnificent Andes mountains topped by snow dominated the landscape. We visited numerous wineries near Mendoza, all very interesting and all striving to improve their quality in difficult conditions due to the high altitude and dry climate. Among others, we visited Norton, a large estate owned by Swarovski, the luxury glass manufacturer; Fabre Montmayou, founded by a Bordeaux *négociant* and his wife, Diane; O. Fournier in the Uco Valley, whose bodega looks like a spaceship just landed; and Finca Abril, a boutique, family-owned estate, also in the Uco Valley, producing outstanding Malbec wines from vineyards planted in 1922. A side trip was made to San Juan, a viticultural area just north of Mendoza, on an extremely cold day. We struggled through the snow to reach one of the highest vineyards in Argentina at over 1,500 metres (4,900 feet).

On another day we took a bus through the Andes up to the border with Chile. The sky was clear and the views breathtaking with the dramatically coloured rock formations and rare condors flying overhead. The road was choked with trucks for over 80 kilometres (50 miles) all trying to reach the port of Valparaiso in Chile from as far away as Brazil, Uruguay, and Buenos Aires, the snow on top of the pass over to Chile making the journey very treacherous. The following year we sent our daughter to Argentina where she accompanied the Cellarworld team on their work with various wineries during the harvest.

My second visit to Argentina was my first overseas journey with the Académie Internationale du Vin in March 2013. Every year the Académie organises an overseas trip to a different wine-producing territory. We started in Buenos Aires where we were lectured on the Argentinian wine scene before the inevitable evening outing to a tango bar. The next day we flew to Mendoza and spent the remainder of the trip being royally received and entertained by some of the most prestigious wineries in the area.

Guided by Roberto de la Mota, member of the Académie, owner of Mendel Winery and one of the most respected enologists in Argentina, we visited numerous wineries, almost too many to take in the wide diversity of wines from Mendoza. To start we were hosted at the Moët Hennessy–owned Cheval des Andes for a polo match followed by a tasting. The next day we were taken to Trapiche, one of the largest bodegas in the country with a capacity of 10 million litres (2,641,720 gallons), then to Roberto's own boutique winery, Mendel, at Lujan de Cuyo. The visits and tastings continued all day, some of the bodegas showing us wines from their friends and neighbours as well as their own. Noteworthy was a superb outdoor lunch at Bodegas Norton followed by a visit to another renowned Moët-owned winery, Terrazas de los Andes. The following day we drove to the Valle de Uco, some 120 kilometres (75 miles) south of Mendoza. There we visited O. Fournier, the second time for me, then went on to Salentein with their spectacular modern winery and vineyards at an altitude of 1,700 metres (5,577 feet). The visit included a tasting of Salentein's remarkable Chardonnays and Pinot Noirs. We then proceeded to Clos de los Siete, a winery founded by Michel Rolland, the eminent Bordeaux-based enologist, with six friends. Then we moved on to the famous Catena Zapeta winery for a tasting and a light meal. The final day was spent visiting Bodega Ruca Malen followed by an excellent lunch on Susana Balbo's terrace before flying back to Buenos Aires. A very intense four days!

I was most impressed by the high standards of quality at the numerous wineries we visited and even more impressed by the fraternity between producers and their common efforts to further improve the quality and prestige of the region. Difficulties for the future could well arise due to climate change and the chronic lack of water. Producers have to rely almost entirely on irrigation from the melting Andean snows. This said, remarkable wines of world-class quality are being made, especially from the Malbec grape which thrives locally, contributing to the singular flavours of the wines from the Mendoza region.

URUGUAY

While in South America I also made a brief stop in Uruguay for an unsuccessful search for an importer for Vega Sicilia. It was early days for the dynamic wine scene of today in Uruguay but I was impressed by a visit to Bodegas Carrau near Montevideo and the drive to Punta del Este, the famous resort. Today the country is producing world-class wines with a special focus on the Tannat grape of Madiran fame.

CHAPTER 12

SOUTH AFRICA

Stunning Wines in
Scenic Splendour

Without doubt the scenery in South Africa is among the most spectacular of all the world's wine-producing nations, especially the Western Cape, in and around Cape Town, with Table Mountain dominating the city and the precipitous mountains plunging into the ocean.

I have had the pleasure to visit South Africa on two occasions. The first was with my wife and longtime friend Janake Johansson from Sweden. Janake, a first-rate personality with a great sense of humour, was our agent and importer for Sweden and has strong connections to South Africa. So much so that he purchased a house in Stellenbosch in the heart of the Cape wine country. Janake represented a number of quality estate wines, his company being one of the leading importers of South African wines in Sweden. A few years back Sweden imported more wine from South Africa than from any other country. Today the country continues to be an important source for the Swedish retail monopoly.

My wife with Janake Johansson at Stellenbosch, South Africa, in 2011.

The estates we visited were mostly exported through Cape Legends, a division of the operator and producer Distell. Each morning, Distell's chauffeur, Abdul, would collect us at our hotel with Janake who told us the morning news before broaching the subject of the day's visits. We have fond memories of tastings at numerous estates in the Stellenbosch area. Among the most memorable was a visit to Hempies du Toit, a great character and ex–international rugby player. We'd had dinner with him and Janake a few years before in Bordeaux with his glamorous wife. He received us in his cellars accompanied by his huge St. Bernard dog but not his glamorous wife who apparently had moved on. The wines were pleasant but his main claim to fame was as a supplier to the royal family of Monaco. Hempies is friends with Charlene, the South African Olympic swimmer and Prince Albert II's wife. Hempies' Merlot was poured during the wedding dinner with a special label branded "Chalbert".

Another entertaining visit was to the Dalla Cia winery and grappa distillery run by Giorgio Dalla Cia, an entertaining character who revels in his Italian roots. His business is located in the station yard at Stellenbosch and here we were treated to an excellent pasta lunch in his trattoria, followed by a visit to the distillery with a tasting of his wines and exquisite grappa.

Other wineries visited in the Stellenbosch area included the traditional Jacobsdal and a tasting of the elegant wines from Le Bonheur. Excursions were made to Constantia, on the east side of Table Mountain, famous for the legendary and historic Constantia dessert wines that were the rage in the late eighteenth and early nineteenth centuries. Few wines have had so much prestige and royal patronage with the possible exception of Tokaj in Hungary. We tasted at Constantia Uitsig, better known for their excellent dry red and white wines.

Although based in Stellenbosch, another side trip was made to Swartland to visit the Sadie Family Winery, arguably the most successful of the South African wineries in the export markets making exceptional wines. Eben Sadie has greatly contributed to South Africa's reputation for world-class wines. Swartland, north west of Stellenbosch, not far from the Atlantic, is source of some of the best wines made from Mediterranean grape varieties, notably, Grenache, Mourvèdre, Cinsault, and the inevitable Syrah. Sadie's Columella blend with these varieties is among South Africa's most prestigious red wines. From the numerous old-vine vineyards in the area, Eben makes single-vineyard cuvées, mostly intense, rich white wines from the Chenin grape with some Semillon and Palomino, for his Old Vine Series.

Another vineyard we visited was Allesverloren on the edge of Swartland. Established in 1690 this is one of the oldest farms in South Africa. Planted mostly with Portuguese varieties, the winery used to be famous for their Port wine. Today this large estate also has cereal crops and a small game park. The winery specialises in dry red wines, made from the Portuguese varieties, and a Douro blend sold at very reasonable prices. *Allesverloren* translated from German means "all is lost". The first owner was a German widow who had to go to Stellenbosch from time to time to buy salt, tools, and go to church. These journeys took a few weeks on horseback since there were no roads at the time. Returning from one of the trips, she found the farm burnt down and her cattle either dead or lost. She cried *"Allesverloren!"* All was lost, hence the unusual name.

Many of the wineries we visited had their own restaurants, usually very elegant and of a very high standard. Wine tourism is big in South Africa and a major source of income. In this respect they are well in advance of their European counterparts. After several days of tasting, we were ready for a change. Returning to Cape Town we took the Blue Train to Pretoria, an expensive but a once-in-a-lifetime luxurious experience. The train leaves Cape Town at about 10.00 a.m., passing through the spectacular scenery of the Western Cape and the vineyards of Paarl before climbing to the high central plateau. The meals in the elegant dining car were sumptuous and the wine selection from the most prominent producers. During the night we passed through Kimberley and arrived in Pretoria the next morning about twenty-five hours after our departure. The following two days we visited a nearby game park before returning to Cape Town via Johannesburg. Another spectacular excursion from Cape Town is to the Cape of Good Hope with breathtaking views along the Atlantic coast, returning along False Bay where excellent restaurants can be found with the added advantage, if lucky, of observing whales in the bay.

PART THREE

SUPPLY

Sourcing the Finest Wines

CHAPTER 13

FRANCE

Classic and More
Humble Appellations

🏵 BORDEAUX 🏵

Tradition and Diversity

Europvin's commitment to selling Bordeaux wines has been ongoing since the very beginning of our existence in 1978. I have already described how important Bordeaux was to our new venture. Thanks to our geographic presence, access to stocks, and a favourable commercial climate for Bordeaux, the company survived the first years and even became profitable from the very early days.

Being a new company, we had difficulty with access to the Bordeaux open market, known as La Place de Bordeaux, and the Grands Crus, but this was resolved thanks to the generous participation of Pierre Dourthe of Dourthe-Kressmann, a leading *négociant*, who purchased the wines for us and shared the profit margin. Later, as we became stronger, we had direct access to the open market for the Grand Crus Classés which continues to this day. Of course, over the years there have been ups and downs as the market, the quality of the vintages, and the world economies have fluctuated. At one time we were extremely active with the opening up of the Asian markets, specifically in Taiwan and Thailand, where we were pioneers and an important source for several importers.

There have also been variations in our active participation in the *en-primeur* or futures market. Speculation makes this aspect of the business somewhat dangerous. On the one hand, you have to commit to the stocks to maintain your allocation and you may not be able to sell your stocks if conditions are unfavourable. We always limited our liability in this field to about 10% of our turnover. This has meant that, on occasion, we have had to reduce or forego our allocation from a specific château, meaning we would have reduced or no access to future allocations. This situation only changes when the overall market is so depressed that the châteaux were willing to review a renewal of an allocation on request.

Sometimes the châteaux change strategy. This caused us considerable complications with Château Latour, who, on release of the well-publicised 2005 vintage *en-primeur*, decided they would not give us an allocation in spite of our commitment to the château and the market visit to Brazil we organised for Frédéric Engerer, the director. This last-minute decision caused us, and some other *négociants* in the same situation, considerable embarrassment with regular customers. Today Latour has ceased trading *en-primeur* and is only offering stocks in bottle after a few years' ageing.

However, we established a strong position with some of the leading chateaux, specifically the First Growths: Lafite Rothschild, Margaux, Haut-Brion, Mouton Rothschild, and, to a lesser extent, Cheval Blanc. Also, over the years, we established links with numerous other leading châteaux including Lynch-Bages, Léoville Barton, Cos d'Estournel, Calon Ségur, Talbot, Gruaud Larose, Léoville Poyferré, Montrose, Beychevelle, Giscours, Grand-Puy-Lacoste, La Mission Haut-Brion, Angélus, Canon, Le Pin, Vieux Château Certan, and L'Eglise Clinet, to name but a few.

From Sauternes and Barsac, we purchased Château Climens, while for Château Rieussec and Château Coutet we were under discrete pressure to buy in order to maintain our position with Lafite Rothschild and Mouton Rothschild respectively. Our other more exciting activity in Sauternes was the relationship with Château Gilette and Château Les Justices, owned by the Médeville family. One day in the early 1980s, driving on the main road near Barsac, I spotted a small stand on the roadside selling wine. I stopped to investigate and noticed some 20–30-year-old bottles. This was the start of a long relationship with these very special wines. Château Gilette is unique in Sauternes due to the method of ageing for at least ten years in concrete vats before release without any oak ageing. The wines are sublime, full of freshness, with a wonderful vanilla-like flavour that is unique to this wine. Furthermore, the ageing capacity is legendary. I have tasted bottles back to 1949 and 1937 that are still bright and youthful. In lesser vintages such as 1956 and 1958 they produced semi-sweet wines under the Château Gilette label. Again, these wines are special; with less sugar content there is no better companion for foie gras. Even today, after more than sixty years, the bright, subtle flavours are spectacular and unique. Château Les Justices is the second wine without the same concentration but with similar flavours and a potential for long ageing.

Regrettably, due to a decline in interest for sweet wines, the great dessert wines of Bordeaux have become difficult to sell, meaning that stocks back up with the *négociants* or remain in the hands of the châteaux for marketing at a later date. Many châteaux are now making excellent dry white wines to complement their less successful Sauternes offerings.

Like most Bordeaux *négociants* we also had an ongoing trade with lesser-known châteaux, also known as Petits Châteaux, properties with which we had a direct contact and with whom we built long-term relationships. The selection is based on quality and compatibility with the owner, working closely to build a strong distribution network. At Europvin we selected a number of châteaux, sometimes with recommendations from the renowned enologist and consultant Michel Rolland. I have already mentioned Château Sénéjac. We had similar relationships with, among others, Château Siran, an excellent Cru Bourgeois in Margaux; Château de Malle in Sauternes and their red Graves Château Cardaillan; Château Cap Léon Veyrin in Listrac; Château La Vieille Cure and Château Villars in Fronsac; and the previously mentioned Château Tertre de Launay in the Entre-deux-Mers for their crisp, dry white wine. These châteaux, as long as their pricing strategy remained reasonable, gave us continuity, especially in countries such as Japan where we had a very loyal customer base.

One of our least successful ventures in Bordeaux was our association with Xavier Copel, an enologist who decided to produce his own wines under the Primo Palatum label. In the mid-1990s, thanks in part to the following created by Robert Parker, it was fashionable to produce rich, intense wines with plenty of oak and extraction. Xavier's strategy was to make wines that had been aged in new oak twice.

The wines were from Bordeaux and other areas of South West France, even including one from Priorat. He carefully selected reputable producers and created his wines with their assistance, following his instructions. White wines from Sauternes and Jurançon were also part of the collection. The wines were indeed spectacular, smooth, and rich with great depth but many of them needed many years of ageing before reaching perfection and being ideal for consumption. This and the pricing made them hard to sell, eventually leading to Xavier abandoning the project. Furthermore, by the end of the 1990s, consumers were looking for lighter, more approachable wines with freshness and elegance. Xavier is now a consultant selling oak casks to producers in France and Spain. I understand he does still dabble in winemaking but with a different focus.

The Bordeaux trade never really understood Europvin's activity. Only about 30% of our turnover was with the wines of the region. We were the first, and for a long time the only, Bordeaux-based *négociant* to offer wines and spirits from all parts of France and other countries. Bordeaux was nevertheless the backbone of our business, continuing to this day.

🏵 BURGUNDY 🏵

Riches Inherited from the Monks

CÔTE D'OR – *The Golden Slope*

After our separation from Becky Wasserman in 1986 we continued to have enough activity in Burgundy to warrant having a resident member of our Europvin team based full-time in the region. For a number of years, Tony Taylor was our local representative and contributed to the expansion of our presence in Burgundy as well as taking care of our importers when they came to visit. We were receiving numerous customers from all parts of the world and most wanted to visit Burgundy.

We continued to represent a number of estates with whom we were working before the existence of Cannan & Wasserman. These included Domaine Henri Boillot, François Germain at Château de Chorey-les-Beaune, Aubert de Villaine's estate in Bouzeron, Jean Defaix and Louis Pinson in Chablis, Hubert de Montille in Volnay, and Marcel Vincent at Château Fuissé.

We also needed to restructure our Burgundy portfolio and find new sources. In the coming years we signed up Dugat-Py, Sylvie Esmonin, and Harmand-Geoffroy in Gevrey-Chambertin; Hubert Lignier and Robert Groffier in Morey St. Denis; Jean Gros and Anne Gros in Vosne-Romanée; Robert Chevillon and J.J. Confuron in Nuits St. Georges; Chandon de Briailles in Savigny-les-Beaune; Antoine Jobard and Robert Ampeau in Meursault; Louis Carillon in Puligny-Montrachet; and Marc Morey in Chassagne-Montrachet. We also continued to receive allocations from the celebrated Domaine des Comtes Lafon in Meursault.

Many of these estates were not available to us for the US but were very successful in Japan, Singapore, Australia, New Zealand, the UK, and Ireland. Each year we would accompany our importers for tastings at the wineries, having visited all the domaines during the previous winter to negotiate allocations for the next available vintage. Indeed, unlike Bordeaux, quantities are very restricted, sometimes just two or three casks of one wine being produced. These visits were not always pleasurable. In mid-winter Burgundy can be quite a hostile place, icy cold with snow on the ground and the cellars damp and very cold – sometimes so cold it was hard to taste the wines, most of which were still in cask with the malolactic fermentation unfinished. But still the welcome from the growers was always friendly and the negotiations successful up to a point. We were frequently unable to reserve the quantities we required for our customers. This said, I have a great love for Burgundy: both the Pinot Noir and Chardonnay from the Côte d'Or are among my favourite grape varieties. Visiting Burgundy and tasting in the cool cellars is systematically a thrilling experience; the tasting unfolds from a simple Bourgogne Rouge through the *villages* wines and winds up with the sensational Premier and Grand Crus. Comparing the different crus and understanding their precise geographical origin and terroir is always fascinating.

Over the years Domaine Henri Boillot in Volnay became Europvin's largest source in value. We were originally introduced to the domaine in the late 1970s by my friend Gérard Jaboulet of Hermitage fame and, as time went by, our allocations increased and we were able to purchase serious quantities, notably of their magnificent Puligny-Montrachet, Clos de la Mouchère, a monopoly for the domaine.

DOMAINE DE LA ROMANÉE-CONTI

There is no doubt that the most noteworthy of my Burgundy experiences was our involvement with the Domaine de la Romanée-Conti. I have already mentioned my early connection with the domaine during my time with Frederick Wildman. Over the years I maintained contact with Aubert de Villaine and sold sizeable quantities from his own family estate in Bouzeron, Domaine A & P de Villaine, specialised in the Aligoté grape. The conditions for growing Aligoté in Bouzeron are so favourable that Aubert was able to propose a specific appellation for the village denominated initially Aligoté de Bouzeron and now just Bouzeron.

The Domaine de la Romanée-Conti is owned by two families, the Leroy and the De Villaine families. From 1974 until 1992 Aubert de Villaine and Lalou Bize-Leroy ran the domaine together. For reasons concerning commercial strategy, Lalou resigned from her role in January 1992. Having been involved in sales, the departure of Lalou left Aubert in charge of sales as well as all technical aspects.

Shortly afterwards I visited Aubert in Bouzeron and we discussed their global distribution network. The strategy Aubert wanted to follow was to have an exclusive importer in each country. The domaine already had a strong presence in the US but there were some markets with no presence. Aubert offered us the distribution in Brazil, Spain, and the island of Malta.

Availability was very strictly controlled. We were given specific allocations of each wine in each market on the release of every new vintage. We acted as a commission agent so they could maintain complete control, not only of the exclusivity but also the pricing, and to make sure that the wines were not re-exported for speculative reasons.

The prestige of Vega Sicilia in Spain made Pablo Alvarez

With Pablo Alvarez of Bodegas Vega Sicilia at the Romanée-Conti vineyard.

the ideal partner with access to the finest restaurants and most creditable consumers in the country. For Brazil we worked with our importer, Otavio Piva de Albuquerque at Expand, for a number of years. For Malta the sixty or so bottles were made available to Philippe Martinet, an importer on the island. Brazil received a good allocation although Otavio was always pressuring for more. The wines were mainly sold to local collectors and prestigious restaurants until Expand ran into financial difficulties. The agency has since been transferred to another importer.

In Spain in 2002, Aubert treated us to a vertical tasting of ten vintages of La Tâche, a monopoly for the domaine and their most prestigious wine after the famed Romanée-Conti. The event was organised with the assistance of Pablo Alvarez for the Fundación para la Cultura del Vino in the magnificent ballroom of the Casino de Madrid. The foundation was created in 2001 by a group of historic bodegas in association with the Ministry of Agriculture to spread the history and culture of wine to a wide audience. The vintages shown to a carefully chosen group of trade and press members ranged from 1999 back to 1971, including 1997, 1996, 1995, 1993, 1991, 1990, 1989, and 1988. It was an extremely well-organised and memorable event, with all the wines served at the correct temperature and showing beautifully in spite of the youth of some of the vintages.

The following day a lunch was arranged at Vega Sicilia with a small group of high-profile restaurant owners and collectors with more great bottles from the domaine. I was seated next to Juli Soler, partner with Ferran Adrià of the famous El Bulli restaurant on the Costa Brava. This happy connection earned me a reservation for a memorable dinner with my wife at El Bulli. Reservations were hard to obtain with a waiting list of a full year. Once seated, the sommelier asked us which wine we would like to choose from the extensive list. He did not approve of our choice to go with the food. He then discovered who we were and who had arranged the reservation. After that a different wine was opened for each of the twenty or so different food preparations! I have no recollection of how we returned to our hotel! El Bulli is now closed and Ferran Adrià is working on other projects.

One great attraction of the relationship with the Romanée-Conti was being able to participate in the distributor meetings at the domaine every two years in January. Since Pablo Alvarez did not speak French and was often unable to attend, I was invited to participate on behalf of Spain. This was a special privilege since I was the only attendee who was not actually an importer. The event took place over two days and included a summary of the market conditions, details on activities at the domaine, and usually a lecture on technical and cultural aspects from well-known experts such as Claude and Lydia Bourguignon on the subject of terroir and biodynamics, and Pierre-Marie Guillaume of the famous vine nursery.

The highlight of the event was of course the tastings. During the first afternoon we would go down to the cool cellars and taste the full range of wines about to be released in bottle after more than two years ageing in cask and bottle. This was followed by the next vintage still in cask. These were very young wines but gave us an idea of the potential of the vintage. All the wines had that wonderful velvety texture that is the signature of the Romanée-Conti estate and clearly showed the differences between the various *crus*.

The following day, after a general business meeting during which issues concerning parallel exports and counterfeit bottles were discussed, another tasting would be organised. These were very special. In my first years of participation the tasting would be held on a table, about 30 metres (100 feet) long, in the Romanée-Conti cellars. It was impossible to put a pin between the sea of glasses spread out over the table, a truly impressive sight in this spectacular setting. The procedure was very serious with complete silence during the tasting and impeccable service of the wines by the Romanée-Conti staff. The last two tastings I attended took place in a restored town house belonging to the domaine. I recall a vertical tasting of La Tâche and twelve vintages of Echezeaux from 2004 back to 1990. Another unforgettable tasting was of fourteen vintages of Montrachet from 2003 back to an amazingly fresh and firmly structured 1969, without doubt the most sensational tasting of white wines in which I have ever had the privilege to participate. More recently there was a comparison between six vintages of Richebourg and six

Tasting at the Domaine de la Romanée-Conti.
Aubert de Villaine (left) and Pablo Alvarez (right) in the foreground.

vintages of Grands Echezeaux, evaluating the 2009, 1999, 1989, 1979, 1966, and 1959 vintages. All were remarkable wines, the 1959s in magnums being a special treat, still young, fresh, and in all their glory. The last I attended was in 2015, a vertical tasting of ten vintages of the legendary Romanée-Conti. The vintages ranged from 1971 back to 1919 and included 1966, 1964, 1961, 1959, 1955, 1952, 1943, and 1935, finishing with the 1919. For me this was a tasting of a lifetime, an experience no wine professional or amateur can ever forget. The wines were all phenomenal; even the 1919 was still alive with fruit and remarkable freshness.

Lunch after the tastings is always in the Romanée-Conti *salle de vendanges*, roughly translated as the harvest room, where the grape pickers have their lunch. A local Michelin-star chef takes care of the food and another range of remarkable wines is served blind. Attendees are asked to guess the Cru and the vintage. It is no easy task, but the Canadian agent from Quebec is nearly always correct in his evaluations. After lunch we are given the opportunity to taste the most recent vintage in cask. The wines, being only a few months old, many without having completed their malolactic fermentation, are not easy to taste so it is more like an early assessment of riches to come.

CHABLIS – *Chardonnay and Minerals*

Chablis, known for its crisp, minerally, dry white wines, has always been a favourite of mine and an important source for Europvin. The Chardonnay grape in this northerly climate performs particularly well on the chalky, clay soils, producing profound wines with ageing potential, especially at the Premier Cru and Grand Cru level. Demand for Chablis is particularly strong in Japan and was no doubt, with the UK and the US, our largest market for the appellation. In the UK no serious wine list can be without a Chablis. We had several sources and I paid frequent visits to the region. I have already recounted my time with J. Moreau & Fils in the 1970s and after the foundation of Europvin we continued to work with Moreau until the company was sold to the Boisset group. Our main focus was, as usual, single-estate wines, and among others we worked with Jean-Paul Droin, Louis Pinson, Jean Defaix, Daniel Dampt, Jean Dauvissat, Louis Moreau, Moreau-Naudet, Domaine Servin, and Sylvain Mosnier. At the well-established cooperative La Chablisienne, we selected our own cuvée and called it Chablis La Porte d'Or. Chablis has been called La Porte d'Or de la Bourgogne for centuries, being the most northerly outpost of Burgundy when coming from Paris.

On a memorable visit to Chablis with Pablo Alvarez of Vega Sicilia and his technical team, stops included William Fèvre, unforgettable tastings from casks and bottles with François Raveneau, and another with Vincent Dauvissat – the two most reputed names when Chablis is discussed.

Chablis has changed remarkably over the years. In the 1950s there were only 500 hectares (1,200 acres) planted. Revival started in the 1960s and today there are more than 5,000 hectares (12,000 acres) under vine. The climate is the cause of much anxiety. Frequent spring frosts can provoke extensive damage, although today measures have been taken to counter this threat. Another concern is global warming which appears to be changing the style of classic Chablis: the wines seem richer and less focused than in the past, losing some of their appealing crispness and charm. This said, there are still some remarkable wines being made by the top producers who endeavour to maintain the unique interpretation of the Chardonnay that makes Chablis so special. A recent visit to Domaine Pinson showed remarkable progress by the new generation, making crisp classic Chablis in the traditional style. As in other regions, there is a movement towards organic and biodynamic practices by the new generation, exemplified by Thomas Pico at Domaine Pattes Loup, a rapidly rising star.

BEAUJOLAIS – *The Home of Clochemerle*

In spite of declining popularity, Beaujolais was always important to Europvin. We had several sources and always enjoyed visits to this alluring region with its rolling hills and long-distance views towards the Alps and the Mont Blanc. We chose to work with various wineries reflecting the different Beaujolais Crus and their specific terroirs, especially those on granite and volcanic soils, giving more focus and complexity to the wines. Our main sources were Château du Moulin-à-Vent, Georges Boulon in Chiroubles, Jacky Janodet in Chenás, and Dominique Piron in Morgon and Fleurie. Europvin supplies the Beaujolais Villages from Dominique to Fortnum & Mason under their own label. We dabbled in Beaujolais Nouveau when it was popular but rarely with success due to the highly competitive nature of this unique activity. We did however send a few cases to Japan every year.

Happily, Beaujolais is coming back in vogue and demand is once again increasing for these attractive, lively wines from the Gamay grape, chock-full of bright fruit and charm. Beaujolais, and the image of the Gamay grape, has long been in the doldrums, partly due to the poor image that the Beaujolais

Nouveau campaign gave to the region with rather indifferent quality. Today, this situation is improving with the commitment of a few star growers devoted to biological and biodynamic farming. They are beginning to change this negative image and show that the Gamay grape can produce great wines with a potential to age. Domaines to look out for are: Guy Breton, Jean-Paul Thévenet, Jean Foillard, Claude Geoffray at Château Thivin, and Marcel Lapierre to name but a few.

❧ RHÔNE VALLEY ❧

From the Continental North to the Mediterranean South

SOUTHERN RHÔNE – *The Pope's Legacy*

The Rhône Valley is another very important chapter in the life of Europvin. From the very early days we were exporting Rhône wines to the US and other countries and were early enough in the game to be able to secure some very prestigious estates for our portfolio. In the Southern Rhône, this included a big commitment to Châteauneuf-du-Pape where, among others, we represented Château Rayas, Domaine du Vieux Télégraphe, Domaine de la Janasse, Domaine de la Vieille Julienne, Le Clos du Caillou, Domaine de Beaurenard, Domaine Chante Cigale, La Bastide St. Dominique, Domaine Roger Sabon, Les Cailloux from André Brunel, Bosquet des Papes, and the more traditional Domaine Lucien Barrot. We also shipped some Château de Beaucastel to Canada in the early 1980s.

One of our Châteauneuf stories was the difficulties encountered with Domaine du Vieux Télégraphe in the 1980s. We represented this celebrated estate in all the US except for California where Kermit Lynch was the importer. Normally the wines from Vieux Télégraphe were lightly filtered before bottling but Kermit requested bottles with no filtration to keep as much of the fruit and flavour as possible. At the time there was a lot of discussion over filtration or non-filtration fuelled by Robert Parker and other luminaries in the trade and press. My view is the decision should be entirely in the hands of the producer and that it is not the role of the importer to impose a technical issue on the grower. Hence for a time, as Kermit expanded his distribution throughout the US, there were two cuvées of Vieux Télégraphe on the US market and much discussion as to which was the better of the two. The vote usually went to the non-filtered cuvée since, just after release, the wine did indeed show more lively fruit and freshness. The filtered cuvée was more closed at the outset but after a year or two the effect of filtration had disappeared and the wine showed more stability with a better reflection of the terroir. In short, after some bottle age, I found the filtered version the better of the two. The discussion became so heated that it began to damage the brand name among consumers. The Brunier family, owners of Vieux Télégraphe, finally decided they could only ship one cuvée to the US and gave the agency to Kermit. In spite of the turmoil over this issue we continued our relationship with the Brunier family, exporting their wines to Asia and Australia. They also honoured me by inducting me into the venerable Echansonnerie des Papes, the local *Confrérie* (or Brotherhood); an event that took place twice a year, at that time, in the basement of the ruined papal château at Châteauneuf-du-Pape.

Château Rayas, Henri Bonneau, Beaucastel, and Clos des Papes are without doubt the most prestigious estates of the Châteauneuf-du-Pape. It took us a number of years before we could receive an allocation from Château Rayas. Jacques Reynaud, the owner in the 1980s and early 1990s, was very shy and did not enjoy receiving visitors. I have heard that he occasionally disappeared when he did not feel like receiving a visit. However, he was always kind to me and allowed me to taste from his ancient casks, many of which dated from the early twentieth century. Occasionally I could also taste a few bottles that were open. Eventually he gave us an allocation of both the red and white Château Rayas with his other wines, Pignan and Château de Fonsalette. After Jacques died in 1997, his nephew, Emmanuel Reynaud, took over, adding to the portfolio his excellent Château des Tours in Vacqueyras. Europvin has continued to receive allocations of all the wines every year. It is not only the traditional winemaking or the dated equipment at the domaine that make

Rayas so special. It is the sandy soil that gives the wines, produced from 100% old Grenache vines, their supreme elegance and persistence. It is arguably the best example in the world of the potential of this grape variety to produce world-class wines with a capacity to age over decades. This observation is also reflected in my joint venture with René Barbier, Espectacle, from 130-year-old Grenache vines in Montsant. More on this subject in a later chapter.

With the representation of so many domaines from Châteauneuf-du-Pape in so many countries it was obviously an area of great importance to Europvin. The region also enjoyed the enthusiastic support of Robert Parker who has a special place in his heart for these rich and elegant wines. The consequence was tremendous popularity for the appellation, especially in the US. On one occasion, in a retail store in Orange County, California, I counted twenty-three different Châteauneuf-du-Papes on the shelves. The result of this popularity and some adverse weather conditions, leading to smaller crops, has led to an increase in prices and less demand for these attractive, easy-drinking red wines. One difficulty was the obsession of some growers with making super-extracted, concentrated wines, in order to try to obtain high scores from the press. This has turned out to be a failure as most of these wines have not shown a capacity to age. On the other hand, we are witnessing an increasing interest for white Châteauneuf-du-Pape, which has improved tremendously in quality in recent years and now has more freshness and grip thanks to earlier harvesting.

The Southern Rhône is much more than Châteauneuf-du-Pape. Another treasure we paid a lot of attention to was the appellation Gigondas, located about 20 kilometres (12 miles) east of Châteauneuf towards Mont Ventoux and foothills of the Alps. This is a spectacular region with the vineyards rising up the slopes, topped by the dramatic rock formations of the Dentelles de Montmirail. Our main partner in Gigondas was Domaine Saint Gayan, belonging to Jean-Pierre and Martine Meffre. It was Robin Yapp's book that put me on the scent of this beautiful property and its rich inventory of old Grenache vines, some dating back more than one hundred years. My first visit to the domaine was in 1981 and the Meffre family have remained friends and a significant source ever since. On one occasion, with our children, we were taken up the mountain to hunt for truffles. These we found by observing the movement of a special reddish-coloured fly that indicated the location of the truffles by laying eggs on the same spot. Following the hunt, we enjoyed the truffles over a sumptuous lunch at the property. Saint Gayan is renowned for its age-worthy Gigondas; a good vintage has the potential to age sublimely for twenty years and more.

The estate also produces other wines worthy of mention, including a rich, intense Rasteau, a vivid white Sablet, and a Côtes-du-Rhône representing extraordinary value since the source is exclusively Côtes-du-Rhône Villages vineyards but at the price of a Côtes-du-Rhône. I continue to visit Saint Gayan every year as, apart from purchasing wines, Jean-Pierre is a fascinating source of technical information with a gift for explaining complicated details in a simple manner.

Europvin has other important sources in Gigondas, including the energetic Yves Gras at Domaine Santa Duc; Domaine Les Pallières, belonging to the Brunier family at Vieux Télégraphe; and the dynamic Louis Barruol at Château de Saint Cosme. This property claims to be the oldest in the area with the ruins of a Roman-era viticultural centre to prove it. All three estates are considered leaders within the appellation, producing wines that can easily rival many from Châteuneuf-du-Pape, and at more reasonable prices.

Other parts of the Southern Rhône are also producing remarkable wines in serious quantities. It is without doubt the source for many of the best-value red wines in the world. A number of the villages are gradually obtaining their own individual appellations, starting with Gigondas in 1971, followed by Vacqueyras in 1990, and more recently Rasteau, Cairanne, and Vinsobres. Others will follow, demonstrating the qualities of specific terroirs within each appellation. Commercially this may not be easy, since consumers are unfamiliar with the new appellations, and it may take many years of promotional work to establish these villages as household names.

NORTHERN RHÔNE – *The Kingdom of Syrah*

The list of prestigious growers in the Northern Rhône we represented over the years at Europvin is long, and important with regard to the performance and future of the company. From 1981 we started signing up estates for export to various markets, the initial list including Emile Champet, Pierre Barge (now Gilles Barge), Bernard Burgaud and the late Albert Dervieux in Côte Rôtie, Georges Vernay and Château de Rozay in Condrieu, Bernard Gripa and Jean-Louis Grippat in Saint Joseph, Gérard Chave (now Jean-Louis Chave), Henri Sorrel (now Marc Sorrel) and Fayolle in Hermitage, Auguste Clape and Thierry Allemand in Cornas, and Domaines des Remizières and Combier in Crozes-Hermitage.

Later on, other wineries of note were added to the portfolio. In Côte Rôtie these included René Rostaing after the passing of Albert Dervieux, his father-in-law; and Domaine Jamet and Patrick and Christophe Bonnefond thanks to the suggestion of Robert Parker. In Condrieu we worked with Yves Cuilleron and more closely with Domaine André Perret from his very first vintage. For a short period, before the property was sold, we purchased a few cases of the legendary Château Grillet, a unique property benefitting from its own appellation within the Condrieu demarcation. In Saint Joseph we added André Perret, Pierre Gaillard, and Domaine Courbis. Until Gérard Jaboulet's untimely death in 1997, we purchased a range of Northern Rhône wines under the André Passat label, essentially the same wines as Jaboulet but for commercial reasons sold with a different label.

In 1984 we received a letter from the late Alain Graillot on the recommendation of Jacques Seysses at Domaine Dujac in Burgundy. Alain had fallen in love with the Syrah grape variety and planned to start his own winery in Crozes-Hermitage, the first vintage being 1985. He was looking to establish a distribution network and offered Europvin the rights to export to the US (except California), Australia, Brazil, and a few Asian countries. Europvin continues to benefit from a sizeable allocation to this day. Alain, and his late wife Elisabeth, were always delightful and generous hosts and we enjoyed many meals at their home, sometimes with Robert Parker, who came to Alain's winery for regular tastings of Europvin's Rhône selections. Domaine Alain Graillot now produces one of the most sought-after red wines from the Rhône Valley, the classic non-destemmed Crozes-Hermitage. It has always sold at sensible prices, deserving a higher price for the quality in the bottle. This, and his considerable social network within the trade, have contributed to the immense success of the brand, selling over 200,000 bottles of each vintage. Some years, the domaine produces a special cuvée, Crozes-Hermitage – La Guiraude, that merits longer ageing, and a Saint Joseph from the granite slopes on the opposite bank of the Rhône. The day-to-day running of the estate is now in the hands of his sons, Maxime and Antoine, both doing an excellent job following in their father's footsteps. Alain became one of the most vocal advocates of non-destemming in France, resulting in wines a little more austere when young but with a capacity for long ageing and more complexity once in bottle.

With some time on his hands after his sons took over, Alain started consulting and winemaking in some unusual places including Morocco, the lagoon of Venice, mountainous Andorra, and Bierzo in northwest Spain. And, for the past ten years, we were fortunate to have had Alain as consultant at our Clos Figueras winery. He visited us twice a year to assist with the final blends for our three red wines, an invaluable contribution to the quality and prestige of our wines. More recently Alain launched Domaine de Fa, an estate in Beaujolais, close to his family home, including a Beaujolais AOC, Fleurie, and Saint-Amour. Alain was very popular, with great knowledge of the trade, both in the technical and commercial fields. His sudden and untimely death in March 2022 was a great loss to his numerous friends and family.

E. GUIGAL – CHÂTEAU D'AMPUIS

I first met Marcel and Bernadette Guigal back in 1976 while working for Frederick Wildman and remember enjoying a bottle of Georges Vernay's Condrieu with them in their small office (Guigal did not produce Condrieu

With my daughter Anne-Josephine at Château d'Ampuis.

in those days.) The object of the visit was to discuss the American market and Wildman's interest in representing Guigal. This was not possible due to an earlier commitment, leading to my close involvement with Paul Jaboulet Ainé, and signing up for the exclusive distribution of these wines for the US instead, an agreement that lasted more than forty years.

After founding Europvin, I maintained contact with the Guigal family, exporting a few cases of their wines to countries where they were not already represented. In the early 2000s, Pablo Alvarez of Vega Sicilia asked me to take his winemaker, Xavier Ausàs, and his vineyard manager to the Rhône to study white grape varieties and white winemaking in warmer climates. Vega Sicilia had planted some experimental white varieties on the estate and was making some experimental wines, a project later abandoned, Pablo not being convinced by the potential of the quality expected for Vega Sicilia. We visited all the domaines making white wine we could think of, one of them being Guigal, with white wines representing 30% of their production. After a long and enthusiastic conversation on the subject, Marcel suddenly asked me if Europvin might be interested in representing Guigal in Asia. I almost fell of my chair! What an opportunity! Guigal's previous agent, Kit Stevens, had died suddenly a few months earlier and there was an opening. This was the start of a long and exciting relationship with this successful and eminently professional family. Over the years and continuing today, Europvin diligently promotes Guigal in China, Hong Kong, South Korea, Thailand, Malaysia, Singapore, Indonesia, Australia, New Zealand, India, the Maldive Islands, and Dubai. The work includes winemaker's dinners, masterclasses for the trade, staff education for the importer's sales teams, and trade tastings. Meetings are frequently held with the importers at trade fairs, specifically Vinexpo and ProWein. On the Friday before Vinexpo when it was in Bordeaux, the Guigal family invited all their importers for a two-day event with tastings, a gala dinner, and an outing in the vineyards or sometimes on a boat floating down the Rhône, admiring the hillsides of Côte Rôtie and Condrieu from the river while drinking glasses of Guigal's Condrieu.

Guigal is a leading *négociant* in the Rhône Valley, producing almost seven million bottles each year, about 60% of which is an excellent Côtes-du-Rhône Rouge. They also have extensive vineyard holdings in the Northern Rhône, specifically in Côte Rôtie, Condrieu, Saint Joseph, and Hermitage. The purchase of the Jean-Louis Grippat estate in 2000 gave Guigal a foothold in Saint Joseph and Hermitage with some of the best vineyard sites. More recently Guigal has purchased Château de Nalys in Châteauneuf-du-Pape, after many years of searching for a suitable property in the appellation. Also, even more recently, they bought the famed Château d'Aqueria in Tavel, an appellation devoted to producing some of the most elegant and concentrated rosé wines in France. However, the company is best known for what is called their "La La" range of wines from Côte Rôtie, three specific sites that produce superlative quality: La Mouline, La Turque, and La Landonne. Made in small quantities and aged for three-years in new oak casks before bottling and release, these wines are the object of much speculation among collectors and

Philippe and Eve Guigal
(second right and second left)
in San Sebastian.

are frequently found on the international auction market at many times their release price. Guigal sells the "La La" wines on a strict allocation basis, linked to the volume of other wines purchased by the importer. I understand a fourth "La La" wine is on the drawing board.

Today, Europvin continues to represent Guigal in all the countries mentioned. With my daughter I represent Guigal in Spain in close collaboration with the importer, Castillo de Perelada. Our activities to promote Guigal are much the same as those for Europvin in Asia. Philippe Guigal visits the market occasionally, helping us introduce the wines to the most prestigious restaurants in Barcelona, Madrid, and San Sebastian. Promoting French wines in Spain is no easy feat since 97% of all wines consumed in Spain are Spanish, nevertheless, Guigal is gradually gaining more recognition, especially in restaurants.

OTHER NORTHERN RHÔNE WINERIES

Winery visits in the Rhône were full of happy experiences. I remember visits to the late Auguste Clape every year since 1981 and observing his commitment to the little-known appellation of Cornas. Auguste almost single-handedly put Cornas on the map as a world-class wine, and merits a statue in his name in the town centre. Later he was assisted by his son, Pierre-Marie, and grandson Olivier, who continue the good work today. On some visits I was welcomed by all three generations in the old cellar under his house which has remained unchanged since my first visit. I have rarely met a more genuine and generous personality, able to convey the love for his work on the land with such humility and modesty, than Auguste. He claimed that Cornas required ten years of ageing before reaching its prime. Invariably, at the end of each visit, a ten-year-old bottle was produced from a corner of the cellar covered in black mould. The wine consistently had wonderful purity with a mineral touch and great elegance.

Visits to Gérard Chave and his cellars in the small town of Mauves were also always memorable. To find his address one has to look out for a barely legible, rusty little sign that seems to have been untouched since the war. Like Auguste Clape, Gérard is modest and humble, in spite of being one of the world's greatest winemakers. In the 1990s, Gérard's son, Jean-Louis, gradually took over the domaine and has kept his father's open mind and attention to detail, resulting in ever more spectacular wines. It took some time to obtain an allocation and quantities were always small. At Europvin we assigned the few cases we had to importers in Asia and Australia.

Although Mauves is located on the right bank of the Rhône within the Saint Joseph appellation, it is for their wines of Hermitage that the domaine is best known. Most of the Hermitage vineyards are owned by large *négociants*, Paul Jaboulet, Chapoutier, Guigal, and Delas; the remainder are controlled by the cooperative at Tain l'Hermitage and a handful of small growers of whom Chave is by far the largest and most prestigious. The domaine was founded as far back as 1481. During visits we were privileged to taste from cask wines from vineyards in the specific plots on the Hermitage hill, especially Bessards, L'Hermite, and Peléat. We also tasted the white wines from Rocoules, Péléat, and L'Hermite. Before bottling, the wines from the different plots are blended to make just one cuvée each of the Hermitage Rouge and Blanc. In special years, when conditions permit, about 2,500 bottles of Hermitage Rouge Cuvée Cathelin are produced from the best casks. This wine is more intense and powerful than the normal cuvée, although essentially made the same way from the same sources. The rarity of this wine is such that the prices on the international market are stratospheric. Wines not required for the final blends are sold off in bulk to the local *négociants*. Today I am fortunate in being able to meet Gérard and his wife, Monique, frequently since he is an active member of the Académie Internationale du Vin. Technical conversations with Gérard are most rewarding, with his gift for simplifying what is really quite complicated.

Other visits in the Northern Rhône were equally rewarding. We had to leave plenty of time to visit Jean-Paul Jamet in Côte Rôtie while he explained in detail the merits of each wine we tasted. With André Perret we could taste a wide range of red and white wines, his single plot Condrieu, Côteau de Chéry, being the quintessence of the appellation in its full aromatic glory. Tasting the silky Syrah cuvées from Côte Rôtie and the aromatic Viognier wines from Condrieu is always gratifying. Many growers are most generous with their time and proud to show how well their wines age, finishing a tasting of young wines in cask with the opening of a much older bottle.

On a more personal note, I can say that the Northern Rhône red wines are among my most preferred wines in the world. They certainly have a dominant presence in my cellar with Hermitage, especially from Chave and La Chapelle from Jaboulet, as my all-time favourites. When mature, these wines show a class and elegance which, in my view, is unrivalled. It seems surprising that this appellation does not receive more attention, perhaps this is due to its small size and consequent rarity.

🎋 LOIRE VALLEY 🎋

The Land of Kings and Châteaux

The Loire Valley has always been one of my favourite regions, not only for wine. The lush green countryside, and the scenery of rolling hills and chalk cliffs dotted with the famous châteaux, is a tourist destination that is not to be missed. For wines it is the variety that is so inspiring, ranging from the crisp, dry white wines from Muscadet to the gorgeous, sweet wines of Anjou from the Chenin grape; the enchanting red wines from Saumur, Chinon, and Bourgueil; the profound dry, semi-sweet and sweet wines from Vouvray and Montlouis; and, further east, the unrivalled Sauvignon Blancs from Sancerre and Pouilly Fumé. A number of lesser-known, but no less-interesting appellations, such as Cheverny, Quincy, Reuilly, and Menetou-Salon, located in between the better-known names, are also worth mentioning.

I have been visiting the Loire Valley since my first bicycle trip in 1966, but it was from 1973 that I began making regular visits to the region, first for Frederick Wildman and later for Europvin. The Loire visits were always the first of the year since in January you can already have a good idea of how the new wines will develop. I would start in Muscadet and travel eastwards to Anjou, Touraine, and finally to Sancerre and Pouilly-sur-Loire, stopping to visit and taste with our suppliers along the way. Tasting the tart, dry Muscadet wines in a cold cellar at nine in the morning in January was not always a pleasurable experience. The soils in Muscadet vary from clay to schist and granite, leading us to choose to work with different producers reflecting the local soil characteristics. These included Domaine des Dorices in Vallet on clay and Marc Olivier at Domaine de la Pépinière at Maisdon-sur-Sèvres on granite and schist. Other interesting growers we represented were Jean Dabin at St. Fiacre, who had another profession making strange-shaped flat-topped *foudres* (large wooden casks for fermenting and ageing wines), and Joseph Hallereau, a great character, much loved by Jasper Morris at Morris & Verdin, who made full, rich Muscadets that are better served with fish in the local *beurre blanc* sauce than with oysters. Normally oysters are the natural accompaniment for these delightful, crisp, undervalued, and under-appreciated wines from Muscadet.

Moving on to Anjou, there's a full spectrum of wines ranging from dry, semi-dry, and sweet white wines from the Chenin Blanc grape, to dry and sweet rosé wines and the captivating red wines from Saumur made with Cabernet Franc. The soils vary from the schist and slate in Savennières and l'Aubence to the chalky clay of Saumur. It is lamentable that the great, sweet white wines from Côteaux du Layon, Quarts de Chaume, and Bonnezeaux are not more appreciated. Made from the Chenin grape, they have bright acidity and a remarkable ageing potential. When young they have an uplifting freshness and balance which contrasts with the rather heavier, richer wines of Sauternes. Some of the most spectacular tastings I experienced were at Château de Fesles in Bonnezeaux, belonging, at the time, to the aptly named Monsieur Boivin. After a tasting of his younger wines, he would invariably open bottles from the 1940s. The 1947 vintage was especially remarkable, still a very fresh and complex golden nectar with many decades of life to come. Occasionally Monsieur Boivin would allow us to purchase some of his older vintages. The little-known Château de la Guimonière in the Chaume appellation had similar stocks which were equally remarkable. The owner would also open old bottles in wonderful condition, going back to the 1930s.

For dry wines from Anjou our main source was Savennières, a small appellation on the right bank of the Loire producing elegant, mineral wines from the Chenin Blanc grown on schist and slate soils. The official yields are low, resulting in wines with good concentration and long ageing potential. Sometimes, when young, Savennières can be tight and austere but with ageing, breed and complexity come forward, making for some of the most intellectually interesting dry white wines from France. The most notable producer is Nicolas Joly, famous for his pioneering work with biodynamic production methods. I met Joly at his Coulée de Serrant estate in the 1980s and for a time we exported his wines to Luxembourg. I still recall a long conversation in his study, or rather a monologue, on the merits of biodynamics in the vineyard. Today, Nicolas Joly is a world authority on the subject, having written books and conducted lectures in numerous countries. Our other suppliers for Savennières over the years have been Château d'Epiré and Domaine du Closel. Savennières has never been easy to sell, in spite of being a world-class dry white wine with an amazing capacity to age for decades.

Saumur is best known for the soft, fruity red wines from, dominantly, the Cabernet Franc grape variety. White wines from the Chenin Blanc are also produced but are more often converted to the excellent sparkling wines from the region. The soils are chalky and some producers stand out, making some of the most sought-after red wines from the Loire Valley. The best known is the Saumur-Champigny from Clos Rougeard but we worked with the Filliatreau family and Château de Targé for many years, and were particularly successful in the UK with a wine from Filliatreau.

A few kilometres further east we come to the red wine districts of Chinon and Bourgueil. The soils here are varied but the grape variety is the Cabernet Franc again. Since the 1990s the two appellations have benefitted hugely from global warming. Back in the 1960s and 1970s the wines were light in alcohol, rather tart, and austere, due to the difficulty of gaining full ripeness of the grapes in this northerly climate. Today the wines enter the world-class category with some of the finest and most expressive examples of the Cabernet Franc grape. We successfully exported the wines from Charles Joguet, Olga Raffault, and Bernard Baudry in Chinon and those from Domaine Lamé Delille Boucard and Pierre-Jacques Druet in Bourgueil. Like the Chenins from Anjou, these red wines have a remarkable capacity to age. I recall tasting many older vintages from Joguet and especially from Lamé-Delillie-Boucard who, for some reason, had kept back a large stock of the 1969 and 1976 vintages, which they frequently opened for visitors to the domaine and at trade fairs. The wines remained bright and fresh with great complexity, not something that could be achieved with every vintage during those decades.

Moving east again, Vouvray was always an important appellation for Europvin, so much so we launched our own label in the 1980s with the appropriate name La Coulée d'Or (the ripple of gold). This was a cuvée we selected from the Monmousseau-family company and like most good Vouvray, the wine was slightly off-dry and very appealing. Our most illustrious source for Vouvray was from the previously mentioned Domaine Huet, no doubt the most prestigious estate, with a large collection of wines from their three main plots. The style ranged from very dry to quite sweet depending on the vintage and the harvest date. Tasting at the domaine was always a revelation, with the varied styles of extraordinary depth and complexity, once again, with an amazing capacity for ageing for many decades. Huet's wines would certainly be candidates for being among the world's greatest examples of Chenin Blanc. In the 1980s and 1990s, we had limited success with the wines from Prince Poniatowski. His best cuvée was the Clos Baudouin. The property has since been sold and is now in the capable hands of François Chidaine, a rising star from nearby Montlouis. Another source in Vouvray is Domaine Bourillon Dorléans. Frédéric Bourillon is a great character and a passionate winemaker. His spectacular cellars stretch back in a labyrinth of chalk caves carved out of the rocks in the fifteenth century under some of the best vineyards. The same cellars are a cultural destination with frequent sculpture exhibitions. Frédéric has vintages dating back to the 1920s, still in fine condition, never having been moved from the caves. Another of my favourite individuals in the Loire was the now-retired Bernard Fouquet at Domaine des Aubuisières. Not only did he produce floral and precise Vouvray of a rare elegance, he was also a great supporter of Europvin, handing over the contact details of importers wanting to purchase his wines, helping us to expand our distribution network.

We dabbled in other wines from Touraine but our main focus shifted east again towards Sancerre and Pouilly-Fumé with a stop in the small but not insignificant vineyards of Quincy and Reuilly. On clay soils with a limestone base, the Quincy and Reuilly appellations are known for their crisp, dry Sauvignon Blanc white wines, often called the poor man's Sancerre since the style is similar and the price more accessible. Although some of the wines are excellent, few have the class of a well-made Sancerre. Almost since the first years, Europvin purchased the wines from Domaine Mardon in Quincy and have never been disappointed after nearly forty years.

Both Sancerre and Pouilly-Fumé have been a priority for Europvin since the earliest years of the company. These two appellations are household names in the wine trade, producing outstanding dry white wines from the Sauvignon Blanc on both silex and chalk soils. Red and rosé wines are also made in Sancerre from the Pinot Noir grape of Burgundy fame. Silex soils are found closer to the Loire and in this sector we worked with Domaine Vacheron, a large family domaine, also well respected for their red wines. On the southern edge of the Sancerre appellation, Europvin purchased thousands of cases from the previously mentioned Jean-Max Roger estate in the village of Bué where he is owner of some of the best historical sites, notably Le Chêne Marchand and Le Grand Chemarin. Another producer I always enjoyed visiting was Philippe de Benoist at Domaine du Nozay, brother-in-law to Aubert de Villaine of the Romanée-Conti. He is a bon vivant and a good friend who spent much of his winter months hunting wild game locally and in Africa. Today the domaine is in the capable hands of his sons. I was also in close contact with the Bourgeois family in Chavignol, purchasing their famous Sancerre, La Côte des Monts Damnés, and at one time close to negotiating a joint marketing venture in the US. From all these producers the style of the wines varies greatly. Jean-Max with the warmest microclimate makes full, rich Sancerre wines with focus and delightful gooseberry flavours. The Vacheron wines on silex are more mineral, and the Domaine du Nozay, on chalky clay at the northern edge of the appellation, makes classic Sancerre with good grip and a floral touch.

On the opposite bank of the Loire in the Pouilly-Fumé appellation, the two main sources are in the village of Les Berthiers. Like Jean-Max Roger, the Chatelain family became one of Europvin's largest suppliers, the shipments often going to the same customers, predominantly in the UK and Ireland. The other source was Serge Dagueneau and his daughters. Chatelain produces rich complex wines on silex soils with a perfect balance and the gunflint minerality of a classic Pouilly-Fumé. Serge Dagueneau makes wines of a slightly different style that appear to be a little sweet but are in fact perfectly dry. No doubt his handling of the fruit gives the wines the impression of a touch of sweetness. Needless to say, both styles are very successful. Both Sancerre and Pouilly-Fumé enjoy worldwide recognition as the definitive source for some of the finest Sauvignon Blanc wines in the world. It is here that the Sauvignon offers us the finest expression of the variety, with a perfect balance between the fruit and refreshing acidity. Having met Jean-Max Roger, Jean-Claude Chatelain, and Serge Dagueneau prior to founding Europvin in 1978, they continue to be suppliers to the company, since those very early days.

ALSACE

The Land of Flower-Decked Villages

Alsace is another of my favourite regions. Each vineyard area has its charms and diverse landscapes but Alsace must be among the most alluring, stretching along the foothills of the Vosges mountains on the left bank of the Rhine, just opposite the Black Forest in Germany. The villages that were not destroyed during the two world wars are among the most picturesque in France. Constructed in the fifteenth and sixteenth centuries, Riquewihr, Ribeauvillé, and Kaysersberg are perhaps the most attractive with their old, half-timbered houses and courtyards decorated with multiple window boxes full of red geraniums and vines that crawl over the walls. They are also the location of some of the best vineyards.

Alsace was always important for Europvin. Over the years the company exported wines from various producers starting with Jérôme Lorentz in Bergheim, Schlumberger, Rolly Gassmann, Albert Mann, and René Muré. Our closest relationship, though, was with the late Jean Meyer at Josmeyer, with our remarkable success with his wines in Japan. Tastings in his cellars were a delight to the senses, the expression of the terroir around the town of Wintzenheim with the different grape varieties being a voyage of discovery. Like with all Alsace producers, multiple wines are made according to the grape variety, sugar content, and location of the vineyard. Almost all Alsace wines are from single grape varieties, the main grapes being Riesling, Gewurztraminer, Pinot Gris, Pinot Blanc, and Sylvaner. The tastings lasted all morning and concluded with late harvest wines and the outstanding Grand Cru Hengst vineyard of which Jean was part owner. All his wines have a floral and mineral touch and are profound, vibrant, and quite structured, ideal with food. The Pinot Blanc and Sylvaner suffer from being classed as lesser varieties but, in my view, when well made by the likes of Josmeyer and other prominent Alsace producers represent some of the best values in France for white wine.

Another close relationship was with Philippe Blanck at the Paul Blanck winery in Kientzheim. A larger-than-life personality, he is an ambassador not only for his family winery but for all Alsace. A tireless traveller, he can be seen in any number of the world's best restaurants successfully convincing the sommeliers of the merits of Alsace wines with their food. As with Jean Meyer, tasting the wide spectrum of the Paul Blanck wines is always an education on the merits of the specific terroirs and Grands Crus in his neighbourhood.

On a personal level, I am most fond of the dry white wines from Alsace that convey the true flavours of the variety. However, there is a tendency for many to be quite sweet and even very sweet. I am not talking about the Vendanges Tardives or Sélection des Grains Nobles, which rank with the great sweet wines of the world, with a capacity for decades-long ageing. It is the classic varietal wines, with or without the name of a specific site, that pose a problem since, when purchasing a bottle, it is impossible to know if the wine is bone dry or semi-sweet. Fortunately, this issue is being addressed and an indication of sweetness is beginning to appear on the labels – this will only improve the commercial prospects for these delightful wines.

CHAMPAGNE

Gastronomy and Celebration

Champagne needs no introduction and has always been on the Europvin list. With chilled Fino Sherry, it is my favourite aperitif. In the early years we worked with the exemplary Mailly Champagne Cooperative, shipping large quantities to Germany. Soon after we included the Venice Simplon-Orient Express cuvée mentioned in an earlier chapter. At Vinexpo one year I visited the stand of Bruno Paillard, a new producer in those days. We started selling his carefully crafted Champagnes with attractive artist labels in Holland and the US. We continued with Bruno for many years until he decided to purchase the clientele from us so he could have better control of his marketing strategy as his company grew. Today Bruno is at the head of the Lanson-BCC (Boisel, Chanoine Champagne) group and the Bruno Paillard brand ranks with the leading houses for quality and prestige. In the early 2000s Luis Caballero, owner of the Caballero Sherry group and Emilio Lustau, was looking for a Champagne house for representation in Spain. Under the guidance of Bruno, we visited Champagne together. After an extensive visit and negotiations, we signed up Lanson Champagne, also part of the BCC group, for the Spanish market.

Later we focused on grower Champagnes, notably J. Lassalle in Chigny-Les-Roses, which we continue to buy for our restaurant at Clos Figueras. Lassalle is now in the hands of three generations of women, producing full-flavoured and focused cuvées from Premier Cru sites on the Montagne de Reims. Other growers were André Jacquart in Le Mesnil and Pierre Gimonnet, with some of the best sites in the Côte des Blancs. Gimonnet makes savoury Champagnes with all the elegance and focus of a Blanc de Blancs. More recently we have worked with Nicolas Maillart in Ecueil who also supplies our restaurant. His vineyards are scattered among Premier Cru and Grand Cru sites and include an ungrafted patch of Pinot Noir. A touch of oak adds to the complexity of these exciting Champagnes with their fine texture and ample finish.

The most famous name we had some involvement with was Champagne Salon in Le Mesnil. We shipped small quantities of this superb and very special vintage Champagne to various destinations. Salon's sister company, Champagne Delamotte, was another source and one of my favourite Blanc de Blancs.

❧ OTHER FRENCH WINE REGIONS ❧

Distinction and Innovation

One of the specialities at Europvin was to seek out the best wines we could find in what might be termed as the lesser-known areas in France. These days some are becoming more significant in the scheme of French viticulture, in particular the wines from the Languedoc Roussillon. This region was never our speciality but we always promoted the very dependable Corbières from Château Etang des Colombes. In the Minervois we worked with the Domaine Sainte Eulalie and Domaine Gros Tollot, a venture launched by Anne Gros of Vosne-Romanée and her husband Jean-Paul Tollot of Domaine Tollot-Beaut in Chorey-les-Beaune. In the Roussillon we purchased wines from Domaine Gauby and from Domaine Sarda-Malet. From Banyuls and Collioure we listed the wines from the Parcé family, unfortunately with little success for these special wines. Today the region is shaking off its poor image as a producer of vast quantities of indifferent, everyday table wine of the past with a new generation of motivated growers taking advantage of the ideal climate, low yields, and perfectly suited grape varieties, including the Grenache, Carignan, and Mourvèdre. Organic and biodynamic practices are now commonplace, with a conscientious study of the diverse terroirs, especially at higher altitudes.

The Southwest, though, was more important for Europvin, especially when we were selecting large volumes for Le Club Français du Vin in the 1980s. We covered most of the sub-regions including Madiran with the powerful, structured wines from the Tannat grape. Suppliers included Alain Brumont, Domaine Laplace, and great value from Domaine Barréjat. In Cahors we worked with Domaine Jouffreau, Clos Triguedina, and Château Lamartine. Cahors deserves much more attention than it receives. These rich, spicy red wines are made predominantly with the Malbec grape, locally called Cot, and have a remarkable capacity to age. In Jurançon our sources included Cru Lamouroux and Clos Uroulat. Both the delightful dry and sweet wines made from the Gros Manseng and Petit Manseng varieties deserve a wider audience.

One important source in the Southwest was Château du Tariquet, an Armagnac producer but better known for the huge quantities of well-made dry and off-dry white wines now found in supermarkets the world over. This is an amazing success story. Due to high taxation and a lack of coordinated promotion, Armagnac was becoming hard to sell in the 1980s. Yves Grassa at Château du Tariquet seized the opportunity to make simple but alluring table wines from the Ugni Blanc grape, while continuing to make very fine Armagnac. My first visit to Tariquet was in the early days of this project, when production was small and in an experimental stage. The family have since substantially increased their vineyard holdings and are now producing millions of bottles of these appealing white wines at very reasonable prices. Europvin has worked with the Grassa family ever since the beginning of their table-wine venture, for many years supplying Taillevent's prestigious wine shop in Paris as well as numerous importers worldwide.

Other wines from the Southwest included Château Bellevue La Forêt in the Frontonnais near Toulouse. A pleasant, easy-to-drink red wine from the local Négrette grape variety that proved to be very successful in the UK. Château de Padère in Buzet was a source of volume for Le Club Français du Vin. This region, on the left bank of the Garonne, grows classic Bordeaux grape varieties, dominated by the Merlot with some Cabernet Sauvignon and Cabernet Franc. The Southwest is exciting in the variety and striking differences in the wines from each sub-region. The distances are large, the grape varieties varied, and the source of diverse flavours, very different from nearby Bordeaux.

Another part of France of interest to Europvin was the Jura, where we were an early prospector. From the early 1980s we exported wines from Domaine Rolet and Château d'Arlay, mostly to Singapore where restaurant owners from the Jura wanted to serve wines to match the food from their home province. Today the distinctive wines from the Savagnin grape have become fashionable, with a number of growers making truly exciting wines. Names to look out for are Domaine André et Mireille Tissot; Domaine du Pélican, founded in 2012 by the Marquis d'Angerville of Volnay fame; and Domaine Ganevat with a huge range of wines available on allocation at steep prices.

Chardonnay is also planted extensively and producing wines to rival nearby Bourgogne Blanc. A recent visit to the Jura with the Académie Internationale du Vin was very enlightening.

Alain Graillot introduced us to Domaine de L'Idylle in the Savoie, another up-and coming-region that used to supply the local alpine ski resorts almost exclusively. Now the distinctive flavours of the local Roussette and Mondeuse grapes are capturing the interest of enthusiastic sommeliers. Quantities are being put aside for export to the more mature markets with fine-dining venues.

Sales of rosé wines from Provence have increased out of all recognition in the past decade. Ever since the 1980s, Europvin has exported the wines from the Savatier family at Château du Rouët in the Esterel hills. Quantities were small until suddenly the New York market started purchasing thousands of cases. This was repeated every spring and continues to this day. Other states and countries now perpetuate the fashion for rosé wines from Provence. After decades in the doldrums, the refreshing, light-coloured dry rosés have become a priority for many importers.

Europvin's activities in France included spirits and products distantly related to wine, such as a Vermouth de Chambéry from Dolin, the only remaining producer from a long tradition in the town of Chambéry. Their dry white vermouth was always a favourite. Macvin, an aperitif from the Jura made from fermenting grape juice with the addition of the local marc, was also on the list. Similarly, Pineau des Charentes and Floc de Gascogne, made from grape must with the addition of Cognac and Armagnac respectively.

Another successful project was natural cider from Normandy. One evening in Seattle a retailer gave me a bottle of Duché de Longueville cider from near Dieppe. I tasted it in my hotel room and was most impressed, especially when I learnt they were making ciders with specific apple varieties, whose attractive names appear on the label, for example Antoinette and Muscadet de Dieppe. These ciders are completely natural and have a small amount of alcohol, varying from 2.5 to 4%. I soon discovered they were also making a sparkling

Ordre du Mérite Agricole.

non-alcoholic cider. On my return to France, I visited the plant and decided to design our own label for the range of products. This proved to be a long-term success and for years we were shipping full containers of non-alcoholic cider to Oregon, and smaller quantities to many other states in the US and other countries. The business continues for Europvin to this day. Spirits were also important, especially Cognac, Armagnac, and Calvados.

On the 22nd February 1999 I was nominated Chevalier de l'Ordre du Mérite Agricole by the French Minister of Agriculture for my services to the export of French wines.

CHAPTER 14

SPAIN

The Iberian Metamorphosis

From the very early days, Spain was part of Europvin's DNA, eventually to the extent that our future was dominated by our close relationships with some of the most prestigious producers. I made frequent trips to Spain and gradually built a network of suppliers and relationships in the key production areas of Rioja, Ribera del Duero, Priorat, Toro, Rueda, Navarra, and Jerez. Before Spain joined the European Union, we had great difficulty in bringing samples back from the wineries to show to our clients when they visited the Bordeaux office. If we were stopped at the frontier, which was a frequent occurrence, we would have to pay taxes and duty. This was not much of a problem but an immense amount of time would be wasted in going to the local authorities to pay the taxes. If it was a weekend, we would have to wait until the Monday morning for the tax office to open. Thanks to our friendship with Txomin Rekondo, an esteemed restaurant owner in San Sebastian who possesses a spectacular cellar with over 100,000 bottles under his restaurant, we found a solution – all our samples were sent to his restaurant. Before each trip to Spain, I would call Txomin and he would order several cases of Bordeaux Grands Crus Classés in different bottle sizes. I recall Château Yquem in large formats was a special favourite. I would load up my car with these cases and once at the restaurant, I would make the delivery and collect my samples to take back to France. Sometimes a customs officer would stop me but usually the subsequent negotiation was cut short when I gave them a bottle of lesser value for their lunch! This excellent arrangement with Txomin became unnecessary after Spain became a member of the European Union. We still visit his excellent restaurant and occasionally he continues to buy some wines from Europvin for his amazing collection.

🎋 RIOJA 🎋

The Ebro and Rioja Rivers of Wine

Through our activities in Bordeaux, we purchased sizeable quantities of wine from Château Larose Perganson, a Haut Medoc vineyard, part of the Château Larose-Trintaudon property, belonging at the time to the Forner family of Spanish origin. In the 1970s, Enrique Forner decided he would create a new Rioja house from scratch in association with the cooperative in the centrally located Rioja town of Cenicero. With permission from the Marqués de Cáceres, Enrique had a suitable name for his wines. He proceeded to enlist the technical advice of Emile Peynaud and create a distinctive dark-red label, now well known to all Rioja lovers the world over. I was particularly fond of the 1973 vintage, which I believe was one of the first on the market. As previously mentioned, we exported some serious quantities to the UK and Australia. As time went on Marqués de Cáceres grew rapidly and required marketing on a scale way beyond our means as a new company. We therefore created our own label for the wine with the brand Grandeza, which we used until we had problems with the brand name.

From the early 1980s we began searching for other sources in Rioja. It was at this time I first visited the classic houses in Haro: López de Heredia, La Rioja Alta S.A., Bodegas Muga; La Granja Remelluri in nearby Labastida, and my old contacts at CVNE (Compañía Vinícola del Norte de España). In those days there were few quality-orientated Rioja producers and almost no single-estate wines apart from Remelluri. We soon added to our portfolio the wines from Muga and Remelluri and were successful with both houses in the US. We also purchased small quantities from López de Heredia for our friend and importer in Holland, Theo van Broekhuizen.

Muga was quite a large company, making classic Rioja wines but gradually modernising their style, little by little replacing their American oak ageing casks with French oak. I became very friendly with the Muga family and we enjoyed a good relationship until suddenly, one summer evening, just before leaving for a holiday, we received a telex advising us we could no longer sell their wines in the US since they had given the agency to Jorge Ordóñez, another importer. This was quite a shock since we had put a lot of effort into selling Muga and were beginning to have good results. It was also the first time we had lost an important agency, consequently an emotional setback. We had similar problems with Remelluri, a spectacular estate high on the mountain above Labastida, for which we were also beginning to have good results. I recall a stormy meeting with Jaime Rodriguez, the owner, who failed to comprehend that time was needed to establish a new brand and could not understand why his native Basque country was purchasing more wine than New York! From CVNE we purchased small quantities, mostly for the Canadian market.

LA RIOJA ALTA S.A.

With La Rioja Alta we had more luck and by 1984 we were exporting small quantities to the US. La Rioja Alta was founded in 1890 and has stuck to the classic Rioja style, using American oak for the ageing of all their wines. Their brands, notably Viña Alberdi and Viña Ardanza, are to be found on almost all the good wine lists in Spain. The company owns more than 500 hectares (1,235 acres) of well-located Rioja vineyards and possesses 45,000 casks, each of 225 litres (60 gallons), for ageing at any one time. Long ageing in bottle before release assures drinkability on the day of purchase. Over eight million bottles are currently ageing in their cellars. I say the style is classic but over the years they have ever so slightly tweaked the winemaking, giving their wines a little less time in cask and consequently a little less oak influence and brighter fruit. This has propelled the company to the top league of great wines of the world, making distinctive, unmistakably Rioja wines of great elegance and charm. Their top cuvées, Gran Reserva 904 and Gran Reserva 890, have a remarkable capacity to age for forty years and more. They are wines that can rival the best of Burgundy, with a wonderful silky texture and a harmonious balance between the oak and fruit.

During our relationship with La Rioja Alta they acquired some other wineries, becoming an important part of our portfolio. The first was Torre de Oña, with Remelluri, one of the first single-estate Rioja wineries to be established after the Franco era. Here the wines are rather different in style to the classics from La Rioja Alta, with the use of some French oak in the blend. It is perhaps a more modern approach but equally appealing. Shortly afterwards in 1988, the company acquired a magnificent estate, Lagar de Cervera in Galicia, producing dry aromatic white wines from the Albariño grape. At the time Spain was not known for white wines but it soon became apparent there was potential in Galicia to make world-class white wines of great appeal. The vineyard is unique for the spectacular views overlooking the Minho river estuary and the ocean beyond with the mountains of Portugal on the opposite bank. Later, in 1990, the company acquired land in Ribera del Duero and created Bodegas Aster, now ranking with the region's most prestigious wineries.

Our relationship with La Rioja Alta became stronger after the arrival of Guillermo de Aranzabal, the new managing director in 1986. A member of one of the founding families, Guillermo understood that time was needed to establish his brands in the US and had confidence in our capacity to promote his wines through our distribution network. The year 1990 was a milestone. First the company celebrated their centenary in great style, inviting me and several of our importers to the event which included tastings, vineyard visits with a barbecue in one of their vineyards, and sumptuous lunches and dinners.

1990 was also the year we created Europvin Iberia with La Rioja Alta, Vega Sicilia, and Emilio Lustau. The association of the three prestigious bodegas helped create a momentum, putting Europvin on the map as a specialist for the finest Spanish wines. The association was also effective in Japan, where we represented all three bodegas. As previously mentioned, several market visits were organised in the US and Japan with the usual activities, including masterclass tastings and winemaker's dinners. Sales improved over the following years reaching about 15,000 cases in the US in 2010. At that time Europvin was owned by Vega Sicilia and the Caballero group, owners of Emilio Lustau. Caballero wanted to sell some of their Europvin shares and found CVNE as a future partner. The co-ownership with CVNE, being a neighbour and competitor of La Rioja Alta, created a conflict of interest and so with much regret Europvin had to abandon their representation of La Rioja Alta after nearly twenty-five years of a successful relationship. Nevertheless, I continue to visit the winery and purchase their wines for my own consumption.

OTHER RIOJA PRODUCERS

Europvin has other suppliers in the Rioja. The Caballero group owns Viña Herminia in the Rioja Oriental, making wines of a rather different style than La Rioja Alta. The bodega is located in the southeastern corner of the Rioja with a more Mediterranean climate. The Grenache grape dominates in this area, producing very pleasant, easy-to-drink wines while maintaining the Rioja character. These wines, full of fruit and charm, were priced very reasonably, creating a good following.

In Rioja Alavesa we represented Bodegas y Viñedos Artadi in Brazil and some other countries. The winery, situated in the attractive medieval town of Laguardia in Rioja Alavesa, produces intense rich wines of a modern style. They are best known for a special vineyard named Viña El Pison producing just 8,000 bottles from 2.20 hectares (5.4 acres). This wine, after receiving 100 points from Robert Parker for the 2004 vintage, has become an icon in the

Spanish wine world. The owner, Juan Carlos López de Lacalle, is a member of the Académie Internationale du Vin. He arranged a memorable visit for the Académie back in 2015. We visited this small vineyard and admired the soil structure before heading for a sumptuous dinner in Laguardia prepared by the Michelin-star restaurant Elkano from the Basque fishing port of Getaria.

Although we have done very little business with them, our greatest friends in Rioja are Maria José López de Heredia and her husband, José Luis Ripa. Their winery has been in the hands of Maria José's family since 1877 and little has changed since. A visit to their cellars is a trip into the past, with multiple rows of old American oak barrels and bins chock-full of blackmould–covered bottles, the oldest being from the 1893 vintage. The wines are extraordinary, the brands household names in Spain and, as for La Rioja Alta, appear on almost every wine list of merit in the country. Each brand represents a vineyard belonging to the family. The best known is Viña Tondonia, a spectacular vineyard dominating a wide bend of the Ebro river. There is also Viña Bosconia, also on the banks of the Ebro, Viña Zaconia, and Viña Cubillo. Being aged exclusively in American oak, these are classic Rioja wines in the old style, dating back to the late nineteenth century when the French merchants established a presence in Rioja after phylloxera had destroyed their vineyards in France. Phylloxera came to Spain later with equally catastrophic results, but the winemaking process had been established and was maintained throughout most of the twentieth century, and continues today at López de Heredia. I have been fortunate to be able to taste Viña Tondonia of various vintages back to 1954. These are wines of extraordinary freshness and complexity with a capacity to age for more than half a century. They enjoy a cult following in Spain and the export markets. This also applies to their very unique white Viña Tondonia, which is released in small quantities after ten years of ageing in cask and in bottle, another classic style from the past which is now only made at López de Heredia. Maria José, with her lively and engaging personality, is the perfect ambassador for her wines. She is committed to maintaining the winemaking practices of her ancestors, conserving a unique window to the wines of past ages, and refusing to be swayed by fashionable innovations so common in today's communication-driven world.

🐉 RIBERA DEL DUERO 🐉

World-Class Wines on a High Plateau

BODEGAS VEGA SICILIA

Ribera del Duero is a relatively recent DO (*Denominacion de Origen*), founded in 1982. Prior to that very few bodegas existed and most were dedicated to making inexpensive rosé wines. One winery stood out as being exceptional, Bodegas Vega Sicilia. My first taste of this unique wine was in the early 1970s in a small restaurant in San Sebastian with my friend Theo van Broekhuizen from Holland. Vega Sicilia on the wine list, at the ridiculously low price of 1,000 pesetas, was irresistible. We returned on several occasions to eat *angulas* (the delectable baby eels) and drink Vega Sicilia. The restaurant's cellar was down the street and had no lighting, so we never knew which vintage we were ordering! All the vintages were from the 1940s and were sublime. Today Vega Sicilia is no longer on the list and the *angulas* have become unaffordable since the bulk of the catch is sent to Japan where they are a sought-after luxury.

Later, in 1984, while researching for new sources, specifically in the Duero region, I stopped at Vega Sicilia without an appointment on the off chance I could meet the owner and discuss export opportunities. The Alvarez family had purchased the winery from a Venezuelan investor in 1982 and had appointed Pablo Alvarez to run the company. At that stage nothing had changed since the purchase. Pablo was not at the winery but I was well received in a dusty office with stand-up desks by Jesús Anadón, the longtime manager of the estate. He told me I should contact Pablo and not long afterwards Pablo came to visit us in Bordeaux and we started discussing distribution. It turned out there were almost no exports, most of the wine being sold on allocation to private clients in Spain.

Wine has been made at Vega Sicilia since 1864 when Don Eloy Lecanda Y Chaves brought vine stocks from Bordeaux and planted them on rocky limestone slopes on the left bank of the Duero river. It was in the early twentieth century that the wines were first bottled and the unique style developed through long ageing in oak and bottle before release. Three red wines are made at the property: Valbuena, released after five years; Unico, after at least ten years in oak and bottle; and finally the Unico Reserva Especial. Unico is only made when the quality of the vintage reaches Pablo's exacting standards, usually about seven years out of ten. Unico Reserva Especial is a blend of three top vintages, from casks put aside for this purpose. About 15,000 bottles of Reserva Especial are produced each year with the vintages in the blend designated on the label. The ageing is in American and French oak casks, also in large oak *foudres* of about 6,000 litres (1,585 gallons) which are renewed every five years. The American oak barrels are made on the property. The staves are imported from the US and dried for four years before being processed in the winery's own cooperage. The main grape variety is the Tinto Fino, the local name for Tempranillo, and small amounts of Cabernet Sauvignon, Merlot, and Malbec.

The Tinto Fino dominates all the blends, with a touch of Merlot for Valbuena and some Cabernet Sauvignon usually destined to complete the Unico blends. The wines are very special, compact, and complex, with power, finesse, and depth, all signatures of a great wine. The fruit is present and carefully enhanced by the long ageing in the small and large oak casks and later in bottle. Thanks to the vibrant acidity, the ageing capacity is amazing. On numerous occasions I have enjoyed the lively fruit of the 1942 vintage. The oldest I have had the privilege to taste was the 1921 vintage, showing its age but still very much alive.

Pablo's attention to detail is legendary. With care and patience, he has transformed Vega Sicilia into a world-class winery with all the modern equipment. No expense has been spared to find the best sources for all the materials, whether for building or winemaking. The offices are of course unrecognisable, a radical change from the dusty office of the early 1980s. In spite of all the changes, apart from being cleaned up, the outside of the main buildings has hardly been touched; even the wines have kept their unique flavours with perhaps just a little less time in oak, giving a touch more fruit and freshness.

We signed up for the distribution in the US, Australia, New Zealand, Japan, and a number of other Asian markets. Pablo wanted to work the European countries directly and we gave him introductions to importers in the UK and Sweden. We soon discovered that Vega Sicilia was almost unknown outside Spain and some promotional work was called for. To many who should have known better, Vega Sicilia was an estate in Sicily. In fact, to those who knew of the wine, few had had the opportunity to taste it. This seems incredible today, now that Vega Sicilia is an icon and immediately comes to mind as the Lafite Rothschild of Spain when Spanish wines are discussed. In the US a few cases had been sent to New York and to a wine shop in South Florida, but in California the trade knew nothing about it. We gradually built a presence throughout our network state by state. Fortunately, we were ably assisted by numerous market visits with Pablo, his winemakers, and his export manager. Furthermore, we showed the wines to Robert Parker in Pablo's presence. His straightforward comment on the legendary 1968 vintage was: "This wine should take its place in wine history beside the greatest clarets of the decade of the sixties." Parker's influence was such that he quickly made the American and worldwide wine trade aware of the existence of this great property.

Initially, before his retirement in 1985, Jesús Anadón accompanied me, with Pablo, on these trips. He was soon followed by winemakers Mariano García, who was born on the property, later by Xavier Ausàs and the energetic export manager, Rafael Alonso. These trips were entertaining. Of course, the importers arranged the usual tastings and winemaker's dinners, however our times with Jesús Anadón and Mariano García were memorable. Both are great characters and very entertaining. Jesus had a store of wonderful anecdotes going back to the Spanish Civil War. Mariano, who hardly drew breath, was an endless source of interesting information. Rafael Alonso's quick wit and lively intelligence also made the trips to the US and Japan unforgettable. Moreover, Pablo's generosity with the wines selected for the meals we had together had no bounds. Frequently he would choose some treasures from a wine list, usually First Growth Bordeaux, so we could compare them with Valbuena and Unico, as referred to in the chapter on Singapore. These tastings were a revelation – surprisingly even the five-year-old Valbuena ranked well with the top Bordeaux. Of course, Unico, having longer ageing, was in a class of its own with its distinctive flavours. Other entertaining journeys with Pablo and his entourage were to Australia, New Zealand, Hong Kong, and Singapore.

In 2000, Bipin Desai, a wealthy collector from Los Angeles, arranged a series of lunches and dinners for his collector friends at three of the most emblematic Los Angeles restaurants, entertainingly assisted by Serena Sutcliffe, Master of Wine and head of Sotheby's wine department. The lineup of Unico vintages back to the 1940s was spectacular, as was the food at Wolfgang Puck and Patina in Los Angeles and Valentino in Santa Monica. It was an unforgettable experience and a wonderful performance by Serena with her quick wit and amusing anecdotes.

One year we arranged a visit to Burgundy with Pablo and his team. The aim was to study the vineyards and the mechanics of biodynamic farming. Apart from a fascinating technical visit with Aubert de Villaine at the emblematic Domaine de la Romanée-Conti, we also spent time with the Domaine Comte Georges de Vogüé, Domaine Bonneau du Martray, Dominique Lafon at Domaine des Comtes Lafon, and Anne-Claude Leflaive at Domaine Leflaive in Puligny Montrachet. Both Dominique and Anne-Claude explained their version and experience of biodynamics with great clarity.

A few years after the purchase of Vega Sicilia by the Alvarez family, Pablo started thinking about expanding the family's wine interests. The first project was to produce another wine in the Ribera del Duero, but in a more modern style than Vega Sicilia. Thus, Bodegas Alión was born in 1991 just 10 kilometres (6 miles) east of Vega Sicilia near the town of Peñafiel. This wine was aged exclusively in new French oak casks of 225 litres (60 gallons). Again, attention to detail has been behind the success of this brand. The wines are very different from those of Vega Sicilia, more modern but firm with bright cherry fruit and classy oak flavours. In good vintages more than 300,000 bottles are produced. Alión became an important item in the Europvin portfolio, with some success, especially in the US.

Further west along the Duero river valley, near the Portuguese border, you come to the arid region of Toro with a wealth of old vineyards, often planted with ungrafted vines of over one hundred years old. Since the style of wine in this region is somewhat different to Ribera del Duero, Pablo decided to build Bodegas Pintia in the village of San Román de Hornija. Another state-of-the-art winery was built, making wines in the classic Toro style with a touch of rusticity but great depth of flavour and, thanks to the careful oak ageing, certainly more class and freshness than most of the wines from Toro. The first vintage was 2001. Since then, Pintia has become a leader in this popular appellation.

The other venture, or should I say adventure, was in Hungary. After the fall of the communist regime, the Hungarian government opened up the economy to foreign investment. One of the activities to benefit were the historic Tokaj vineyards in Tokay, Northeast Hungary. Having such a long and prestigious history, Vega Sicilia was intrigued and later invited to found a winery in the region and purchase some of the best-located classified vineyards, initially as a partner with the Hungarian government. The negotiations were long and complex. An agreement was eventually reached and Tokaj Oremus was founded, Oremus being the name of one of the oldest of the classic vineyards.

With the Oremus vineyard Vega Sicilia also acquired important stocks and 5 kilometres (3 miles) of twelfth-century underground galleries for ageing in cask and bottle. A modern vinification plant was constructed in the village of Tolcsva. Tokay is best known for its botrytis-infected Aszú wines of varying sweetness. The region is also producing distinctive, dry white wines from the Furmint grape.

Under the professional guidance of Andras Bacso, the recently retired manager, and arguably the world's number one expert on Tokaj, Oremus is making a range of exquisite Aszú wines with classic methods but in a fresher, less

Intronisation into the Confrérie de Tokaj.

oxidised style than during the communist era. The development of the unique dry Furmint from Oremus is another success story. I have been fortunate to be able to visit Oremus and other Tokaj wineries on at least four occasions and have been honoured with the intronisation (induction ceremony) to the Tokaj Confrérie (Tokaj Brotherhood). Needless to say, Oremus is a priority within the Europvin portfolio.

Selling Tokaj wines is not easy, mostly due to the current lack of affection for sweet wines generally, but Tokaj has a distinctive character of its own with remarkable freshness and a spicy touch. The wines are gradually regaining the popularity and prestige they enjoyed in the sixteenth and seventeenth centuries in the royal courts of France, Austria, and Russia.

I have always enjoyed visiting this picturesque area of rolling hills, rivers, and forests sheltered by the Carpathian Mountains. The climate is continental, with hot summers and cold winters. In the autumn the climate is soft and just humid enough to provoke botrytis or noble rot in the grapes, essential for the production of the great Aszú wines.

When we opened the capital of Europvin in 2003, our principal partner was Emilio Lustau from Jerez. Soon afterwards Vega Sicilia decided to take a small share in our company. In 2017, after CVNE resigned from the board, Vega Sicilia took a much larger share and now owns 50% of the company and Emilio Lustau the other 50%.

BODEGAS MAURO

The discovery of Bodegas Mauro was pure chance. Again in 1984, I was driving into the village of Quintanilla de Onésimo, 2 kilometres (1¼ miles) west of Vega Sicilia when I spotted a sign on a small warehouse with the words "Bodegas Mauro". I was intrigued and stopped to find out more. It turned out that the warehouse was just a point of sale for the wines but the employee proposed to put me in touch with the late Luciano (Chano) Suárez, one of the shareholders. Little did I know that Mariano García of Vega Sicilia was also a partner and winemaker for this venture. Later I met Chano in a bar in the small town of Tudela de Duero and he took me to a town house across the street. The house had been converted into a bodega with the barriques stored on the first floor and a few fermentation vats at the back. Chano explained that he was an architect, specialised in restoring churches and monuments on the pilgrim road to Santiago de Compostela. He was also a gastronome and wine lover – in fact, a lover of all good things in life – full of exuberant charm and generosity. I have enjoyed many sumptuous meals with him in Valladolid, San Sebastian, and Bordeaux when he came to visit us.

Chano showed me the wines and I was most impressed by the elegance and perfect balance between the oak and rich red fruit. On the palate the wines have a silky texture with freshness and vibrant energy. Needless to say, I requested an allocation but since they were offering the 1979 vintage – only the second vintage from the winery – quantities were understandably small and we were only allowed 1,000 bottles, which were quickly sold in the UK and the US.

For some strange reason Mauro is in an area not included in the Ribera del Duero DO. This is no doubt more due to political reasons than technical, since the area around Tudela on the Duero river benefits from the same soils and climate as the areas classified as part of the DO. Furthermore, the vineyards are the closest to the city of Valladolid, one-time capital of Spain, having a long tradition and a fine reputation for their wines. No matter, because Mauro, without the DO, is now a well-established brand and numerous are the finest restaurants in Spain who list their wines.

During my time with Europvin we represented Mauro in the US and other markets, the volume growing with the winery, which is now producing over 200,000 bottles. The winery has also added two more wines: Mauro Vendimia Seleccionada and the single old-vine vineyard Terreus. Mariano García continues with the winemaking accompanied by his two sons, Alberto and Eduardo. The style has not changed from the refreshing elegance I discovered on my first visit nearly forty years ago. A white wine made from the Godello grape has recently been added to the portfolio. The family also owns a leading winery in Toro called Maurodos, which Europvin listed for the Asian markets.

OTHER RIBERA DEL DUERO WINERIES

In the early 1980s, while searching for new sources, I visited Bodegas Tinto Pesquera, who soon after became famous when Robert Parker called the winery the Petrus of Spain. This assured the long-term success for the owner, the late Alejandro Fernández. I shared some local lamb chops one evening with Alejandro. Later we placed an order for Australia but to our surprise it was cancelled since they had given the worldwide agency to one single importer in Seattle. This absurd situation caused us some embarrassment.

Another well-established winery we worked with was Hermanos Pérez Pascuas, Viña Pedrosa, located at a high altitude near Pedrosa de Duero. The wines are very intense, with a high acidity and plenty of new oak. They benefitted from long ageing and are among the leaders of the DO.

Of course, a priority was Viñedos y Bodegas Aster, 95 hectares (235 acres) of vineyards and a state-of-the-art cellar belonging to La Rioja Alta S.A. The wines receive all the attention to detail that is the signature of this long-established group.

Finally, Europvin also represents the spectacular Abadía Retuerta winery, near Vega Sicilia but not in the DO. With over 200 hectares (495 acres) of vineyards and the restored twelfth-century monastery with a five-star hotel and a Michelin-starred restaurant, the estate has become an obligatory destination for visitors to the area. I have been fortunate to be able to visit this superb estate on a number of occasions.

❧ RUEDA AND MARQUÉS DE GRIÑÓN ❧

Of Aristocrats and Inspiration

Our first contact with Rueda was with the late Carlos Falcó, Marqués de Griñón. Carlos, a grandee of Spain, was passionate about wine. After studying agriculture and viticulture at Davis University in California he decided to plant Bordeaux grape varieties on his estate near Toledo, southwest of Madrid. He also wanted to make a white wine to accompany his red. He chose to work with Antonio Sanz in Rueda and produced a refreshing, well-balanced white wine from a specific plot just south of the town of Rueda.

Rueda is another DO in the Duero valley, although most of the vineyards are some 10 to 20 kilometres (6 to 12 miles) south of the river on gentle slopes descending to the valley, and on rolling hills around the towns of

Nava del Rey and La Seca. The soils are stony on a limestone base and the main grape variety is the Verdejo, although Sauvignon Blanc and Macabeo are also included in the DO. The region had been almost abandoned after the ravages of phylloxera, but was redeveloped from the 1970s when Marqués de Riscal established a winery for a white Rueda to accompany their red Rioja wines.

I first met Carlos Falcó when he alighted from his Jaguar on the main Madrid–Galicia highway just next to the vineyard that was the source for his Rueda. Spain was not known for its white wines but Riscal and Griñón recognised the potential for the region to produce excellent whites with an attractive balance between floral and mineral aromas. The DO was founded as recently as 1980. Today, with regions of Galicia, Rueda is a leading appellation for white wines in Spain.

Later we visited Carlos Falcó's estate near Toledo where he had planted the Bordeaux grape varieties and had enlisted the help of Emile Peynaud, the esteemed Bordeaux-based enologist, for advice on both viticulture and winemaking. For the blending, Carlos would bring his samples to Bordeaux and taste with Emile Peynaud in the Europvin office. We were allowed to participate and listening to Peynaud's comments was always instructive and rewarding. After Peynaud's retirement, Michel Rolland took over as consultant.

At Europvin we sold both the Rueda and his red wines, especially the Cabernet Sauvignon and Petit Verdot, during the 1980s and 1990s with limited success. The reds were outstanding but from an obscure region and Spain had not yet established a reputation for well-made white wines. It is interesting to point out that it was fashionable to plant Bordeaux grape varieties in Spain in the 1970s and 1980s, a decision that many producers regret and have since converted their vineyards, privileging local varieties.

Our other relationship in Rueda was with Belondrade y Lurton. I had met Brigitte Lurton when she worked with her family properties in Bordeaux but it was our mutual friend Bruno Paillard from Champagne that suggested she contact us during Vinexpo in 1995 with a sample of her first wine from Rueda. It was the 1994 vintage, very oaky but with lots of underlying fruit, more depth and complexity than any other white wine I had tasted from Spain. We therefore decided to represent the estate from the very first vintage and Europvin continues the good work today. Brigitte was married to Didier Belondrade, also her partner in this adventure, but later they separated and Didier continued the project on his own and later with their son. The 40 hectares (99 acres) of vineyards, farmed ecologically and split into twenty-two separate plots, produce about 90,000 bottles each year. The wines have gained a worldwide reputation for being among the finest in Spain. They are aged in new French oak casks and maintain all the complexity and class of the earlier vintages, albeit with a perfect balance between the fruit and the oak.

PRIORAT

A Gem in the Heart of Catalonia

My involvement in Priorat is discussed in detail in a later chapter. It is in this unique appellation that I decided, for better or worse, to invest in production.

My first association with the region was in the mid-1980s when I discovered the wines of Scala Dei during a trip to California. Later I met Alvaro Palacios who told me about his new venture in Priorat. Alvaro did not require our services to export his wines but he introduced me to René Barbier of Clos Mogador. René's family, whose origins are in the Southern Rhône, previously owned a winery in Tarragona making quality wines for everyday drinking. The brand now belongs to Freixenet, the Cava producer. René was the initiator, with Alvaro, of what I like to call "the new wave" of Priorat producers. Europvin has successfully represented Clos Mogador since the very first vintage in 1989. During the 1990s we represented a number of other well-known wineries from Priorat, including Mas Martinet, Cims de Porrera, Vall Llach, and Gran Clos. Priorat became an important source for Europvin's Spanish portfolio.

❧ JEREZ DE LA FRONTERA AND THE WORLD OF SHERRY ❧

I have mentioned Europvin's association with Jerez de la Frontera in other chapters. Although we purchased some Sherry in the early years of the 1980s, it was from 1984 that we became associated with Emilio Lustau. Little did I realise how important Lustau would become for the future of my company. It was our importer in San Francisco, Diamond Wine Merchants, who first told me about the Almacenista Sherries. The project was initiated by Rafael Balao, the managing director of this family-owned company. *Almacen* is the Spanish

word for warehouse. An *almacenista* is a person or family who stores fine Sherries in cask over long periods and occasionally sells a cask to the large Sherry shippers to improve their blends before bottling. Rafael's idea was to purchase these casks and bottle them separately specifying the name of the *almacenista* on the label and the number of casks in the solera.

I was intrigued and lost no time in going to meet Rafael Balao at the Lustau bodega, located at the time in the old Moorish town walls of Jerez. In 1984 Lustau had some commitments in the US with an export manager taking care of the market. We therefore decided to

With Rafael Balao, manager of Emilio Lustau in Jerez in the 1980s.

create our own label for our Sherries and the Almacenistas from Lustau. Soon after the export manager left the company and subsequently, I recall a memorable meeting with Rafael Balao on the terrace of the Hotel Jerez when he offered Europvin the exclusivity of the Lustau brand for the US, including access to their existing customers. This was an undreamed-of opportunity and we quickly went to work to establish the brand through our network of distributors. We sent samples to Robert Parker, which took forever to reach him having been misdirected to Ohio. When he finally tasted the Sherries, he was enthralled with the quality and diversity of the range, scoring some of the Sherries with 96 points, helping us put Lustau and Sherry on the map as a producer and product to be reckoned with. His most noteworthy comments included: "simply staggering in quality" and added "Sherries such as these remain among the last great unknown wine bargains of the world. They must be tasted to be believed."

Prior to this moment, Sherry was more often considered a semi-sweet wine consumed by an elderly population with no consideration for quality. Sherry of sorts was made in California, Cyprus, and South Africa until the authorities in Spain were able to protect the name and make it exclusive to the wines of the carefully defined region. With Parker's praise consumers realised there was more to Sherry than the semi-sweet variety. Shortly after Parker's article we arranged a tasting in a Washington DC hotel which was a resounding success and from that day we did not look back. We had no competition in the 1980s and 1990s and established distribution in all the important markets. Few were the serious wine shops who did not carry Lustau and eventually our sales reached a plateau of about 15,000 cases each year. We found it hard to increase the volume until quite recently, when Sherry in cocktails became popular and more consumers understood that fine Sherry is such good value and so interestingly diverse. At Europvin we also represented Lustau in Japan, other Asian countries, Australia, New Zealand, Italy, and Scandinavia.

In the US we organised numerous tasting events, even entire meals accompanied by Sherry exclusively. The versatility of Sherry is such that there is a style that can accompany most dishes. Furthermore, the dry Fino and

Manzanilla Sherries make ideal aperitifs when served cool and are perfect with seafood of any description, including sushi and sashimi from Japan. The Amontillado Sherries are also a good aperitif, especially with nuts and olives in winter, and also go well with white meat and any dish with a light sauce. The Olorosos are richer and perfect with game and Northern Chinese fare. Finally, the creamy sweet Sherries go well with all kinds of dessert, and Parker even suggested pouring the ultra-sweet Pedro Ximenez over ice cream.

In 1990 the Caballero group purchased Lustau from the Lustau family and soon after Rafael Balao left due to illness. This was a sad moment as Rafael had become a close friend. His enthusiasm and ideas had no bounds and his undying support for Europvin resulted in the creation of Europvin Iberia with Vega Sicilia and La Rioja Alta S.A., sealing the future of the company with three of the most prestigious producers in Spain. In the early 2000s Luis Caballero purchased and reformed a beautiful nineteenth-century bodega in the centre of Jerez. The bodega had belonged to Harveys of Bristol, known for their Bristol Cream Sherry. Today these classic cathedral-like bodegas are an unmissable sight for tourists and wine-lovers alike. This bodega was destined for the ageing of the Lustau Sherries. The group is based in El Puerto de Santa Maria, where other bodegas are used for the production of their Fino del Puerto brand. El Puerto, as the town is called by the locals, is a paradise for seafood lovers. On every corner there is a bar serving fresh seafood, straight off the boats in the harbour, with infinite amounts of cool Fino.

I always enjoyed my numerous visits to Jerez, especially the visits to the *almacenistas*. Each one had a very different profile. One was a university professor, another sold motorcycles, there was also a pharmacist, but they all had these old stocks of unique Sherries, mostly dry Amontillados and Olorosos. In Sanlúcar de Barrameda, the only place Manzanilla can be made, we frequently visited *almacenista* Cuevas Jurado, the elderly owner of a grocery business, who had superb stocks of aged Manzanillas and the sublime Manzanilla Pasada, a richer and more intense version of the younger Manzanillas. Lunches on the banks of the Guadalquivir river at Sanlúcar, from where Columbus set out for

America, just opposite the Doñana National Park, were special. The fresh fish with glasses of cool Manzanilla must be gastronomic heaven.

As time went on, with the creation of Europvin Iberia, in association with Vega Sicilia and La Rioja Alta, Lustau became ever more important to Europvin. During the early 2000s we felt the need to establish a full-time presence in the US, which would entail more investment than we could afford. We therefore decided to open up the capital and after long and arduous negotiations sold part of the company to the Caballero group, owners of Lustau. As previously mentioned, Vega Sicilia also took part. Eventually Lustau had a controlling interest in Europvin until they sold some of their shares to CVNE. During this period Europvin purchased Golden State Wine Co. in Southern California. For Europvin, the company became the importer for the entire US and a successful distributor in California.

🦋 OTHER SPANISH REGIONS 🦋

From North to South – East to West

In the US, Europvin became better known for their Spanish selections than their French portfolio. Apart from the close associations mentioned, we filled out our list of producers from other regions in order to cover most of the key denominations. The most important was Catalonia, where we became involved with Priorat in the mid-1980s. We also promoted wines from Galicia, notably the classic Albariños from Granbazan, the spicy Bierzo wines from Bodegas Godelia, the light, spritzy white Txakoli from Ulacia in the Basque Country, and the rich but fresh Mourvèdre wines from Castaño in the Levante. So much has changed on the Spanish wine scene over the past thirty years. In the 1980s only Rioja and the Torres bodega in Catalonia were noteworthy for table wines. Jerez was well known for their fine Sherries but almost no white table wine of any repute was produced. It has indeed been a revolution with the founding of thousands of new wineries in regions and appellations no one had heard of thirty years ago. Spain has been rediscovering its wealth in old vines, some of them on the point of extinction, often in very remote regions where the locals had little idea of how to produce quality wines. This was the case in Priorat, Calatayud, Sierra de Gredos, Salamanca, and many other locations. Many of these regions have been "discovered" and the wines are now sought after by discerning sommeliers.

CHAPTER 15
_____

PORTUGAL

Tradition and Innovation

Portugal is another of my favourite European countries. Apart from the beauty of the landscape and amiability of the people, the wine scene is fascinating. The diversity of grape varieties and wine styles, so different from elsewhere in Europe, is captivating.

At Europvin, our connection with Portugal was primarily with the Douro Valley, however, our involvement with Portuguese table wines was premature. We started research in the late 1980s when the local economy was doing well. The few quality-orientated producers were able to fetch good prices for their wines in Portugal; consequently, prices for export were high and uncompetitive. More recently the demand for Portuguese wines has justifiably grown and there are many quality producers with offerings at more reasonable prices. Once again, we were ahead of our time. Nevertheless, we selected and worked with a few producers in various regions. The results were mediocre but the experience most enjoyable.

❧ DOURO ❧

A Valley of Legendary Beauty

CHURCHILL'S PORT

It was an English importer and friend, the late Jan Critchley-Salmonson MW, who first told me about Johnny Graham and his new port company. Johnny is a member of the Graham family of Graham's Port. Graham's was sold to the Symington group in 1970. Johnny, having been trained as a winemaker and having begun his career in Port with Cockburn's, decided to set up his own company in 1981 with his two brothers, Anthony and William. Churchill Graham Lda was the first new Port house to be established in over fifty years. The brand is named after Johnny's wife, Caroline Churchill.

Johnny rented a cellar from Taylor's in Vila Nova de Gaia, which soon became too small. A plot of land was found nearby and a new cellar with stylishly furnished offices and a tasting room were constructed on the steep slopes of Vila Nova de Gaia, where Port is traditionally aged and bottled.

Initially Johnny sourced all his grapes from three Grade A quintas (estates) belonging to the Borges de Sousa family. Johnny had first choice at harvest for grapes in these ideally situated vineyards in the Pinhão Valley, on the right bank of the Douro, in the centrally located Cima Corgo district. Soon after my first visit I returned to Portugal with my wife for a memorable journey up the Douro Valley in Anthony Graham's Jeep. In those days there was no fast road to the centre of the Douro, the journey taking four hours on narrow and dangerously twisty roads. Today the same trip takes only one and a half hours. We visited all three vineyards and tasted more Port than we should have done. Anthony is a larger-than-life personality out to enjoy the good things in life. Johnny, on a more serious note, gave us an insight into the secrets of the Douro Valley and information on the best sites. The scenery is staggering in its dramatic beauty and, in my view, the steep schistous slopes

My wife with Johnny Graham of Churchill's Port,
tasting Port in the Douro Valley, Portugal.

and meticulously maintained terraces, descending to the Douro river from an altitude of over 600 metres (1,968 feet), are the most spectacular vineyards in the world. Classification as a UNESCO world heritage site is fully justified.

After Borges de Sousa died in 1999, Johnny had to look for other sources for his grapes. Quinta da Gricha, a 100 hectares (250 acres) vineyard on the left bank of the Douro near Quinta de Roriz, was purchased in 1999. A further 12 hectares (30 acres) were added with the acquisition of Quinta do Rio in the Rio Torto Valley and Quinta da Perdiz with 30 hectares (75 acres) nearby. All the quintas are classified Grade A, giving Johnny better control and ample supply for his Ports and his more recent table-wine venture.

In spite of the youth of the company, Johnny, with his talent as a winemaker and master blender, has taken the quality of his Ports to the absolute top level, ranking with the long-established great Port houses. The range includes a delicious, aged white Port, ten- and twenty-year-old Tawny Ports, Crusted Port, and the famous Vintage Ports, some of which are Single Quinta Vintage Ports, usually Gricha. His table wine project is exciting too, showing the potential of the valley for great wines with balance and definition.

Over the past thirty years the demand for Port has stagnated. From the late 1980s a few quintas, and later the Port houses, realised the potential to produce superb table wines from the great variety of grapes in the Douro Valley, the schist soils giving the wines complexity and rich flavours with a mineral touch. Today many Port houses, including Niepoort and the Symington family, are making world-class table wines accounting for about 50% of the production.

At Europvin we introduced Churchill's Ports to the US market with considerable success and in one year, with the outstanding 1987 Vintage Port, the volume reached 4,000 cases. Sadly, by the late 1990s, due to changes in Churchill's shareholding, we were unable to continue the association with the US market. However, we continued supplying customers in France and elsewhere, maintaining the relationship.

QUINTA DE LA ROSA

Quinta de la Rosa was a pioneer in the production of table wines to accompany their excellent Ports. I was intrigued and arranged to visit this beautiful property on the banks of the Douro. For over a hundred years the estate has belonged to the hospitable Bergqvist family of British and Swedish origin. Until 1988 the grapes were sold to the Port houses, notably Sandeman. It was in that year, after the legislation changed with Portugal joining the European Union, that the late Tim Bergqvist and his daughter, Sophia, decided to launch Quinta de la Rosa as a single estate producing and distributing their own estate-bottled wines and Ports. The dynamic Sophia Bergqvist runs the show, which includes the wine cellar, guest houses, and a spectacularly steep, south-facing vineyard of 55 hectares (136 acres) on the right bank of the Douro near Pinhão. Enotourism is an important part of their business.

I recall a number of memorable sojourns on the property. On one occasion with my wife, they invited us to stay for a weekend and a picnic lunch was arranged on the Sunday with a ride in Sophia's speedboat. After the picnic under a eucalyptus tree, some of the party returned to the quinta in the speedboat, which was supposed to come back to collect us and the remainder of the party. They never returned! We waited all afternoon in stifling heat with no phone coverage and had no idea what had happened. It wasn't until early evening that we were collected in a Land Rover that had mastered extremely difficult terrain to reach us beside the river.

In 2006 we were invited to celebrate the one hundredth anniversary of the Bergqvist family at the quinta. The party included many well-known personalities in the wine trade. They took us up the Douro Valley in a bus to visit a new property they had just purchased in the Upper Douro, not far from the Spanish border. The return journey by boat was the highlight of the day, with food and wine served as we negotiated the locks and took advantage of the fabulous scenery. The day finished with a superb dinner served in the garden, with no lack of wine and Port.

Under Sophia's direction with an excellent team, the quinta is making both world-class table wines and outstanding Single Quinta Ports.

OTHER PORT HOUSES AND DOURO WINE PRODUCERS

During the Europvin years, we had on-and-off contact with the delightful and extensive Symington family, owners of many of the most respected Port houses, notably Graham's, Dow's, Warre's, and Cockburn's. They offered us the Quarles Harris label, an old family company founded in 1680 and absorbed by Warre's in the 1920s. Although not as famous as some of the Symington-owned houses, the quality was on a par with the best from the group. I also recall a trip I made to Oporto with Rafael Balao of Lustau. We met with James Symington to discuss the possibility of a commercial linkup of some form but, apart from an enjoyable, visit nothing came of these negotiations. It was a pity because the dynamics of both the Port and Sherry trade are very similar and a joint venture could have been profitable for both companies.

Other producers we worked with in the Douro were Cristiano van Zeller at Quinta Vale Doña Maria, and Pintas founded in 2001 by Sandra Tavares da Silva and her husband, Jorge Serôdio Borges. Sandra was also winemaker for Cristiano van Zeller and for her family at Quinta de Chocapalha near Lisbon. Quinta do Vallado was another source of outstanding table wines at reasonable prices. Vallado belongs to the Ferreira family, famous for their Port house and table wines from the Upper Douro, the best-known being Barca Velha, the Vega Sicilia of Portugal, with similar ageing potential. The Barca Velha winery and Port house are now in the hands of the giant Sogrape group.

MADEIRA

Mountains, Woods, and Flowers

The island of Madeira is paradise on earth, with spectacular mountain scenery and high cliffs dropping straight down to the heaving swell of the Atlantic Ocean. In the spring the island is a sea of flowers lining the roadsides, sharing space with the steep, terraced vineyards. The name *Madeira* is the Portuguese word for wood. When discovered, the island was covered almost entirely by dense forests. Needless to say, it is one of my favourite places to visit.

Madeira wines are very different from Port, being made in a unique way with exposure to heat during the ageing process. They do however have a longer life expectancy. Our main source was the long-established house of Henriques & Henriques. Based since 1850 in Camara de Lobos, near Funchal on the south coast, the company is among the most prestigious of the seven producers on the island. The late John Cossart, owner at the time of my visits, became a family friend resulting in a summer exchange of our two sons of the same age. At Europvin we exported some of the Henriques Madeiras to Japan on a regular basis. This included all the classic styles: Sercial, the driest; Verdelho, off-dry and the most popular in Japan; the richer Boal; and the sweeter Malmsey. These are all named after the specific grape varieties. Another called Terrantez is being revived, having been almost wiped out by phylloxera. Madeira was not an easy product to sell. The logistics of obtaining quantities from the small island are complicated to say the least. Producers often had problems obtaining empty bottles from the mainland and there were further problems of space on the boats carrying the finished product to Portugal.

What is most exciting about Madeira wines is their capacity to age. I have been privileged to taste Madeiras from the early nineteenth century, still in superb condition. On one occasion we were given a bottle of this age to show Robert Parker. The bottle remained open for almost six months after the tasting and never became oxidised. In fact, it was even better after being open for a few days and never declined. This must rank among my most memorable tasting experiences.

On the island I also visited the Madeira Wine Company, which owns several long-established Madeira brands, notably Cossart Gordon and Blandy's. Occasionally, as a special treat, we would stay at the luxurious Reid's Palace Hotel by the sea at Funchal, a favourite of Winston Churchill and numerous other celebrities. Although the island is full of tourists in the summer, it is possible to escape the crowds in the lush forests of the interior. No doubt, the best times to visit are the spring and autumn.

❧ OTHER REGIONS IN PORTUGAL ❧

Rising Stars and Fascinating Diversity

Our first contact with Portuguese table wines was with Luis Pato in the 1980s. Luis was really the pioneer of single-estate wines in Portugal, famous for his wines from the Bairrada district, about 100 kilometres (62 miles) south of Oporto. I made several visits to the winery and enjoyed delicious lunches in Luis's home. However, the local Baga grape produces rather tannic and rustic wines, in a similar vein as Madiran in Southwest France. They were not easy to sell, in spite of Luis Pato's fame and tireless energy in promoting his winery.

In the Vinho Verde district in Northern Portugal we found Quinta do Ameal. The wines from this region used to be very light and sometimes with some spritz, best for local consumption. Until the early 2000s they were not suitable for export. Now, with global warming and much improved winemaking, Vinho Verde has gained worldwide recognition for some exciting, dry white wines that can compete with the best from Spain and elsewhere. The grape varieties, notably the Loureiro and Alvarinho, are responsible for more complexity and depth without losing the charm of a crisp, bright, dry white wine, ideal with seafood of any description.

In the south of Portugal, I visited a number of wineries in the Ribatejo and Alentejo regions. One of the most spectacular was the historic Casa Cadaval, dating back to 1648 when the winery was established by the Duke of Cadaval. Still in the same family, it is a huge property covering 5,400 hectares (13,334 acres) of cork forests, open fields, and 45 hectares (111 acres) of vineyards. Apart from the wines, the property is famous for being one of the oldest for breeding the local and renowned Lusitano horses. In the office, where I was received on one occasion, I could not help noticing the dates on the ledgers behind the desk, going back to the early nineteeth century! The wines are traditionally made with full use of the local varieties: Trincadeira Preta, Touriga Nacional, Aragonês, Arinto, Fernão Pires. Most of these varieties are also planted at Quinta de Chocapalha, previously mentioned as being the home of Sandra Tavares da Silva, winemaker and co-owner of Pintas in the Douro. It is a beautiful property in rolling hills just north of Lisbon, producing some of the best-made and most expressive wines in the area. I visited the estate on a few occasions and was received with great generosity by this charming family in their home.

Recently I received an invitation from the cork producer Amorim to visit their facilities in Portugal. It was a fascinating trip, accompanied by Miquel Compte, our manager at Clos Figueras. On arrival in Lisbon, we were taken to the cork forests and after some searching, located the team that was stripping the trees of their cork, a process that can only take place every eleven years. It is a fascinating sight and an accomplished art. Later we were taken to the processing plant, where the cork is prepared in sheets before being trucked north for the manufacture of the corks. The afternoon was spent driving to Oporto, where we spent the night before visiting the cork-making plant the next day. We were shown how the cork is classified and made for various bottle shapes and wine styles. For the very best wines they showed us a new plant, where they were making corks that guarantee the absence of cork taint in wines. This is an expensive new process requiring twenty seconds for each cork. At the time, only wealthy producers could afford such corks. We were also shown all the procedures in place to avoid cork taint on normal corks for quality wine, but there was no 100% guarantee. Today Amorim is claiming that all their corks are now free of cork taint. After the visit we were honoured by a lunch invitation from António Rios de Amorim, the chairman and CEO.

CHAPTER 16

ITALY

Abundance of Riches

Italy was an important activity at Europvin. We signed up many prestigious producers but never really succeeded in establishing a reputation for Italian wines, being better known for French and Spanish wines. Nevertheless, I had many richly rewarding experiences in my pursuit of making Italy part of Europvin's destiny.

During the days of Cannan & Wasserman in the 1980s I met Neil Empson and his wife Maria. He had set up a company with a similar approach to ours, the selection of the finest estates in each Italian wine region for export, primarily to the US. We shared a few distributors, notably in Florida and Chicago. I wanted to know more about his operation so we visited a few vineyards with him in the Piedmont, the most memorable being to the dynamic Angelo Gaja in Barbaresco. Over the years we maintained contact with Neil and at one point started negotiating a joint venture with him and his team in the US. The discussions went well and together we could have made a strong force in the US market. However, when the subject of a cross-shareholding came up, Neil lost interest and the negotiations came to nothing.

We started visiting Vinitaly, the massive and chaotic annual wine trade fair in Verona, in the late 1980s. Guided by the knowledgeable Drake McCarthy of Diamond Wine Merchants in California, we met a number of well-known producers, notably Paolo de Marchi of Isole e Olena, and Aldo Vajra and Vietti from Piedmont. Later, thanks to the Montreal-based wine critic Michel Phaneuf, I met Cristina Geminiani of Fattoria Zerbina in Romagna. After visits to the respective wineries, others we listed included the Vino Nobile di Montepulciano from Poliziano; the indomitable Elisabetta Fagiuoli of Montenidoli, producing world-class Vernaccia di San Gimignano; Tenuta di Valgiano from near Lucca, a region they like to call "the other Tuscany"; the outstanding Chianti Classico from Riecine; Elisabetta Foradori from the Trentino, famous for her work with the local Teroldego Rotaliano grape; and Alois Lageder from the Alto Adige, arguably one of the best run wine operations I have ever had the chance to visit. In Piedmont I liked to visit Castello di Verduno, where the Burlotto family had guest rooms and their simple but excellent trattoria. I stayed there from time to time and very much enjoyed their wines from Barolo and Barbaresco. They were not well known in those days but the wines are so classic and authentic, they have since come to the attention of the world wine press.

Later, Greg Lemma, our distributor in Oregon, suggested I visit the south of Italy and Sicily. He put us in touch with Robin Woodhouse, a broker for the UK market and ex-employee of Neil Empson. He took me on a memorable journey covering Campania, Basilicata, Puglia, and later Sicily. In Campania we visited the impressive Cantina del Taburno near Naples. In Puglia we called on Cantele and Fellini. For many years after we exported the Primitivo di Manduria from Fellini, the same grape as the Zinfandel of California and excellent value.

In Sicily we visited Firriato in Trapani. After a quick cellar visit, we were taken to the harbour and embarked on a speedboat to be transferred to lunch on a nearby island. Although the ultra-fresh fish was delicious, we were not very reassured. The island is the location of a rather sinister prison located opposite the restaurant. On the boat trip my wife had mentioned that she was studying gemmology. On our return to Trapani the local jeweller was waiting for us on the quayside with his wares!

From Trapani we drove to nearby Marsala to visit the late Marco de Bartoli, an imposing personality who devoted much of his career to the promotion of Sicilian wines, almost single-handedly putting Marsala back on the map as one of the great wines of Italy. He also made a fascinating range of table wines from the local grapes, Grillo and Zibibbo, as well as the finest Marsala I have had the privilege to taste and an excellent Passito di Pantelleria from a small island off the coast of Sicily. Dinner with his large family at his home with the local North-African–influenced cuisine was an experience. He discovered our daughter was called Anne-Josephine. Marco's aunt was called Josephine and had lived in Bordeaux. He named one of his products after her. Knowing it was Anne-Josephine's birthday, even though he had never met her, he picked up the phone and called her to wish her "Happy Birthday"! Marco passed away too young and still in the process of successfully reviving the image of Sicily as a source of some great wines. His family continues the good work at the winery.

The next day we visited Florio, a large Marsala producer making very acceptable products. I still wonder why Marsala has not made more of an impact in the world of fortified wines. Like Madeira, I suppose the reputation was spoiled by rather indifferent wines being sold for cooking and the famous Marsala sauce. Few took the trouble to look beyond this reputation until Marco de Bartoli began showing what could be achieved with well-made fortified wines going through the solera system, like in Jerez. Marco, for a time, was so embarrassed by the image of Marsala, he refused to print the word Marsala on his labels, qualifying his Marsala as simple table wine. This has changed today with the new generation. Part of the problem is no doubt the legislation that has done little to improve the overall quality by allowing large yields.

At about the same time we had an introduction to Riccardo Cotarella, a prominent enologist. We met in a restaurant in Orvieto. After lunch he drove us to some of the wineries he was consulting for in Umbria and a visit to his own winery, Falesco, in Lazio. He was particularly proud that day because Parker had just awarded 100 points to Montevetrano, a Campania-based winery he consulted for. Riccardo was instrumental in us listing Falesco and some of his wines from Umbria, notably the excellent La Palazzolla, today better known for their sparkling wines.

ORCHESTRA

It was in the early 1990s that our Italian activities took on another dimension when I met three enthusiastic young wine-loving entrepreneurs who had formed a company in Treviso that went by the name of Orchestra. The partners were Osman Sultan, Christian Patat, and Roberto Cipresso, a well-known enologist. We met in a small house in Montalcino and discussed their plan of establishing a portfolio of top-quality estates in most of the Northern Italian wine regions. Their focus started in Tuscany where they had a close association with the renowned Ciacci Piccolomini d'Aragona estate in Montalcino. They shared a similar approach and philosophy with Europvin, so it was an easy decision to join forces and introduce their selections to our importers worldwide. In turn they imported some of our French and Spanish selections for sale in Italy. We even went as far as taking a small percentage in their company.

It was an exciting selection of top-rated producers. I recall many fascinating visits to the various wineries. A strong area was Friuli, home of Christian Patat, in the northeast corner of Italy on the border with Slovenia where they represented the rich, silky wines of Borgo del Tiglio; the elegant, precise wines from Le Due Terre; and the cult wines from Miani, only available on a strict allocation basis. The large number of grape varieties in this historic border region makes for exciting wines, especially whites. They include local varieties not found elsewhere such as the Tocai Friulano, Ribolla, Verduzzo, Picolit, and Schiopettino among others. A total of seventeen varieties are permitted for just 2,500 hectares (6,180 acres).

Orchestra's selections in the Veneto were among the most prestigious and included an allocation of the legendary Amarone from Quintarelli and very fine Valpolicella from Marinella Camerani at Corte Sant'Alda. Marinella graciously invited me, with my family, to a memorable and spectacular performance of *The Barber of Seville* in the magnificent Roman arena at Verona. From Soave we worked closely with Stefano Inama, producing crisp, dry white wines from the Garganega grape with the classic flinty/smoky aromas from the volcanic soils. Stefano's single-vineyard Soaves from the hills rank with the best of the Soave Classico DOCG. In Soave we also worked with the Suavia sisters, making elegant wines that are now much sought after. Another source on volcanic soils was Vignalta from the little-known region of Colli Euganei, not far from Venice.

Apart from Foradori, we did not list other wines from Trentino, just a selection of outstanding grappa from Pilzer, a small family distillery producing eaux-de-vie embracing a multitude of flavours from the Alpine plants and fruit. The valleys and mountains of Trentino and Alto Adige are a tapestry of fruit trees of many varieties.

In the Alpine province of Alto Adige, we were introduced to Cantina Terlano, an exemplary cooperative making sublime white wines of great precision and a wonderful combination of floral and mineral tones. We tasted a Sauvignon Blanc that had been aged for more than twenty years in a concrete vat. It was an extraordinary wine with unexpected freshness and great complexity. The wines from this source have a remarkable capacity to age, gaining in complexity and depth. A delightfully fresh Sauvignon Blanc from the 1950s was a revelation. I never hesitate when I find them on a restaurant wine list.

In Tuscany our main source was the previously mentioned Ciacci Piccolomini d'Aragona, a historic winery located in a seventeenth-century palace in the town of Castelnuovo dell'Abate on the southern edge of the Brunello di Montalcino appellation. The Orchestra team had a particularly close relationship with this prestigious winery through Roberto Cipresso, who was the consulting winemaker. The wines are all classic Brunellos with an added dimension of elegance and distinction. Other important Brunellos in the Orchestra portfolio included the now famous Casanova di Neri and Collosorbo.

One of my favourite white wines in the portfolio was from the Marche, a Verdicchio di Matelica from Aldo Cifola at La Monacesca. The Matelica vineyards, located on the Apennine slopes, are well inland from the better-known Verdicchio dei Castelli di Jesi vineyards on the coast. The wines from these well-exposed slopes are richer than the more common Jesi wines but both have a remarkable capacity to age for many years. La Monacesca is considered very much the standard bearer in this small enclave of only about 300 hectares (740 acres). Other wineries from the Adriatic coast included Saladini e Pilastri, famous for their fruit-driven Rosso Piceno red wines from the Montepulciano and Sangiovese grapes. Also, in the same area, we visited the much smaller but very exclusive, organically farmed, Oasi degli Angeli, with their Kurni, a stunning, intense red wine made from Montepulciano grapes, now considered among the elite of Italian wines.

Another allocation from an elite winery, this time from Abruzzo, a little further south, was from Valentini, a winery known to all connoisseurs of Italian wines. We were allocated a small quantity of the Montepulciano d'Abruzzo and the Trebbiano d'Abruzzo, aged exclusively in old oak and a long time in bottle, a similar approach to Château Rayas. These wines have an extraordinary ageing capacity and their freshness after twenty years and more is a revelation, as well as an optimum sensory experience.

Our dynamic friends at Orchestra were talented at selecting wines of exceptional quality, even convincing the likes of Quintarelli and Valentini to part with small quantities of their precious wines. Their dedication and enthusiasm helped their sales both in Italy to Michelin-starred restaurants and in export markets. Unfortunately, their company did not possess a good business manager and, after a few years, costs overran income, meaning they had to close up shop. This was sad and could have been avoided since without doubt they were representing some of the finest and most prestigious wines of Italy. Roberto Cipresso continues his career as a well-respected consultant and winemaker, Christian Patat is working with a winery in Friuli, and Osman Sultan has apparently disappeared from the wine scene.

ALEX BURGE

With the demise of Orchestra, we needed to rethink our strategy for Italian wines. Europvin had enough activity to justify having a representative based in Italy and thanks to Sean O'Callaghan, the winemaker at Riecine, I was introduced to Alex Burge. In July 2000 I flew to Florence to meet him and discuss our plans. My flight to Florence took me via Paris. While waiting on the runway for takeoff there was a terrific roar and I saw a Concorde passing the nose of our aircraft. From my seat I could see the Concorde hurtling down the runway but something seemed wrong – too much smoke and flames were issuing from the undercarriage. The plane took off and a minute later there was an explosion and a gigantic plume of smoke that did not subside for what seemed a very long time. We waited on the runway for at least an hour without the pilot telling us what had happened. We learnt that it was an emergency and were told we would hear more when we reached Florence. In effect I had just witnessed the Concorde catastrophe, which would later lead this superb aircraft to be grounded forever.

Alex lives in Tuscany and had previously worked for Neil Empson. He was a great asset to Europvin, continuing the coordination with our suppliers in Italy. We became stronger in Piedmont, where Orchestra was rather weak. We continued working with the classic and prestigious Vietti Barolos, representing them in various Asian countries for a time. We also started working with the Brovia family nearby and in Barbaresco with a small winery in Neive called Ugo Lequio. Ugo is specialised in the Barbaresco Gallina cru, making traditional wines aged in Slovenian oak casks. Even though production does not reach 30,000 bottles, Ugo has created a reputation as being a leader in the appellation for harmonious wines in the classic style. I continued visiting the Burlotto family at Castello di Verduno, full of admiration for their wines, in spite of the lack of recognition as a topmost producer of classic wines in both Barolo and Barbaresco. They also produce a delicious wine from the extremely rare Pelaverga grape, a variety only found at Verduno. The grape almost disappeared in the 1970s and even today there are only 15 hectares (37 acres) planted, making a delightful wine, light in colour but full of fruit with a peppery touch.

In Tuscany our main sources were in Chianti Classico. At Riecine in Gaiole in Chianti we worked with three successive owners: the Englishman, John Dunkley, who sold the property to an American, Gary Baumann, and today with the Frank family who have invested heavily in the vineyards and cellar. John Dunkley insisted that only Sangiovese be planted on his estate, which boasts some of the best-located vineyards of the entire Classico appellation. John hired a young winemaker, the previously mentioned Sean O'Callaghan, in 1991, who has left his mark on the Riecine style with a deep, rich, and vigorous Chianti Classico of great charm. The site of the property is special, high up in the hills above Gaiole, with panoramic views from the terrace and not a single building in sight. Europvin was instrumental in Fortnum & Mason choosing Riecine as the source for their own label Chianti Classico.

Another long-term association was with Paolo de Marchi at Isole e Olena, a beautiful property on the western edge of the Chianti Classico appellation. Paolo, with his engaging and inquisitive personality, produces some of the most interesting wines of Tuscany. Always expressing consistency and balance, the wines are undoubtedly among the most sought after by Chianti lovers. The property is large and covers the two abandoned hamlets of Isole and Olena. Apart from Sangiovese, Paolo produces an excellent Syrah, a refreshing and well-structured Chardonnay, and a Vin Santo to die for. His Cepparello from 100% Sangiovese is on the list of Italy's top and best-known wines. Paolo and his wife, Marta from Uruguay, have become family friends. Before joining Clos Figueras, my daughter worked the harvest at the property, nearly losing her finger in the destemmer. We also enjoyed family lunches in their kitchen. At Europvin we represented Isole e Olena in parts of Asia and in Brazil with Paolo's active and dynamic support. In 2022 the winery was sold and a chapter in the history of this fine estate has sadly ended. However, Paolo will continue to own his winery, Proprieta Sperino, in the foothills of the Piedmont Alps, where he is making sublimely elegant wines with his son Luca.

A fond memory of Tuscany was visits to a very small Brunello di Montalcino winery named Il Paradiso di Manfredi whose owner is a mathematics teacher in Siena. The vineyard covers just 2.5 hectares (6 acres) facing northeast on the slopes below the town of Montalcino. Tastings at the domaine were followed by a delightful family lunch, more like a feast, that often went on until early evening, all the while tasting various vintages of this sublime Brunello. Only two wines are made, the classic Brunello di Montalcino and a Riserva. The wines are traditional in style, restrained and rich without being heavy. Other sources in Tuscany included the prestigious Tua Rita estate that has joined the "Super Tuscan" club of hard-to-find wines from the Tuscan coast.

One of our longest relationships in Italy was with Cristina Geminiani of the Zerbina estate in Emilia Romagna. We worked closely with Cristina and her exciting range of wines in the US and Brazil. Fortunately, she was very supportive, making numerous trips to visit our distributors and promote her wines. Emilia Romagna is better known for inexpensive Lambrusco; however, in a corner of the province near Faenza, on the lower slopes of the Apennines, some excellent wines are made, especially from the Sangiovese grape. Cristina is not only a brilliant winemaker but also passionate about her wines and wines in general. Her husband, Alessandro Masnaghetti, is famous for his very detailed maps pinpointing the vineyards and crus of various appellations, especially in Piedmont and Chianti. Her wines are systematically at the top of the quality tree in Romagna, with her magnificent handling of the local Sangiovese di Romagna for the reds and Albana di Romagna for the whites, including Scacco Matto (check mate), a luscious but focused sweet wine from botrytised grapes.

In Fruili we signed up for an allocation from Vie de Romans, a beautiful property not far from the Gulf of Trieste with a mixture of continental and maritime climate conditions. The wines are made and aged in small oak casks, displaying an elegance and freshness that is fairly unusual for Italian whites. In fact, they are somewhat Burgundian in style and texture. Great attention is taken to detail, putting the winery on the map as one of the leading Italian producers.

VINITALY

The annual Vinitaly trade fair in Verona is a must for anyone involved with Italian wines. We used to visit every year from the late 1980s. In 1991, on the autostrada in pouring rain, just before arriving in Verona, we had an accident which wrote off my BMW. There was congestion in the fast lane and I was able to stop just in time before hitting the car in front. However, the car behind did not stop and crashed into my back end, pushing me into the car in front. No one was hurt but the situation turned out to be complicated, even comical. The car behind was Italian, the car in front had German plates, driven by an Italian on his way to his wedding, and my car had French plates. All this was rather perplexing for the police. Anyway, we were towed to Verona and were made to pay the toll for the autostrada. Subsequently the police car taking me to the garage broke down and I had to help push their car several yards to avoid holding up the traffic!

Vinitaly was important because most of our American distributors would be present. For several years we took a stand and were able to show our selections from Italy, France, and Spain. We were one of the few stands showing wines from countries other than Italy. Of course, Vinitaly was always an opportunity to meet our suppliers and look for new sources. The evenings were very social since so many of our customers and suppliers were in attendance. Our favourite place for dinners, sometimes for up to twenty-five people, was a trattoria in nearby Sommacampagna. Trattoria Al Ponte had the very best pasta and fish from Lake Garda, washed down with the local Lugana white wines. The pasta is delectable, served with local herbs and extra virgin olive oil. The late Greg Lemma, our Oregon distributor, would always order three different pasta dishes and nothing else!

CHAPTER 17

GERMANY

Cool-Climate Gems

The German wine scene is somewhat comparable to Bordeaux. On the one hand you have huge quantities of inexpensive generic wines led by the ubiquitous Liebfraumilch and on the other you have the top estates, many of them members of the VDP (Verband Deutscher Prädikats und Qualitätsweingüter), a private association of top growers founded in 1910 to lobby for vineyard classification and quality-orientated legislation.

Ever since my days with Frederick Wildman in the 1970s, when I was selecting German estate wines for the US market, I had wanted to become involved with exports of some of the finest estates through our network. Unfortunately, time was not on my side. We initiated some negotiations for a joint venture with David Schildknecht, a wine critic and acknowledged expert on German wines based in Kentucky, but made little progress. As we expanded our activities in France and Spain, I felt we were ill-equipped to do a sufficiently good job for a selection of German estates.

Nevertheless, my love for Riesling got the better of me. For a time, we represented the emblematic and historic Dr. Bürklin-Wolf estate in the US.

Covering more than 100 hectares (247 acres) of biodynamically farmed vineyards, the property is at the pinnacle of the German wine scene. Located in the heart of the Pfalz, their vineyards are spread over several villages, including such well-known names as Wachenheim, Deidesheim, and Forst. Back in 1994, the owner, Bettina Bürklin von Guradze, disillusioned with the confusing German classification system oriented more to sugar levels than quality, made the decision to focus exclusively on 100% dry Rieslings, based on the Burgundian appellation system, with four levels of quality: basic estate wines, named village cuvées, single-vineyard Premiers Crus (the letters PC on the label), and single-vineyard Grands Crus (the letters GC on the label). After studying some historic documents, Bettina discovered her system was almost exactly the same as the Royal Bavarian Vineyard Classification of 1828.

With the advantage of the mild climate of the Pfalz and the ideal soils, composed of basalt, limestone, sandstone, and a unique concentration of black volcanic basalt in Wachenheim, the estate systematically produces dry Rieslings of great elegance, harmony, and depth, of a very different style to the focused and sharper Rieslings of the Mosel. The Premiers and Grands Crus are rich and intense without being heavy, showing the potential of the Pfalz to produce some of Germany's greatest wines with decades-long ageing capacity.

Unfortunately, despite the quality and friendship with Bettina, and great support from the winery, we had difficulty in selling these superb wines in America. Germany was not a popular source at the time, even though many wine lovers professed their love of Riesling. After a few years we regretfully had to abandon our one German venture.

We had other relationships in Germany, and recent highlights include memorable visits to Egon Müller of the famous Scharzhofberg in the Saar, also to the Prüm family of J.J. Prüm, who we occasionally met at joint tastings in Singapore. I recall joining them for a family lunch on their terrace overlooking their magnificent vineyards on the Middle Mosel. Hermann Dönnhof in the Nahe, Heymann-Löwenstein in the lower Mosel, also Schloss Schönborn in the Rheingau, were other unforgettable occasions.

With Frau Prüm (right) of J.J. Prüm on the Mosel.

CHAPTER 18

SPIRITS

Treasures from the
Highlands and Lowlands

As part of our pursuit for quality products at Europvin, we became involved with spirits in the very early days. I was always looking for family-owned distilleries producing the very best spirits authentically, and being representative of their origin. Jean-Claude Vrinat, of the Michelin-starred restaurant Taillevent in Paris, was instrumental in my becoming more involved with this fascinating sector.

Early on we represented Château de Beaulon, a family estate and historic seventeenth-century château owned by Christian Thomas and his family since 1965, producing refined single-estate Cognacs aged substantially longer than required by the legislation. The Cognacs are superb but the estate is better known for their sublime five- and ten-year-old red and white Pineau des Charentes, a well-respected local aperitif made with grape must, fortified with Château de Beaulon Cognac. The relationship with Europvin is now nearly forty years old, supplying the same customers since the early 1980s.

Other long-term Cognac suppliers included Logis de la Mothe, another family-owned single estate ideally located in the centre of the Grand Champagne district. For many years this was the source of the Fortnum & Mason Cognac with their own label, supervised by Europvin. Regrettably the estate has now ceased production for inheritance reasons.

Another Cognac we launched in the US in the 1980s was Leopold Gourmel, with their range of stylish Cognacs with names reflecting the character of each blend, like Age des Fleurs, Age des Fruits, and Quintessence. These were very pure and natural. The owner at the time, Pierre Voisin, was fanatical about the ageing process and put Leopold Gourmel on the map as a prime producer of some of the most elegant Cognacs available. We represented Leopold Gourmel in the US for a time and travelled with Caroline Voisin, Pierre's enthusiastic daughter, to help us promote the brand.

For Taillevent's own label we worked successfully with Hine Cognac – I have fond memories of my meetings with the energetic Bernard Hine and their sublime Cognacs – and the Château de Lacaze Armagnacs selected for the Taillevent label were outstanding.

This leads me to the subject of rare Early Landed Vintage Cognacs. This activity was special as, until recently, Cognac was not permitted to have a vintage date. The only exception were casks of Cognac from a single vintage sent to the UK for further ageing for about twenty years in damp underground cellars. The specialist in this field is John Barrett, owner of the Bristol Brandy Company and an expert in fine spirits of all descriptions. We worked closely with John, first selecting the Early Landed Vintage Cognacs, usually from Hine and Delamain. Taillevent was our main customer but small quantities were also exported to the US and Japan.

Due to the long ageing in such damp conditions in the cool climate of England near Bristol and now in Scotland, these Cognacs take on a softness not found in Cognacs bottled at source. Light in colour, without reduction or additives of any description, they are smooth, elegant, and quite delicious, very much to the English taste. The tradition dates from the nineteenth century when the merchants imported nearly all their wines and spirits in cask and bottled them on their premises.

The Bristol Brandy Company was also the source of some superb Caribbean rums aged and bottled in Scotland. They came from various islands and countries including Jamaica, Guyana, Guatemala, Nicaragua, and a host of small islands. Again, the ageing for long periods in damp conditions somehow took the edge off the spirits, making them softer and more elegant but keeping all the flavour of each individual cask.

John Barret accompanied me to Scotland and, after a short flight from Glasgow in a small plane, we met with the owners of the Springbank malt whisky distillery at Campbeltown. Springbank also bottled malt whiskies from other sources under the Cadenhead label. Tasting so many whiskies was quite a challenge. The key is to evaluate the quality of the aromas before actually tasting the whisky. Certainly, it was a fascinating experience. Springbank has been owned by the Mitchell family since its foundation in 1828 and is one of my favourite malt whiskies. There are many blends aged in different types of casks but generally they are creamy and elegant, with finesse and a touch of spice. I was so enamoured that I purchased a cask of Springbank in 1990 for £342.00. I sold it back to the distillery in 2005 for £2,067.00. Today, seeing the current prices for similar whiskies, I wish I had kept the cask!

While in Scotland I visited other distilleries in the Highlands and selected our own label blended whisky from the family-owned whisky producer and wine importer Inverarity Vaults, who also became a customer for some of our French selections.

I returned to Scotland at a later date with Gordon Hue, a close family friend and our distributor in Ohio and Kentucky. Gordon is also a specialist in spirits. In the late 1980s he purchased a large quantity of Bourbon whiskey under the Van Winkle and Hirsch labels and we imported small quantities for Taillevent and others. I still have two bottles of this very special Bourbon. While visiting a wine store in Kentucky in 2018 I noticed a bottle with the same label and could not believe the price tag of $2,000! I thought it was a mistake until I was told otherwise. I shall now have to decide with whom to share these precious bottles. In Scotland with Gordon, I visited Springbank again for another extensive tasting. We learnt about the history of the distillery, the only one of thirty in Campeltown to survive the prohibition era in the 1920s. Since the 1970s the Mitchell family have revived two other Campeltown distilleries, Longrow and Hazelburn. Gordon was also kind enough to take me to visit the Maker's Mark distillery in Kentucky, opening my eyes to a completely different approach to the production and ageing of whiskey.

Other spirits we represented included the Calvados from the Dupont family, another long association with Europvin over more than thirty-five years. Dupont has been family owned since 1834, producing Calvados found in most of the Michelin-starred restaurants in France. Although Etienne Dupont also produces Pont L'Evêque cheese from the cattle on his farm and some excellent cider, his real passion is the distillation and ageing of his Calvados. He is so fond of his stocks he always seems reluctant to part with them! Only about 10,000 bottles are released each year from stocks going back forty years and more. Dupont owns 30 hectares (74 acres) of orchards planted with 6,000 trees of various apple varieties, well adapted to the production of the finest Calvados.

In Armagnac we worked closely with Domaine d'Ognoas, a meticulously run estate owned by the *département* of the Landes. The location is ideal, in the heart of Bas Armagnac at Arthez d'Armagnac. The Armagnacs are very pure with intense flavours and great distinction. Only 15,000 bottles are produced each year from 44 hectares (109 acres) of prime vineyards with sandy soils planted with Folle Blanche, Colombard, Ugni Blanc, and Baco Noir grape varieties.

In the chapter on French wines, I have already mentioned our relationship with Domaine Tariquet and their excellent Armagnacs, sold alongside their successful table wines. Laberdolive was another emblematic producer we visited, purchasing a few bottles for export, as was Darroze, especially when a specific vintage was required. Darroze owns a collection from about forty different producers with stocks of almost every vintage back to the 1950s. The Darroze family seeks out individual casks from families that have aged their Armagnacs over decades. The quality is phenomenal and the brand needs no introduction among fans of fine spirits.

From Alsace we purchased some liqueurs and eaux-de-vies from the perfectionist Jean-Paul Metté, a distiller based in Ribeauvillé. The lineup is bewildering, with at least forty different liqueurs from what appears to be all the plants and fruits from the slopes of the Vosges mountains and surrounding countryside. The quality is of course outstanding, justifying Metté's reputation as the leading distiller in Alsace, with his products available in most of the Michelin-starred restaurants.

In the mid-1990s I was invited to dinner with the late Michel Couvreur, from Belgium but living in Burgundy, and producing some very fine whiskies distilled in Scotland, with rare ingredients in the process, including a special low-yielding barley from the Orkney Islands called bere barley. Much to his disappointment, and although the products were fascinating, we never succeeded in selling his whiskies – however, we did end up sending him a large number of used Sherry casks from Emilio Lustau for ageing them.

PART FOUR

PRODUCTION

*The Foundation of Wineries in
Priorat and Montsant*

CHAPTER 19

PRIORAT AND CLOS FIGUERAS

A New Adventure

Back in 1991 I wrote the following text in a fact sheet for the Scala Dei winery. At the time, it was part of the Europvin portfolio and the only family-owned estate in Priorat exporting their wines:

> *Because of the difficult conditions there are very few producers in Priorat. Scala Dei is currently the only winery whose entire production comes from their own vineyards. They are, without question, the most reputable source for fine Priorat wines. Due to the potential of the area, it is probable that new investments will be made in the years to come. Perhaps this will draw attention to an appellation which produces world-class wines of enormous concentration and originality.*

Little did I know at the time that I was to become one of those investors and the region would go on to achieve worldwide recognition for outstanding quality and originality.

Priorat being close to the ancient Roman capital of the Iberian Peninsula, Tarraco (Tarragona of today), it is no surprise that vineyards have existed in the region for more than 2,000 years. It is believed that many of the surviving terraces were initially built by the Romans.

During the Middle Ages the entire region was dominated by the Carthusian monks at the monastery of Scala Dei, the prior of Scala Dei exercising his authority over several villages, hence the name Priorat or priory in English. The monks controlled the local economy and all cultivation, including vineyards, olive groves, almonds, and hazelnuts; the only agriculture able to adapt to the poor schistose soil in this Mediterranean enclave.

In 1835 the Spanish state expropriated the monasteries, many of which were destroyed and the land given over to smallholders. During the nineteenth century the Priorat vineyards extended over 9,000 hectares (22,240 acres), mostly devoted to supplying the French wine trade, severely afflicted by the onslaught of phylloxera in the 1880s. Subsequently phylloxera struck Priorat at the end of the century, causing ruin and massive emigration. What with political upheavals, the Spanish Civil War, and the Franco dictatorship, it was not until the latter part of the twentieth century that Priorat began to revive. In the 1970s only about 600 hectares (1,483 acres) remained under vine.

During the 1980s a group of inspired enthusiasts fell in love with Priorat and saw the potential to produce very great wines. The group was led by René Barbier and Alvaro Palacios from Rioja. In 1989 their first wine was produced with a few other friends in an abandoned chicken farm outside the village of Gratallops. The presence of very old Grenache and Carignan vines in the unique slate-schist soils called *llicorella*, helped by some recent plantings of international varieties such as Cabernet Sauvignon and Syrah, showed the way to making wine of world-class quality with the minerality, elegance, and the distinctive freshness of the Priorat character. Also, the wines showed the potential to age for decades, thanks to the acidity derived from the rocky soil. It was not long before the international wine press was falling over themselves to expound the virtues of this rediscovered territory, rapidly putting Priorat on the map as one of the great wine-producing regions of the world.

In the past Priorat was better known for rather rustic high-alcohol red wines, often exported in bulk for blending purposes in France and other countries. Today the region enjoys the coveted *Denominación de Origen Calificada* appellation which, in Spain, is shared only with Rioja. The wines have to be made and bottled within the appellation territory.

I had already discovered the potential of Priorat back in 1983 when I was given a bottle of the 1974 vintage Priorat from Scala Dei by a retailer in San Francisco. Tasting the wine that same evening with a Californian winemaker, it turned out to be excellent and extraordinarily good value at $4.00 a bottle! We said to each other, "How can a wine of this quality cost so little?" A large quantity of the 1974 Scala Dei was produced and some bottles, still encountered today, are in good condition.

Shortly after my return to Europe I met Manuel Peyra, owner of Scala Dei, and started exporting these distinctive wines to various countries including the US and Japan.

Later, in 1988, I met Alvaro Palacios at the New York Wine Experience. Alvaro informed me briefly of his plans and invited me to dinner in Logroño where he enthusiastically explained the project to produce world-class wines from old vineyards in Priorat. At the end of the conversation, Alvaro told me he did not require our services at Europvin but he proposed an introduction to René Barbier at Clos Mogador who does not speak English and was looking for distribution for his wines. A few weeks later René turned up in Bordeaux in his old Peugeot and a few samples of his Clos Mogador. At first, I was sceptical: the wine was excellent but the price was high for an unknown product. Nevertheless, a couple of years later, I decided to show the wine to Robert Parker at one of his regular tastings in Europvin's Bordeaux office. Parker did not wait long to write an article to show his enthusiasm. It was after he published his subsequent issue of the *Wine Advocate*, with exceptionally high scores, that the trade finally took notice of what was happening in this remote corner of Catalonia. Since then, Europvin has been exporting Clos Mogador and other Priorat wines to numerous countries in North America

The signpost to Clos Figueras.

and Asia. Initially the other producers included Mas Martinet, Gran Clos, and Cims de Porrera. Later we added Vall Llach to the portfolio. Priorat has not looked back. Today over 2,000 hectares (4,942 acres) are in production and over one hundred bodegas are shipping their wines worldwide.

It was one day in July 1997 that René Barbier showed me, and my wife Charlotte, an abandoned vineyard just north of Gratallops called Figueres, named after the two magnificent fig trees on the property. The same day the entire Cannan family jumped into their car and followed René to Barcelona. It was on a pavement café beneath Gaudi's La Pedrera building on the Paseo de Gracia that we met a charming widow and schoolteacher, owner of the vineyard. Negotiations were rapid and easy, land values being very reasonable at the time. For the modest sum of £40,000, recently inherited from my mother, we purchased 10 hectares (25 acres) of land with the classic *llicorella* soil. By October 1997 the paperwork was completed and the hard work commenced. At the outset René Barbier and his vineyard team agreed to take care of the estate which we called Clos Figueras. Clos, because it consisted of 10 hectares (25 acres) all in one block and because it was the prefix to most of the new wines on the Priorat scene. The true translation of the word clos is a vineyard surrounded by a wall. We do not have a wall around our vineyard but it is all in one piece, and our justification for using the word Clos is that our winery and restaurant buildings and garden are entirely surrounded by a wall.

The location of the vineyard is ideal, with magnificent views of the Ebro river valley and the Montsant mountain. Not all the land is fit for planting vines. Some parts are too steep and others are covered by forest and olive groves. The microclimate is strongly influenced by the Ebro river valley with plenty of wind, which helps avoid diseases. Orientations are towards the east, west, and north, avoiding the direct sunlight on southerly exposed slopes. Initially the terrain had to be prepared for planting and, having been abandoned for eight years, there was much work to do on the terraces. The centuries-old olive trees and a few rows of mostly 20-year-old Carignan vines were recuperated but most of the remaining hectares had to be replanted. With my conviction that biodiversity is paramount for the future of our planet, we left the forests and olive groves untouched. The land in the forests had been planted with vines in the nineteenth century, since the remains of the terraces are still visible among the trees.

I travelled to the Southern Rhône to visit a specialised nursery and select the vines to be planted after grafting on to American root stock. I gave priority to the local Grenache Noir, also Syrah, Mourvèdre, a few Cabernet Sauvignon vines, and a little Viognier to complement the Syrah as it does in Côte-Rôtie.

An amusing anecdote relating to the purchase of these vines occurred when two years after planting, I received repeated phone calls from René Barbier asking how many Cabernet Sauvignon and how many Viognier vines we had purchased. Indeed, the few grapes on the supposed Cabernet vines were not changing colour! After careful examination of the leaves, it was discovered that nearly all the Cabernet was in fact Viognier. What was to be done? On consultation with the nursery, who admitted a mistake, 2,000 Cabernet

Sauvignon vines were sent free of charge. All we needed to do was to decapitate the Viognier at ground level and graft the Cabernet onto the Viognier roots. In this process one year's production would be lost but compensated for by the nursery. However, when the Cabernet vines arrived, the Viognier looked so healthy it was decided to leave the vines where they were and plant the Cabernet elsewhere. As a result, Clos Figueras now has an excellent dry white wine, Font de la Figuera Blanco, composed of Viognier complemented with Grenache Blanc and Chenin Blanc, planted at a later date, undeniably a happy accident!

In early 2000 a handful of owners of adjacent vineyards, on mostly cooler north-facing slopes, proposed selling their holdings to Clos Figueras. The transaction took place without difficulty and gave the estate access to some old Grenache and Carignan vines, which have since been an important ingredient for Clos Figueres, the principal wine of the estate. The acquisition added another 10 hectares (25 acres) to the property, making a total of 21 hectares (52 acres) all in one block, of which 11 hectares (27 acres) are planted. One of the slopes has a classified Roman wall running diagonally across the terraces, no doubt the border of a long extinct Roman roadway.

Initially the wines were made in the Clos Mogador cellar outside Gratallops. The first wine was just 1,200 bottles of our second wine, Font de la Figuera 1999. It was a pleasant wine which was sold and consumed quickly. In spite of the rather indifferent quality of this vintage, I was immensely proud to finally have my own wine to sell. For my entire career I had been selling wines made by others. What a difference it makes when proposing to customers one's own creation! With the 2000 vintage the first serious wines were made – the Clos Figueres 2000 and Font de la Figuera Tinto 2000 were highly rated by the specialised press and sold well. With the 2001 vintage, Clos Figueres was awarded 96 points by Robert Parker, putting the estate rapidly in league with the top names of the fast-emerging Priorat appellation. In the following years Robert Parker awarded Clos Figueres 94 points for every vintage, with the happy exception of the 2005 with 96 points.

In early 2002, with space running out at Clos Mogador, an independent vinification cellar was purchased in Gratallops. A disused chicken barn was converted and made ready for the 2002 vintage. To help with costs, part of the cellar was rented out for vinification to two other new producers, Trio Infernal from France and the Osborne family from El Puerto de Santa Maria, one of the Sherry-producing towns in Southern Spain. They are well known for their Sherries and especially their Brandy. For ageing the wines in cask, space was rented in an ideal, humid underground cellar beneath the adjoining building. This part of the building belonged to a group of eight young friends led by René Barbier Jr. and Sara Pérez of Mas Martinet. They produce a wine called La Vinya Del Vuit, with *Vuit* being the Catalan word for the number eight. Only eight barrels were made each year, so there was plenty of room for our wines from Clos Figueras to age in their cellar.

Throughout the decade the reputation of the estate became established in numerous export markets. Some clients outside Europe are taken care of by Europvin with a presence in Asia, especially Japan and Korea. In Europe, the US, and parts of Asia, sales are made directly from the bodega with the US and Switzerland being the principal markets. Additionally, the wines are also sold in Germany, Austria, Poland, the Czech Republic, Sweden, Denmark, Holland, Belgium, Luxembourg, England, Ireland, Australia, New

Clos Figueras Priorat, 2005,
was awarded 96 points in the Wine Advocate.

Zealand, Singapore, Hong Kong, China, the Philippines, Canada, Mexico, Brazil, Costa Rica, and Guatemala – and one of our collector friends even found a bottle of Clos Figueres in Bhutan! In Spain there are numerous local customers, especially at top-rated restaurants in Barcelona and the Costa Brava, as well as a presence in Madrid and Malaga. Founders of a new winery sometimes forget the importance of having a sales network in place. It takes many years and extensive travels to establish the reputation of a new winery and, without a network, even longer. I was fortunate in having my contacts from Wildman and Europvin days to help launch Clos Figueras, as well as the impact of the positive press.

Today we produce three red wines and two white wines: Clos Figueres from the old vines, the classic Font de la Figuera Tinto from the vines planted back in 1998, and the more recently launched Serras del Priorat, a fruit-driven wine for early consumption that still maintains all the Priorat characteristics. The whites include the Font de la Figuera Blanco from the mistaken Viognier and our Serras del Priorat Blanco made from white Grenache. Some years a late-harvest sweet wine aptly named Sweet is made in small quantities: 100% Grenache lightly fortified to stop the fermentation and keep the natural sugar from the grapes.

At Clos Figueras a total of between 35,000 and 40,000 bottles are made with single-minded passion and commitment to the highest quality possible. The style has always been orientated towards elegance and freshness, unlike the over-extracted and often over-oaked Priorats of the 1990s. To assist in this achievement I enlisted my friend, the late Alain Graillot of Crozes Hermitage fame in the Rhône Valley, to help with the blending and give welcome advice.

In 2011 Clos Figueras was finally able to purchase the previously mentioned part of the neighbouring building from *Los Vuit*, including the attractive centuries-old underground cellar for ageing the wines. Furthermore, in August 2011 the remainder of the building was purchased. This was initially a restaurant owned by René Barbier Jr. and Sara Perez called Les Irreductibles.

Clos Figueras also produces an Extra Virgin Olive Oil with the Siurana DO from 135 olive trees of the celebrated Arbequina variety. Many of the trees are more than 300 years old. Finally, some beehives have been installed in our vineyard with the bees busily making our own Clos Figueres honey and contributing to the ecological balance in the vineyard.

The vineyard and olive groves have always been farmed with ecology in mind and are now officially certified organic by the CCPAE (the official Catalan body for organic certification). The vines are planted at various altitudes stretching up from the north-facing slopes above the Montsant river valley and other cool locations chosen to slow down the maturing of the grapes. The views over the wide Ebro valley to the mountains beyond are stunning, with the hill where the famous L'Ermita vineyard is located, and Montsant mountain to the rear, protecting the site from the cold northerly winds.

Clos Figueras in the village of Gratallops, in the Priorat.
The winery is the long, low building on the edge of the village, below the church.

The Clos Figueras vineyard.

As can be imagined, owning a vineyard is not a ride without emotions. It is a costly and challenging hobby and in Priorat, even more so, since the yields, thanks to the poor rocky soil, are so low. As is well known in the trade, owning a vineyard is an expensive proposition. With the low yields in the Priorat, an

Amidst the schistous terroir at Clos Figueras.

average of 12 hectolitres (317 gallons) per hectare (2.5 acres), a new producer must have a lot of patience and the means to invest over a long period before becoming profitable. In the Priorat this can take at least ten years. Luckily, I had the proceeds from the sale of Europvin to keep me afloat. Even after a decade of spending, all profit continues to be ploughed back into the estate to finance new plantings, new equipment, new barrels for ageing, and all the misfortunes that happen along the way with small harvests, adverse weather, including occasional hail and torrential rain destroying the terraces. Like everywhere, we depend on the climate. While it is always hot and the grapes can ripen without difficulty, there are other challenges. Drought has been a significant problem for a number of years, further reducing the yields and forcing us to purchase grapes for our Serras del Priorat entry-level blend. We have had to install sophisticated irrigation, especially for the young vines during long periods of drought. In this respect, we have ample water supply

Alain Graillot assisting with the blending at Clos Figueras.

from clean, underground mountain streams, which is an enormous advantage. Other problems have included the overnight disappearance of 1,000 litres (264 gallons) of Viognier from the vat during fermentation, an unsolved mystery. However, when all is said and done, it is worth it and nothing

With Anne-Josephine in the Clos Figueras cellar.

gives more satisfaction than the moment when the wine is finally bottled, labelled, and recognised by experts of being of a quality to rank with the world's finest wines.

We are fortunate with our winemaking team, which comprises my daughter, Anne-Josephine, after completing her enology studies and practice in Australia, Italy, and Argentina; our on-site enologist, Silvia Puig, a meticulous and talented winemaker; and the late Alain Graillot of Crozes Hermitage fame, our well-respected consultant until his sudden death in 2022. Our manager, Miquel Compte, has been with us almost since the founding of the winery. With his cautious financial management and experience running restaurants he is an essential part of the team. His natural charm has made him a favourite with our visitors, doing much for our image. Anne-Josephine is very active with the Women in Wine movement, at first organising successful tastings for women winemakers from Priorat at Clos Figueras and now, on a more national scale, in Barcelona with plans for Madrid. She is also very active with the sales of our wines in Spain, especially in Barcelona where she is now an expert on the restaurant scene.

As previously mentioned, in 2011 we were fortunate in being able to acquire the remainder of the building of which our winemaking facility is part. This consisted of the underground cellar which we had rented over the past nine years, and a restaurant which had previously belonged to René Barbier Jr. and his wife, Sara Perez of Mas Martinet. It used to be called Les Irreductibles and had an excellent reputation. The restaurant, now named Les Figueres, is a huge asset, with a large wisteria and vine-covered terrace, a spacious garden with fruit trees, stunning views, and enough seating for seventy people. Also, we have our own vegetable garden and a few chickens. We are lucky to have a great team in the kitchen and on the floor. Some of the restaurant clientele is local or from Barcelona, especially at weekends. During the week we receive

Miquel Compte (left), our loyal manager at Clos Figueras.

many foreign visitors. Working closely with half a dozen travel agents in Barcelona, specialising in winery tours for overseas visitors, has been a great success. We offer them and their clients a cellar visit followed by a tasting and lunch. In normal years our small shop and the restaurant account for the sale of about 20% of our production. The remainder is exported or sold to distributors in Catalonia and Madrid. Covid-19 posed some problems for the restaurant with fewer foreign visitors. However, in the summers of 2020 and 2021, the restaurant and guest rooms were full every weekend, with visitors from Barcelona and nearby Tarragona, looking to escape the cities at the earliest opportunity.

Initially, running a restaurant was quite a challenge. We had no experience and at first planned to serve only simple cold food to accompany the wines. However, our wonderful chef, Maria-José from Ecuador, had other ideas and soon wanted to make more sophisticated dishes. This contributed to our growing reputation and Les Figueres has become a restaurant for all-comers, whether interested in wine or not. There are few restaurants in Priorat at this time, and only one or two other wineries having a restaurant is also a factor.

The winery and restaurant at Clos Figueras.

Clos Figueras vineyard and its scenic background.

This is likely to change in the future as the region gains more of a reputation as an outstanding destination for enotourism.

The first floor of the two parts of the building we acquired in 2011 had been abandoned for many years. In 2014 we cleared out the debris and constructed three comfortable guest rooms with great views over the mountains and vineyards, also an office and a small apartment. This bed-and-breakfast activity has also grown rapidly and is open year-round with more than 50% occupation. Of course, the summer months see more activity than in winter.

For the future we are clearing and planting other parts of the vineyard. White wine currently represents only 5% of the Priorat production but is becoming popular and increasing, the soil being well suited to the white Grenache and Viognier, among other varieties. At Clos Figueras more planting of white varieties and the traditional Carignan are planned. As the years go by, we expect to sell more wine directly from the cellar door but, at the same time, in spite of the difficulties with distribution, I have always wanted a presence on at least some of the world's best wine lists, giving the winery a more international perspective and reputation.

CHAPTER 20

MONTSANT

A Missed Opportunity

The Montsant DO almost completely surrounds Priorat. Imagine a fried egg with the yoke being Priorat and the white component Montsant. The climate, altitude, and grape varieties are similar but the topography is different, with wider terraces and less-precipitous slopes. The soils are also different, clay dominating with pockets of sand, chalk, and even some schist, leading to larger yields than in the Priorat.

My history in Montsant goes back to 1999 when, with René Barbier, we recognised the potential of the region to produce outstanding wines with grapes purchased from carefully chosen vineyards. At the time the region was not called Montsant but DO Tarragona sub-zone Falset, since the DO Montsant was only created in 2001. Tarragona-Falset being a complicated name and the wines so much better than the majority from the Tarragona DO on the Mediterranean coast, the authorities in Falset negotiated the separation of what is now the Montsant DO from the Tarragona DO.

After an extensive vineyard research and finding a suitable building in Falset, the commercial centre for the area, we created Europvin-Falset with the brand name Laurona for the wines. The name I found in a nineteenth-century wine book on the history of wine, with Pliny the Elder mentioning the Roman town of Laurona, not far from Falset, in a now lost location on the Mediterranean coast.

The building was part of a disused factory built by a long-departed German company. The negotiations for the acquisition of the building with the mayor of Falset were long and complicated. Nevertheless, once the purchase was complete, we were able to install the vats and casks in time for the 1999 vintage. Soon after the building was purchased, we learnt that a new factory, a subsidiary of a Barcelona chemical facility, was going to be constructed on the opposite side of the road. This caused great concern because, if chemicals were involved, they could prejudice the quality of our wines. I recall driving to Barcelona with René and wandering round the mother factory, sniffing the air to see if we could detect some adverse aromas. In the end the factory was dedicated to fabricating lifts for multistorey buildings!

We made two wines, Laurona and 6 Vinyes de Laurona, from six old-vine vineyards. As in Priorat the dominant grape variety was Grenache, with the addition of Cariñena (aka Carignan), some Syrah, Merlot, and Cabernet Sauvignon. The wines are aged in 500-litre (132-gallon) French oak casks for over a year before bottling.

Our first vintage was 1999, a difficult year with rain during the harvest. Nevertheless, we made a good wine that sold quickly through the Europvin network and in Spain. The subsequent vintages had no such problems with harvest conditions and good wines were made every year, the 6 Vinyes being not far off world-class quality. We received excellent press from Robert Parker and achieved a place in the Top 100 list for the 2001 vintage in the *Wine Spectator*.

As the years went by Europvin continued to establish Laurona as a leading brand from the new DO Montsant, quickly gaining recognition as a source of excellent wines of a style different from that of Priorat. René was making full, rich wines with plenty of fruit and freshness, good grip, and acidity too, but not the distinctive mineral character of Priorat. Furthermore, yields from the more diverse soils are higher and consequently production costs lower, making for wines of excellent value.

During the sale of Europvin to the Caballero group in Jerez, the question of what would become of Europvin-Falset came up. Caballero was prepared to invest in the company but I felt the relationship with René Barbier would not be compatible, so I decided to purchase the company with the proceeds from the sale of Europvin. This turned out to be a mistake as I was hoping that René would take a larger share in the winery and reduce his sizeable consultancy fee. This was not to be. Then the financial crisis hit in 2008 and sales dropped to near zero. With the crisis, I also felt the need to launch a less expensive wine, and possibly a white wine as well, but René, in his role as winemaker, was not interested in extending the range. This situation and the financial crisis were fatal to the profitability, so I decided to sell the company. An entertainment group from Barcelona purchased the now-named Celler Laurona and part of my share in the Espectacle project (more on this subject to follow). Recently the company has been sold again to the competent Fischer family from Switzerland.

This was a sad moment in my history in the wine trade and such a pity, since Laurona had the potential to be a leader for the Montsant appellation. The quality of the wines made by René is without question superb and he continues to make excellent wines to this day. With the sale to the Barcelona group, the new owners had no commercial expertise in wines and did not attempt to maintain the relationship with Europvin. The brand soon became eclipsed by newly established rising stars in the DO. Today Celler Laurona is endeavouring, and will no doubt succeed, in re-establishing a worldwide presence with the new and capable Swiss owners.

CHAPTER 21

ESPECTACLE

A Vinous Wonder

This project has its origins in the Laurona adventure. With the careful selection of vineyards for 6 Vinyes de Laurona we sourced some excellent Grenache grapes from the village of La Figuera, the highest village in the Montsant DO, where the old vineyards are almost exclusively planted with Grenache. One of the vineyards stood out as being very special. On visiting the site with René, we were amazed by the condition of the vineyard, with century-old vines and breathtaking views in all directions. On some days the distant Pyrenees are clearly visible, with views up the Ebro Valley on the left, and a stunning side view of the Montsant mountain on the right. It has never been easier to find a name for a wine. We said to each other, "This is spectacular – now we have a name!" Thus, Spectacle Vins was born and the wine named Espectacle. Initially we were three families in the partnership, hence the three chairs on the label designed by Isabelle Barbier, René's late wife. The original painting only had two chairs but with three families involved a third chair had to be added! The founding partners in the project include René Barbier and his wife; Fernando Zamora and his wife Marta, both enologists from Tarragona University; and finally me with my wife Charlotte.

The project was launched with the 2004 vintage, a very elegant and complex wine that was awarded 99 points by the *Wine Advocate*. This immediately put Espectacle on the map as a world-class wine, ranking with the finest examples of Grenache-based wines from Châteauneuf-du-Pape and elsewhere. The impact from this positive press also helped publicise the new Montsant DO as a potential source for some outstanding wines.

At an altitude of over 650 metres (2,133 feet), the vineyard is located on a dangerously steep slope at the highest point of the Montsant and Priorat appellations. The vines date from the early twentieth century, immediately after the phylloxera plague, and some are so old their branches are propped up by stones. The vineyard covers less than 2 hectares (5 acres) and produces only about 4,000 litres (1,057 gallons) in good vintages. The altitude and the exposed, windy location signify a late harvest starting in early October. The grapes are taken to Falset for vinification in just one new 4,000-litre (1,057-gallon) French oak vat. This same vat is used for the whole winemaking and ageing

A view of the steep Espectacle vineyard in Montsant.

process and sold after the wine has been bottled. A new vat is then purchased for the next vintage. A total of about 5,000 bottles are made each year and allocated to various markets throughout the world. In Spain the wines are sold exclusively and directly to leading restaurants.

The resulting wine is very special, with extraordinary complexity and balance. The colour is a deep ruby with the depth and clarity of a great Pinot Noir. The aromas start out with intense but subtle floral notes hinting of roses and orange blossom but after a few minutes the fruit comes forward with blackberries and raspberries dominating.

Close-up of vines and terraces at the Espectacle vineyard.

On the palate, Espectacle is smooth and intense with velvety tannins and a never-ending finish, expressing the aromatic nuances of this great wine. To show the full potential, we always recommend the wine be decanted an hour or so before being consumed.

Year after year the trade press has awarded top scores to Espectacle, assuring a place in many of the world's best private cellars and wine lists. The partnership has been slightly modified over the years and today includes the Fischer family, the Swiss owners of Celler Laurona, where the wine is made by René Barbier.

PART FIVE

RETIREMENT

CHAPTER 22

CRUISES

A Relaxing Diversion

One never really retires from wine. Every year the vine produces a new vintage and the wine has to be made, aged, bottled, and sold. My years in retirement have been, and continue to be, devoted to Clos Figueras with frequent travels to the vineyard from my Bordeaux base and numerous foreign trips to promote and sell the wines. This is rewarding work and has gradually contributed to the profile of the estate and a presence in more than twenty-three countries.

Other activities have included lecturing on cruise ships, which has provided a relaxing and enjoyable interlude. Celebrity Cruise Lines asked me to participate in their so-called wine cruises. The starting point was a UK port with stops in Le Havre, Le Verdon for the Bordeaux vineyards (the ship being too large to cruise up the Gironde and Garonne to the port of Bordeaux), Bilbao for Rioja, Vigo in Galicia for Albariño, and Oporto for the Douro and the Port wine houses. On board all I had to do was conduct a tasting on the days the ship was at sea. The cruise line purchased our wines from Clos Figueras which I showed alongside other wines from Priorat. I also gave a lecture on fortified wines with samples of Sherry, Port, and Madeira. I was not remunerated but all expenses were paid with a comfortable sea-view cabin, meals in the best restaurant, and a $100 voucher for wine in the evening. This was enough to select some very fine bottles. On the downside I soon noticed that very few of the passengers had much interest in wine. From the 3,000 passengers, only about twenty attended the lectures. After the second cruise I decided that a crowded ship, with few passengers interested in purchasing quality wines, was not an ideal method for promoting our Clos Figueras. On the plus side I had the opportunity to visit Bilbao and the Guggenheim Museum, the city of Oporto and picturesque Honfleur, including vineyard visits to Albariño vineyards in Galicia and a Txakoli estate near Bilbao.

CHAPTER 23

L'ACADÉMIE
INTERNATIONALE DU VIN

In Defence of Authenticity

Much more appealing during my retirement years have been activities with L'Académie Internationale du Vin which I joined in 2013. The previously mentioned Swiss-based organisation was founded back in 1970 by Constant Bourquin. Members include personalities from the world of wine, many of whom are household names in the trade. They include producers such as Angelo Gaja; Jean-Pierre Perrin of Beaucastel; Willi Bründlmayer from Austria; Gérard Chave; Dominique Lafon; Alvaro Palacios; Carl von Schubert of Maximin Grünhaus in Germany; Jacques Seysses of Domaine Dujac; Jean-Noël Boidron, one of the founding members; Alois Lageder; Maria José López de Heredia; Michael Silacci of Opus One; Paul Draper; and many more. The journalists included the late Steven Spurrier; also Michael Schuster; John Salvi MW; Raoul Salama; Michel Bettane; Victor de la Serna; and Juancho Asenjo. Then there are the specialised technicians such as Claude and Lydia Bourguignon, the terroir specialists; José Vouillamoz, co-author of Jancis Robinson's Wine Grapes and specialist in the DNA of vines; and the late Jacques Puisais, famous for his books on taste with food and wine compatibility. Finally, there are some collectors and wine traders such as Quim Vila from Barcelona and Fiona Morrison MW, author and importer in Belgium. Jean-Pierre Perrin is the president and Raymond Paccot, who owns the reputed Domaine La Colombe vineyard in La Côte near Lausanne, the chancellor. Other Swiss producers include Raoul Cruchon, Emilienne Hutin Zumbach from Geneva, and Corinne Clavien-Desfayes from Valais.

The object of the Académie is to defend the interest of the so-called noble wines, or wines made with the minimum of intervention and bottled at the estate, in contrast to the industrially produced branded table wines that were dominating the market in the 1970s. Today the Académie is a forum for the defence of fine wine encompassing production, distribution, consumption, and all aspects surrounding the culture of wine.

The Académie meets twice a year. In December the annual general meeting takes place during which a series of lectures are conducted on various wine-connected subjects, both general and, often, quite technical. New members are also requested to give an introductory presentation on a subject of their choice and approved by the chancellor. The meetings used to be held in Geneva but more recently other cities have been chosen including Lausanne, Berlin, Barcelona, Vienna, and Lyon. Apart from Berlin, the advantage of changing cities allows an extra day to visit producers and vineyards in the neighbouring appellations. Locations visited have included Lavaux and La Côte near Lausanne with Raymond Paccot and Raoul Cruchon; Wachau and Kamptal near Vienna, organised to perfection by Willi Bründlmayer; and the Beaujolais near Lyon with Claude Geoffray of Château Thivin, Dominique Piron, Michel Bettane, and Pierre-Henry Gagey. From Barcelona, I organised a day in Priorat with a lunch at Clos Figueras followed by visits to Recaredo and Can Rafols del Caus in the Penedès.

The other session is a tour to a production area somewhere in the world. I have been fortunate to be able to participate in trips to Argentina, Hungary, Rioja, Sicily, South Africa, Tuscany, Switzerland, Bordeaux, and Ribera del Duero. I have to pay special attention to all that is said and tasted since I am usually appointed to write the report on each trip for the Académie website, a role that gives me much pleasure and motivation to learn as much as possible.

ARGENTINA

During these tours we are invariably treated like royalty, being systematically spoilt with sumptuous meals and extensive, well-conducted tastings. The schedules are quite intense with several winery visits each day. Already broached in a previous chapter, the travels in Argentina in March 2013 were focused on Mendoza and the Valle de Uco, visiting, among others, Catena Zapata, Cheval des Andes, Terrazas de los Andes, Zuccardi, Norton, O. Fournier, Salentein, Ruca Malen, Susana Balbo, and Bodega Mendel, owned by Roberto de la Mota who capably organised much of the expedition. During the stopover in Buenos Aires, we were received at the Palacio San Martin, the Ministry of Foreign Affairs, for a tasting and presentation of Argentinian wines from other areas including Patagonia, San Juan, and Cafayate.

HUNGARY

The following year we visited Hungary in the capable hands of Robert Cey-Bert and Erik Sauter. This trip was split into two parts, one for table wines and the other for Tokaj. After a general presentation in Budapest, we proceeded by bus to the attractive Lake Balaton region where we had our first introduction to the local grape varieties, notably the Olaszrizling, Kéknyelü, and ubiquitous Kékfrankos. The next day we drove to Villány, in the south of the country, arguably the best region for red wines and where Erik Sauter has a joint venture in a winery. Here the Bordeaux varieties dominate, notably Cabernet Franc, Merlot, and Cabernet Sauvignon, sometimes blended with local varieties. Returning to Budapest a stop was made in the region of Szekszárd, on the right bank of the Danube, where the Kadarka grape is king with the inevitable Kékfrankos. During the bus rides Robert Cey-Bert gave us a detailed and fascinating account of the history of wine in Hungary.

The trip to Tokay was memorable and included visits to the most dedicated and prestigious producers. We started with the Royal Tokaji cellars and then moved on to spend time with István Szepsy, considered to be the leading and most respected winemaker in Tokay. Here we were treated to a lengthy and fascinating tasting of dry wines made with the Furmint grape from different plots and soil types. We tasted various vintages from 2011 back to 2006. The wines were sublime with a strong mineral presence thanks to the volcanic soils. We also tasted Szepsy's classic sweet wines, Aszú 6 Puttonyos, 2003 and 2002, wines of great complexity with layers of flavour. In short, wines for meditation. Other cellars visited included Disnókö, owned by AXA Millésimes, where we tasted numerous Aszú 5 and 6 Puttonyos wines back to 1993. It was a fascinating experience which displayed the complexity and finesse of these great dessert wines. Finally, we were well received at Tokaj Oremus, owned by Vega Sicilia. Here we were treated to another extensive tasting which included the famous Eszencia from the 2003 vintage. This wine is very rare and only made in small quantities when conditions permit. Eszencia is so thick and intense one is reminded of black treacle. With only 2.8% alcohol they can survive for centuries. The flavours are something else, with huge complexity and, at this stage, dominated by aromas of orange peel, like English marmalade.

The visit to Tokay included a side trip to the Hortobágy National Park on the Hungarian steppes with herds of wild horses said to have been used by the armies of Attila the Hun. Returning to Budapest we stopped in Eger to visit the area responsible for the famous Bull's Blood red wines. It was somewhat of a disappointment after the allure of Tokay.

RIOJA

In 2015 Rioja was the destination with an impeccably organised schedule devised by Maria-José López de Heredia, Alvaro Palacios, and Juan Carlos López de Lacalle of Bodegas y Viñedos Artadi. Visits were made to Bodegas Marqués de Riscal and La Granja Remelluri, owned by the Rodriguez family, and where we enjoyed a superb buffet lunch accompanied by a range of the Telmo Rodriquez selections. Bodega Vivanco and their spectacular wine museum, Marqués de Murrieta, Bodegas Franco Españolas, and Viñedos del Contino were also included in the schedule. The highlights were the visits to Bodegas López de Heredia, Bodegas y Viñedos Artadi, and the vineyard, La Montesa, owned by Alvaro Palacios.

The visit with Alvaro included an extensive tasting in the vineyard, with Alvaro describing the virtues of the Grenache grape in the Rioja, especially in the Rioja Oriental with a more Mediterranean climate. This was followed by an entertaining rustic bullfight in which Alvaro participated as a toreador!

At López de Heredia we were treated to a sumptuous lunch in the bodega, surrounded by century-old oak fermentation vats and served with a lineup of historic wines including the Viña Tondonia Blanco Gran Reserva 1964, Viña Tondonia Tinto Gran Reserva 1964, and the extraordinary Viña Tondonia Gran Reserva 1954. All the wines were in remarkable condition, bright and fresh with gorgeous, complex flavours, great depth, and elegance. Without doubt showing perfection in the classic Rioja style, displaying just how well these wines can age.

Finally, at Bodegas y Viñedos Artadi, we were shown the emblematic El Pison vineyard followed by a dinner with fresh turbot brought directly from the Basque fishing port of Getaria and prepared by the Michelin-starred restaurant Elkano of the same village. A choir of Basque singers only added to the ambiance.

SICILY

The following year Sicily was the destination for a short, two-day visit. Based in Taormina we toured the southeastern part of the island near Vittoria and Noto, stopping first at Feudi del Pisciotto, a large winery, fascinating due to the remains of a Greek and subsequently Roman wine cellar around which the modern cellar has been constructed. It was also our introduction to the charms of the ubiquitous Nero d'Avola grape variety. We moved on to the Planeta winery where we were well received by Alessio Planeta. Over lunch in the cellar, we tasted wines from their different wineries around the island. Planeta initiated their operations in the western part of the island and later constructed wineries in Etna, Vittoria, and other locations, becoming the largest fine-wine producer in Sicily. After visiting the historic town of Noto, we returned to Taormina.

The next day was spent on the flanks of the Etna volcano, visiting wineries on the south, eastern, and northern slopes. The wines from Etna have gained worldwide recognition thanks to the volcanic soils producing wines of great finesse and elegance. The reds have the colour and texture of a fine Pinot Noir from the Côte d'Or. The main grape for red wine is the Nerello Mascalese, while for the whites it is the Carricante. We called on Scammacca del Murgo in Santa Venerina, Barone di Villagrande in Milo, and Graci at Passopisciaro, a winery on the northern slope and also part of a joint venture between Angelo Gaja and Alberto Graci. Our main regret was the trip was too short, not allowing us time to visit the western part of the island around Marsala and some of the most emblematic producers, notably COS and Arianna Occipinti in Vittoria, and Terre Nere and Tenuta de Passopisciaro on Etna.

SOUTH AFRICA

My second visit to South Africa was with the Académie Internationale du Vin in February 2017. Like the previous visit we called on numerous wineries where we were received as VIPs, several well-known producers and trade members being among us. On arrival we were whisked up to the top of Table Mountain in a cable car where a glass of Klein Constantia sparkling wine awaited us with some tapas. South Africa produces some excellent sparkling wines made in the same way as Champagne and is labelled as Méthode Cap Classique (MCC). Of course, the views from the mountaintop were amazing, taking in the whole of Cape Town and the ocean beyond.

The first night was spent in Constantia and the following morning we visited Klein Constantia, an emblematic winery belonging to Bruno Prats, president of the Académie at the time, and Hubert de Boüard of Château Angelus in Saint Emilion, among others. A tour of the vineyards on the flank of Table Mountain was very instructive, the granite soils and rainy climate providing ideal conditions for the Sauvignon Blanc, yielding elegant, dry white wines. The estate is however better known for their classic dessert wine called Vin de Constance. As mentioned previously this is a historic wine, a favourite of Napoleon during his exile on Santa Helena. Made from late-harvest grapes of the Muscat de Frontignan variety, and not being too alcoholic at 14.5%, the flavours are complex and exquisite with a touch of citrus on the palate. An extensive tasting was followed by a delicious lunch under a huge oak tree in the garden.

We only visited two wineries the following day, the most impressive being Mullineux & Leeu in Franschhoek. Here we were hosted by Chris and Andrea Mullineux, two very competent young enologists. In the past Franschhoek benefitted from many immigrants of French origin who brought viticulture and expertise to the valley. Notwithstanding, most of the grapes vinified by the Mullineux couple come from Swartland. We tasted a range of red and white wines from two soil types, granite and schist; comparing the two soils with a Chenin for the white and Syrah for the red was a fascinating exercise.

Returning to Stellenbosch we stopped at the DeMorgenzon winery. The vineyard, planted on decomposed granite soils, benefits from the continuous broadcasting of Baroque music without repetition for a whole week! Being close to False Bay with windy conditions it is questionable how effective this strategy can be. Certainly, the wines, mostly Syrah, Chenin Blanc, and Chardonnay, are highly regarded.

Since we were a group of about thirty-five Académie members we travelled everywhere in a forty-seater bus. The next day we drove to Hermanus, about 160 kilometres (100 miles) from Cape Town on the South Coast, stopping at a penguin colony at Stony Point on the way. Facing the Southern Ocean and the Antarctic, the climate around Hermanus is particularly cool, ideal for the Burgundian grapes, Pinot Noir and Chardonnay. We called on two wineries in the Hemel-en-Aarde valley, just inland from the coastal town. The best-known being Hamilton Russell, specialising exclusively in the two Burgundian varieties. Anthony Hamilton Russell treated us to an extensive tasting and a sumptuous buffet lunch in his home overlooking the surrounding vineyards and valley. Further up the valley we visited the more recent Newton Johnson winery. Founded in 1997, the estate is run by two brothers, Bevan and Gordon Newton Johnson. To our surprise the first wine we tasted was an Albariño, a variety rarely seen outside Galicia in Spain. It showed well with the classic aromatics and freshness of the variety. There followed an extensive tasting of Chardonnays and Pinot Noirs, wines that can convincingly rank with the best from outside Burgundy.

We returned to Stellenbosch via the inland route and the next day made another trip to Franschhoek where we visited the somewhat strangely named and historic Boekenhoutskloof winery, founded in 1776. This is a large winery selling over seven million bottles under various brand names. We were only shown their most prestigious wines, notably their Semillon, Syrah, and Cabernet Sauvignon.

One full day was devoted to tourism with a long drive down the Cape Peninsular to the Cape of Good Hope. The breathtaking scenery and sighting of wild animals, mostly baboons, made for a most agreeable trip. We lunched on fish at Kalk Bay by the sea with a glass of Saronsberg Viognier and Kanonkop Pinotage and a colony of seals basking on the rocks below us.

We wound up the trip with a few more winery visits. The most memorable were Backsberg in Paarl for their old wines dating back to the 1970s and Anwilka, near Stellenbosch, which belongs to the same partners as Klein Constantia and run by Hans Astrom, the competent Swedish manager for both estates and now also a member of the Académie. Finally, a delicious lunch at the 96 Winery Road restaurant, belonging to the Ken Forrester winery, was a special treat with a tasting conducted by Ken Forrester himself with tremendous enthusiasm, regaling us with his superb Chenin Blanc wines, Rhône variety reds, and his insuppressible sense of humour.

In spite of the political situation and extremely dry climate, the wine scene in South Africa is both exciting and stimulating. Huge and constant efforts are being made to improve quality. We were welcomed everywhere by very capable and qualified producers who do their best to transmit their knowledge and devotion to making South Africa a source for world-class wines.

TUSCANY

In 2018 we returned to Italy for a short stay in Tuscany. The trip was efficiently organised by the charming, soft-spoken Donatella Cinelli Colombini, member of the Académie and owner of the Casato Prime Donne in Montalcino. I participated with my daughter, Anne-Josephine, on this occasion. On the first day we drove from our base in Florence to Montalcino. After a visit to the impressive Casanova di Neri winery, much admired by the American press with 100 points from Parker in 2015 and the *Wine Spectator* Wine of the Year in 2006, we moved on to Donatella's winery nearby. As the name suggests, the winery is run exclusively by women – even the blending team from various countries is all female. Donatella is producing some outstanding Brunello di Montalcino from her 17 hectares (42 acres) inherited from her mother in 1988. There is no doubt the feminine touch shows in the elegance and purity of her wines. We were offered an amazing Tuscan lunch and the opportunity to taste various vintages of her Brunellos and wines from another estate she owns in the Chianti Superiore DOCG.

The next visit was a dramatic change. We were received by Marchese Piero Antinori in person at his huge ultra-modern winery dominating the road between Florence and Siena. The architecture is state-of-the-art with the building carefully integrated into the landscape. The wines produced here are the large-volume commercial brands, notably the Antinori Chianti Classico and Villa Antinori Chianti Classico Riserva. After a tasting of a series of

Antinori wines, regrettably not the famous Solaia and Tignanello, we returned to Florence and a superb classic Tuscan dinner in the Il Latini restaurant.

Early the following morning we drove by bus to Bolgheri for a fascinating visit at Ca' Marcanda, Angelo Gaja's Tuscan venture. Angelo, in his usual fine form and bounding with enthusiasm, gave us a tour of the winery and an extensive tasting which included wines from his Barbaresco and Brunello di Montalcino estates. He also gave us a lecture on his version of biodynamics, with a demonstration on how to avoid unwanted insects by releasing a species of ladybird into the vineyards, and a discussion on the planting of diverse crops between the rows of vines.

Just down the road we visited the emblematic and impressive Tenuta San Guido winery where the famed Sassicaia is produced. We were received by Marchesa Priscilla Incisa della Rocchetta, daughter of the founder, Mario Incisa della Rocchetta. Here we admired the vast barrel cellar and tasted two wines, the current 2015 vintage Sassicaia and the Guidalberto 2016, the second wine from the property. The estate is huge, covering some 2,500 hectares (6,178 acres). Apart from vineyards there are olive groves, forests, and fields for crops, cattle, and breeding of thoroughbred horses. The land stretches for 13 kilometres (8 miles) from the sea to the mountains with varied soil types, the most ideal for vineyards being nearer the mountains that rise to 400 metres (1,312 feet).

After a brief conference on the history of wine in Tuscany given by Emanuele Pellucci, a well-respected journalist and wine judge, we returned to Florence and a gala dinner in the Il Locale restaurant, washed down by a selection of wines from other Tuscan producers.

SWITZERLAND

The 2019 journey to Switzerland was special due to the unique opportunity to attend the Fête des Vignerons in Vevey, a spectacular event organised by the association of winegrowers in Lavaux and Chablais which only takes place every twenty to twenty-five years. The show is located in a specially constructed arena of 17,000 square metres (183,000 square feet), seating 20,000 spectators on the shore of Lake Geneva in the centre of Vevey. More than 5,600 actors and 900 choristers take part in a display of sixteen different wine-related themes. The three-hour pageant is magnificent, and sensational in its display of colour, music, and the superbly coordinated performance of each scene. It was a truly unforgettable experience and a privilege to be able to witness such an extraordinary event.

We took advantage of our stay in Switzerland to visit producers in Valais and Lavaux. In Valais we visited wineries in Leytron and Fully. Sadly, the rainy conditions did not allow us to enjoy the magnificent scenery. However, the wines showed well and demonstrated the efforts being made to improve the quality and image of the region. In Lavaux we were luckier with the weather and admired the wines and vineyards that dominate Lake Geneva. The vineyards are classified as a world heritage site by UNESCO. They are indeed spectacular, literally falling into the lake from steep, well-terraced slopes, initially constructed by the Romans. The wines, made almost exclusively from the Chasselas grape, are fresh and mineral, delightful with perch and other fish from the lake.

Our stay in Switzerland included some cultural activities with visits to Chaplin's World, the Charlie Chaplin museum in Corsier-sur-Vevey; a Blancpain watchmaking facility; and a Gruyère cheese producer in the Swiss Jura mountains.

BORDEAUX

In the summer of 2021, despite the Covid epidemic, a very intense three-day visit to Bordeaux was organised by Fiona Morrison MW of Château Le Pin and Véronique Sanders of Château Haut-Bailly. The programme included visits to Château Palmer, a lunch at Château Lafite Rothschild with a taste of the legendary 1949 vintage, a visit to Château Cos d'Estournel followed by a vineyard tour, and a sumptuous dinner at Château Ducru-Beaucaillou. The following day, after a technical visit to the Bordeaux enology faculty, we were treated to lunch at Château Haut-Bailly before visiting Château de Fargues with the Lur Saluces family in Sauternes during the afternoon. The evening was spent at Château Haut-Brion, where another superb dinner was served with outstanding wines. The last day included visits to Château Le Pin, Château Figeac, and lunch in the garden at Château Cheval Blanc, with wines from Châteaux Ausone and Pétrus. The day was concluded by a visit to Pétrus followed by dinner at Château Angélus. Everywhere we were treated like royalty and were able to enjoy some outstanding vintages with excellent meals; a unique opportunity to appreciate the greatness of mature Bordeaux from the most prestigious châteaux.

JURA

Just before a symposium of the Académie in Lausanne in December 2021, a day visiting the Jura vineyards was organised by Guillaume d'Angerville, owner of the renowned Marquis d'Angerville estate in Volnay and Domaine du Pélican in the Jura. Also, Alain de Laguiche, owner of Château d'Arlay, made arrangements for us to taste a wide range of wines from the Jura. Despite the pouring rain we were able to appreciate the fascinating diversity of the Jura wines. At Château d'Arlay we tasted wines from three of the most prominent estates, including Château d'Arlay. It was an opportunity to understand the complexity and merits of such wines as the famous Vin Jaune and Vin de Paille, and appreciate the local Savagnin grape variety.

RIBERA DEL DUERO

In June 2022 I assisted in the organisation of an Académie trip to the Duero Valley, 200 kilometres (124 miles) north of Madrid. With the help of Joaquim Vila of Vila Viniteca, an outstanding wine shop in Barcelona, with the single-most exhaustive selection of fine wines in Spain, I was able to arrange visits to Bodegas Mauro, Vega Sicilia, Cillar de Silos, and Abadía Retuerta, among others. We were fortunate to be able to visit and taste the finest wines from the most prestigious estates in the region. Apart from Mauro and Vega Sicilia, these included Dominio de Pingus, arguably the most expensive and sought-after wine in Spain; Pago de Carraovejas; and rising stars such as Dominio de Calogia and Dominio del Aguila. A tasting of a further selection of ten top wineries was arranged in the remarkable surroundings of the Castillo de Peñafiel, a distinctive fortified castle that features on many of the Spanish tourist brochures. We explored the differences between the wines from different parts of the valley. Among the most exciting experiences were the visits to the fifteenth-century underground cellars at Dominio del Aguila, Dominio del Pidio, and Cillar de Silos in Quintana del Pidio. We enjoyed some outstanding meals but for lunch every day it was ubiquitous *lechazo* or suckling lamb, which is the great speciality of the Duero and quite delicious.

These journeys with the Académie were more than just visits to wineries and local cultural activities. The participants are all interesting and entertaining and each contributes something different to the ongoing conversations. To mention but a few, Claude and Lydia Bourguignon enthusiastically display their knowledge of all subjects related to terroir in an entertaining manner. José Vouillamoz provides in-depth observations on the subject of vine varieties and their DNA. Angelo Gaja gives philosophical speeches with his sense of fun and novel approach to all wine-related subjects. Maria-José López de Heredia shows her interest in history and everything else that crosses her mind, and the late Jacques Puisais conversed on all subjects related to taste with remarkable modesty. Our meals and tastings are always lively and full of intelligent conversations, crowned by the remarkable speeches by our presidents, Bruno Prats and Jean-Pierre Perrin, also chancellor, Raymond Paccot, all very eloquent and brilliant in the art of diplomacy.

CONCLUSIONS
AND REFLECTIONS

So much has changed in the past half century of my career. The world of wine is unrecognisable. From the days when Bordeaux Grands Crus Classés were still shipped in cask to be bottled by importers in Nordic countries, to the modern-day revolution in communications and commitment to quality in the most ideal, environmentally friendly conditions, the changes have been enormous. This is indeed progress, although the question can be posed as to whether the wines have actually much improved over the years, especially after enjoying a glass of 1961 Palmer or 1947 Cheval Blanc.

In the 1960s and 1970s Bordeaux, Burgundy, and Germany dominated wine lists. Over the following decades we witnessed the emergence of the New World as a leading force in the trade, no doubt partly initiated by Steven Spurrier's 1976 Judgement of Paris tasting. Today wine lists include outstanding wines from the world over including more exotic locations, like Georgia, Brazil, and even India.

We have experienced a series of fashionable tendencies over the years. These include the many subjects that come and go in the world of wine with arguments on filtration or non-filtration, to destem or not, the use of more or less oak for ageing, the use of indigenous or cultivated yeasts, the most ideal fermentation vessels, the rise of natural wines with a rather loose interpretation of the meaning, among others.

Interest in wine has been stimulated by the admirable work of the Wine & Spirit Education Trust (WSET) with several thousand students participating from numerous countries. Women now have an important role at the executive level in a trade which was once almost entirely male dominated.

In short, the past fifty years have been nothing short of a revolution. The 1970s was a decade of economic hardship and a series of poor vintages, especially in Bordeaux, very much the leading wine-producing region at the time. Burgundy, apart from a handful of domaines, was dominated by the *négociants*, many of whom were churning out wines of indifferent quality. In the UK a bottle of Nuits-Saint-Georges did not even have to come from Burgundy. Appellation Contrôlée was only applied after the UK joined the European Community. The trade was sleepy and lethargic. The London merchants used to work a little in the mornings then retire to copious wine-drenched lunches that often lasted until it was time to take the train home! An afternoon appointment with an importer was out of the question.

Today, château-bottling in Bordeaux has become the norm. Few *négociants* succeed in establishing successful generic brands and most of those are witnessing declining sales. There are several hundred Burgundy estates producing, bottling, and selling their own wines. A few top *négociants*, such as Louis Jadot, Joseph Drouhin, Chanson, and Bouchard Père et Fils, are making world-class wines. Overall, quality has improved remarkably.

This analysis is similar in the Loire Valley and the Rhône but is even more remarkable in the lesser-known regions from all parts of France and the wine-producing world where Spain, Portugal, and Italy have to be singled out for their progress and an explosion of new producers. London has become the dynamic centre for the worldwide trading of fine wines, with dedicated merchants working round the clock. World-class wines are being made in the New World, albeit with the ongoing search for ideal vineyard locations. Recently Bordeaux has joined London and Hong Kong to become a leading trading centre for some of the world's most prestigious wines from the New World and the Old.

This said, there are problems threatening the future of fine wine, not the least being global warming with the resulting changes in the flavours and structure of wines from some of the best-known appellations. The higher alcohol content is a challenge but can be mastered by careful blending and the use of grape varieties better adapted for warmer climates. The search for suitable terroir at higher altitudes, north-facing slopes, and the appropriateness of more northerly countries such as the UK, Benelux, and even Poland could provide a solution. Scandinavia could also become a producer of good wines.

The rejection of globalisation is another difficulty, with an increasing number of consumers looking for ecologically friendly solutions including avoiding the purchase of products that have travelled long distances. This will mean that markets may become more localised and cellar-door sales will become a priority, leading to the importance of wine tourism and the huge advantage of being able to receive visitors at the winery for tastings and purchases direct from the producer. Food must not be forgotten in the equation and the possibility of opening a restaurant at the winery is a huge advantage. This is already common in the New World but only just getting underway in Europe.

Modern communications, having accelerated during the Covid pandemic, are revolutionising the distribution of wines and spirits. The ability to purchase almost all wines online makes life so much easier for the consumer, meaning that traditional networks will surely suffer, and direct sales from the producer's cellars and specialised online operators will be favoured.

Then there is the phenomenon of so-called Natural Wine, which sometimes means a wine loses its identity and becomes just another drink without a sense of place. This said, all good producers strive to make wines as natural as possible with the minimum use of sulphur to protect the wine for travel, storage, and long ageing in bottle. So, what will natural wine mean in the future or is it just a passing fad?

Regarding a sense of place – an issue to which I have been attached throughout my career – I am perplexed by certain wineries deciding to exit from their control of origin, being in disagreement with the authorities in charge. Admittedly this often concerns well-known estates with established brands, but the consumer deserves to know where the wine is produced and is increasingly requesting information on the precise geographic origin of the wine they wish to purchase and consume. Perhaps this is also a short-term phenomenon, but, at the same time, we are seeing various regions striving to introduce new official classifications of specific villages and vineyards, provoking a certain contradiction.

I am often asked which is my preferred wine. This is the most difficult question to answer. Of course, I have my preferences, notably crisp mineral Chablis for white wines, great Burgundy and Châteauneuf-du-Pape for reds, but a classed growth Bordeaux, when fully mature from a great vintage, is hard to beat. However, all things considered, well-made wines of all origins that have a sense of place are to my liking.

In conclusion, I have been lucky with my career on the whole with just a few setbacks. With my family, too, I am more than lucky with Charlotte, my supportive wife; Edward, our son, who, after a number of years with Moët Hennessy based in Canada and California, is now ambassador for the renowned Saint Estèphe estate, Château Cos d'Estournel, for all of North America and the Caribbean. My daughter, Anne-Josephine, is proving a huge asset at Clos Figueras with her winemaking skills and love of the commercial side of the business. She has two small sons who are already being exposed to the allure of fine wine. Anne-Josephine is also one of the leading personalities in the Women and Wine movement in Spain where she organises regular events.

The past five decades have been a fascinating and enjoyable journey, every day learning something new and always on the lookout for quality and integrity both in the products and the personalities behind each label. I have enjoyed every minute of it – not just the chance to sell many hundreds of thousands of cases of fine wine and spirits but also the wonderful people I have been lucky enough to meet both from the producing and importing sides of the fence. At this point I wish to convey my gratitude to all those who have believed in me and my activities, and have given me the support to make a success of my career in this captivating and engaging profession. It is these people that make our trade magic and unique, not to mention so many fond memories of great meals with unforgettable wines I have benefitted from in vinous companionship.

Our son, Edward, in Burgundy.

GLOSSARY

almacenista: *Almacen* is the Spanish word for warehouse. An *almacenista* is an individual or family that ages stocks of fine old Sherries that are frequently sold to the big Sherry houses to improve their blends or, as is the case for Emilio Lustau, bottled separately with the name of the *almacenista* on the label.

Amontillado: A rich, usually dry Sherry, ideal with nuts, olives, white meat, and consommé soup.

autobahn: German for motorway or freeway.

barrique: A cask of wine holding about 225 litres (60 gallons), usually made from French oak.

Blanc de Blancs: A wine or Champagne made entirely from white grapes. Certain wines and most Champagnes use red grapes that are pressed as soon as they arrive at the winery, giving a white juice, thus avoiding the red colouring which is in the skins.

botrytis (or noble rot): A fungus that shrivels the grape and concentrates the sugar content; it is essential for the production of some of the world's greatest sweet wines. Sauternes and Trockenbeerenauslese from Germany are classic examples.

carbonic maceration: A winemaking technique involving full bunches of grapes fermented in a sealed tank, saturated with carbon dioxide, resulting in light, fruity wines. The classic example is the wines of Beaujolais but the method is widely used elsewhere for light- to medium-bodied wines wines for early drinking.

cask: The barrel used for ageing fine wines. In Bordeaux they contain 225 litres (59 gallons); in Burgundy 228 litres (60 gallons).

Classified Growth: see Grand Cru Classé.

courtier: A broker who is the intermediary between the wine estates and the wine shippers or *négociants*.

Cream Sherry: A sweet Sherry made by blending Oloroso with the ultra-sweet Pedro Ximenez Sherries.

Cru: In French the word *cru* indicates a specific vineyard or plot, especially in Burgundy where the best vineyards are classified as Grand Cru or Premier Cru. In Champagne it indicates a whole village. In Bordeaux it is the classification system.

Cru Bourgeois: Applies to a classification of châteaux in the Medoc that are quality-orientated and not part of the Grands Crus Classés.

Crusted Port: A strongly flavoured Port that has been aged for four years in large wooden vats and bottled without filtration, leaving a sediment (crust) on the inside of the bottle. It is often a blend of two or three vintages, although single vintages do exist. This style is delicious young but has the capacity to age for many years.

cuvée: A specific wine as distinct from other wines in the cellar or in bottle.

DO / DOP: *Denominacion de Origen*; Spain's system for regulating origin and production.

DOCa / DOQa: *Denominacion de Origen Calificada* or *Qualificada* in Catalan. Only two regions in Spain qualify for this superior classification: Rioja and Priorat.

en-primeur: Wines sold on a futures basis, offered and paid for before bottling and release.

Factory House: In colonial times, the Factory House was the gathering place for the British merchants. In Oporto, the tradition survives. The Port community continues to meet for lunch every Wednesday to discuss mutual concerns. The building is also used for receptions, parties, and other events related to the Port trade and other British business.

Fino: A dry Sherry, ideal as an aperitif, also with sushi, sashimi, and shellfish.

First Growth: The leaders in the Bordeaux classification. Today this includes châteaux in the Medoc, Graves, Saint Emilion, and Sauternes.

foudre: A wooden vat, usually made of oak and used for the making and ageing of wines in many countries. The size can vary from 1,000 litres (264 gallons) to about 5,000 litres (1,320 gallons).

Grade "A" quinta: The top classification for single vineyards producing Port wine in the Douro Valley of Portugal.

Grand Cru Classé: Indicates the classification of the Bordeaux châteaux. In the Medoc the classification dates from 1855 and badly needs to be reformed. In Saint Emilion the classification is revised every ten years with much controversy. In Pomerol there has never been a classification.

Liebfraumilch: A mass-produced wine from Germany of rather indifferent quality.

malolactic fermentation: The transformation of malic acid to lactic acid in wine. This usually takes place naturally after the initial fermentation, but not always. Some producers, especially those who make white wines, often choose to prevent the malolactic fermentation to keep more acidity in the wine.

Manzanilla: A bone-dry Sherry that can only be produced in the town of Sanlúcar de Barameda where the sea breezes give the wine a salty tang. Perfect with the local seafood.

marc: The remnants of grape skins and pips which are left in the vat after the wine has finished fermentation and has been transferred to another vat. This cake-like mass is often distilled to produce an eau-de-vie called "Marc". A classic example is "Marc de Bourgogne".

must: Grape juice before fermentation has started to convert it into wine.

negoçiant: A merchant who purchases, blends, bottles, and sells wines of varying origins including their own vineyards. They are not necessarily vineyard owners. Sometimes they purchase grapes to make their own house blends.

negoçiant-eleveur: A merchant who ages and blends wines before bottling and shipping.

Oloroso: A dark rich Sherry, usually dry, ideal for rich food and strong cheese.

on consignment: A supplier delivers goods to a client without payment; payment is made by the client on a date negotiated with the supplier, after the goods have been sold.

Pedro Ximenez: An ultra-sweet Sherry made from grapes dried in the sun before pressing. Ideal with ice cream.

Petits Châteaux: The term used for châteaux in Bordeaux that have no classification. They often represent excellent value.

Place de Bordeaux: An open market for the purchase and sale of wines of all categories through a system of brokers that take care of almost all the transactions between the properties and the *négociants*.

ProWein: A major trade fair for wines and spirits that takes place every year in Düsseldorf, Germany

puncheon: A wooden container of 500 litres (132 gallons), shaped like a barrel and used for the ageing of wines and spirits.

quinta: A farm or vineyard property, particularly in Portugal.

schist: A sedimentary rock which forms in thin layers and breaks easily. Schistous soils are ideal for producing wines with a mineral character. Examples are Priorat in Spain, the Douro Valley in Portugal, and the northern part of Côte Rôtie in France.

second wine: Many of the top châteaux produce a wine of slightly lesser quality at a more reasonable price, keeping the best lots for the top wine. These wines are often excellent and represent good value. Sometimes even a third wine is produced, as is the case at Château Latour.

Sélection des Grains Nobles: Botrytised grapes that are picked one by one for the production of high-quality dessert wines, especially in Alsace.

silex: A hard rock formed from invisible crystals. Silex soils are ideal for producing wines with a mineral character. Classic examples are some of the vineyards in Sancerre and Pouilly Fumé, usually those closest to the river Loire.

solera: A system of fractional blending with the goal to have a product that tastes similar year after year. Soleras can be a hundred years old and more.

stage: An apprenticeship generally lasting between one and three months in the wine trade.

sur souche: A wine that is sold before the grapes are harvested. This practice is rare today.

Systembolaget: The Swedish retail monopoly.

terroir: A French term indicating the environment in which a wine is produced including the soil, climate, and exposure to the sun.

Vendanges Tardives: Late-harvest grapes indicating more ripeness and concentration, and sometimes sweeter wines.

vertical tasting: A tasting with numerous different vintages of the same wine, usually starting with the youngest and going back to the oldest, which could be many decades old.

villages: In Burgundy the term is used to classify wines from a specific village, which are not of the level of a Premier or Grand Cru.

Vin de Paille: A wine made from grapes that have been dried for a few weeks on a bed of straw or in an airy attic to concentrate the juice, resulting in a delicious sweet wine.

Vin Jaune: A wine produced in the Jura region made rather like Sherry, ageing under a layer of yeast for at least six years.

Vinexpo: An important trade fair that used to take place in Bordeaux every two years but is now based in Paris.

Vinitaly: The most important trade fair for Italian wines that takes place every year in Verona.

vin ordinaire: Wine without a control of origin, usually of indifferent quality.

Vintage Port: A single vintage Port that has the capacity to age for decades. Vintage Port is only made when the vintage is of outstanding quality, on average about three years out of ten.

INDEX

Illustrations are indicated by page references in *italics*. In subheadings CC indicates Christopher Cannan. Châteaux, domaines, etc, are listed by their individual names.

ACKNOWLEDGEMENTS

Owing to a lack of time the creation of this book has been in the pipeline for many years. There are many people who have influenced my career. They are too many to acknowledge here but my heartfelt thanks go out to them for making my time in the wine trade so stimulating and interesting. A special mention to all producers who had confidence in my abilities to distribute their wines in many countries, among many others, Aubert de Villaine of Domaine de la Romanée-Conti, Pablo Alvarez of Bodegas Vega Sicilia, Guillermo de Aranzabal of La Rioja Alta S.A. and the late Luis Caballero of Emilio Lustau and the Caballero group in Jerez. Not forgetting the prestigious producers, especially in Burgundy and the Rhône Valley, who agreed to give me allocations of their exquisite wines, even if the quantities produced were minute and the demand acute. Thanks to all the importers in more than fifty countries who had confidence in my selections and ability to export some of the world's finest wines in the best possible conditions.

I also wish to thank those who helped me found Europvin in 1978 and contributed to the success of the company, especially my friend Tim Denison, sales director of one of the leading Cognac producers, who lent me 50,000 French francs to help me get started. Also, the loyalty of Luc Savatier whose administrative skills kept the company on its tracks for thirty-two years and consolidated its continued prosperity today. In this respect, mention should be made of the late Rafael Balao, managing director of Emilio Lustau in Jerez at the time, and Marcel Guigal in the Rhône Valley, who had enough confidence in me and Europvin to give us the agency of their prestigious products in certain key markets, notably the US and Asia for Lustau and most of Asia for Guigal, enormously contributing to the success and prestige of the company.

To be more specific, before starting the book, I contacted Jancis Robinson who kindly invited me to tea in her home and gave me some sound advice. After some busy years had gone by, I contacted James Lawther MW, a resident in the Bordeaux region. He kindly agreed to read a first draft and give me some detailed advice. Later, he read the entire script and corrected my numerous errors and gave me more guidance. Without his assistance and encouragement this book may not have existed.

More words of encouragement came from the late Steven Spurrier who had just launched the Académie du Vin Library. He agreed to read the text and introduce me to the editor. In December 2020 he told me he had read part of the book but tragically he passed away before being able to comment on the text and propose the book to the Académie du Vin Library. Later I learnt the strategy of the Library had changed and an autobiography was not part of their future plans, unless one was a prominent winemaker. They did however suggest I take the self-publishing avenue and put me in touch with Sharon Lucas, a British editor based in the US, to whom I am also most grateful for her invaluable assistance and advice. In turn she put me in touch with Michelle Thomas in Wales who has been so helpful in the production of the book.

Printed by Amazon Italia Logistica S.r.l.
Torrazza Piemonte (TO), Italy

48475740R00179